Churchill's Bodyguard

Churchill's Bodyguard

Tom Hickman

headline

First published in 2005
by HEADLINE BOOK PUBLISHING

4

ISBN 0 7553 1448 4

Cataloguing in Publication Data is available from the British Library

Typeset in Garamond by Palimpsest Book Production Limited,
Polmont, Stirlingshire
Designed by Ben Cracknell Studios
Printed and bound in Great Britain by
Mackays of Chatham plc, Chatham, Kent

Headline's policy is to use papers that are natural, renewable and
recyclable products and made from wood grown in sustainable forests.
The logging and manufacturing processes are expected to conform to
the environmental regulations of the country of origin.

HEADLINE BOOK PUBLISHING
A division of Hodder Headline
338 Euston Road
London NW1 3BH

Photographs courtesy of Linda Stoker unless otherwise marked.

Every effort has been made to fulfil requirements with regard to
reproducing copyright material. The author and publisher will be glad
to rectify any omissions at the earliest opportunity.

www.headline.co.uk
www.hodderheadline.com

Contents

Acknowledgements

In 1999, having sold her three educational publishing and training companies, Linda Stoker wanted something to do. She was browsing in a second-hand bookshop when she found a copy of *Guard from the Yard*, written by Winston Churchill's long-time bodyguard, Walter Thompson – her great-uncle. As a child, Linda had often played 'spot Uncle Walter' when her family watched *All Our Yesterdays*. But she hadn't read anything he'd written. Now she read everything. And with the determination of someone who'd been voted a Woman of the Year and been GMTV's assertiveness expert, she set out to discover all she could, beginning by tracing Walter's large and scattered family.

Philip Nugus is the managing director of Nugus/Martin Productions, an independent television company specialising in historical documentary series and a considerable authority on the Second World War. One day he received a letter from Linda outlining Walter's story. He thought it sounded like a one-off programme, not a series, and wrote back suggesting that BBC2 might be interested. Some months later Linda phoned: would he like to see the material? She turned up with a suitcase on wheels – and Philip quickly changed his mind.

'The suitcase was packed with flimsies – I could smell the 1940s,' he says. 'I read the lot over a weekend. In fifteen years of documentary making I've handled a lot of artefacts but never anything so obviously historically significant – which is why I immediately secured the world TV, publishing and movie rights.

'When you look at previous programmes on Churchill, you see endless head-and-shoulder shots of parliamentary secretaries, diplomats, generals and politicians talking away in cut-glass accents. It's a story told so many times I thought there was nothing new to be told. But here was something entirely different – the classic tale of a little man, a working-class East Ender, tracking the big man against the backdrop of the first half of the century. It was a dramatic new perspective on the big man – and in the little man's own words.'

Churchill's Bodyguard is compiled from the contents of that suitcase, as well as from other research and interviews. I would like in particular to thank Walter's son Harold, whose memories at ninety are still sharp; Harold's younger sister Kathleen Bucknall; Harold's son Peter, who spent fifteen years working out the family tree; and Jan Glass, Walter's niece by marriage, who knew the older Walter so well that she's helped me considerably in trying to understand him.

Walter Thompson may only be a footnote to the history of the twentieth century, but he had slipped from the page. *Churchill's Bodyguard*, in both its book and television versions, attempts to put him back where he belongs.

CHAPTER 1

Getting to Know You

The sun was shining cheerfully one morning in February 1921, but Walter Henry Thompson, a detective sergeant from Scotland Yard's Special Branch, was anything but cheerful as he went up the steps of a house in Sussex Square near Hyde Park in London. This was the home of Winston Churchill, MP, and Walter – Tommy to almost everyone except his family, as Thompsons inevitably are – had just been sent to act as his bodyguard in the face of Sinn Fein threats. 'I was filled with dismay, because there was a belief among us that he was a difficult man to guard and rather uncertain of mood,' Walter would later write. 'Some of my colleagues had survived the detail only a matter of days. As one of my senior officers remarked: "He's a tyrant."'

The brief meeting that followed seemed to confirm it. For a spell, Walter had provided protection for the Prime Minister, David Lloyd George. When Lloyd George first met him he'd smiled and said, 'So you're to be my new guardian angel.'

Churchill, however, 'greeted me almost disdainfully. Looking me up and down, he said, "Well, just don't tread on my heels too often," and went back into his office.' And Walter found himself back on the doorstep, cursing the officer who had suddenly resigned rather than continue looking after the Secretary of State for the Colonies, who was also Minister of Air. Walter also cursed his luck. He'd arrived early at work that morning to deal with some matters concerning the Yard athletics club, of which he was secretary. Quite likely he'd been assigned only because his chief spotted him in the building. Still, he consoled himself, he'd been told the assignment was for only two weeks.

The Sinn Fein danger had been uncovered by the Yard[1] less than three months earlier. A cell in Glasgow had decided to try to kidnap Churchill, Lloyd George and others in reprisal for Britain's continuing refusal to grant Irish Home Rule.[2] Churchill was perhaps the main target. He'd opposed Home Rule almost from the day he entered Parliament. As head of the Admiralty during the First World War, he'd sent warships to Ireland to quell one of the recurrent crises (and thus provoked a mutiny), and after it, as Secretary for War and then Home Secretary, he'd shown an iron fist in a strategy of counter-terrorism against the Irish Republican Army – the previous March he'd established a temporary 'special emergency gendarmerie', the Black and Tans, whose brutality had alienated public opinion on both sides of the Irish Sea. He'd also called for executions (though he acknowledged that 'grass grows over the battlefield but never over a scaffold'). The hanging of eighteen-year-old Kevin Barry, the first since 1916, triggered a wave of atrocities.[3]

Just for good measure, there was also an outside chance of an attempt on his life by someone sympathetic to the Bolsheviks – in his time at the War Office, Churchill had supported the White

Russians with arms and men, declaring that 'Bolshevism must be strangled in the cradle'.

The officer previously in charge of Churchill's protection had taken turns with a detective constable in sleeping at Sussex Square, and Walter should have shared the load. 'But thinking I would only be with him [Churchill] for two weeks, I took only the absolutely necessary interest in my new job, looking upon "Winston" as a routine detail, and let the junior carry on sleeping there each night.' Walter went home to his young family in Sydenham, south London.

*   *   *

The paths of Churchill and his bodyguard had already crossed, the first time ten years earlier at the Siege of Sidney Street in the East End. When news of the siege spread, Walter had dashed there to watch. A gang of Latvian refugees, interrupted the previous night in the middle of breaking into a jeweller's, had shot and killed three policemen trying to arrest them. A number of the gang were now holed up in a house in Sidney Street, with a company of Scots Guards on the scene. Walter 'shouldered through to the front of the excited crowd. Shots rattled from the old house, and rifle fire clattered back into it from the police and guardsmen, some concealed on roofs opposite, others on one knee in the open street like redcoats at the Battle of Waterloo.' In the shooting, another policeman was killed and the house caught fire; two bodies were recovered from it.

Before the billowing smoke filled the street and clouded my view, I saw a gentleman in a black trilby hat and black overcoat with an astrakhan collar arrive and was informed it was Winston Churchill, the Home Secretary. I watched agape as the man who was later to become my boss at Scotland Yard was shot at. Sir Patrick Quinn was standing behind Winston when a bullet from the gunmen was fired through his hat. It was a near miss for Winston, who was well to the front.

For all the excitement, Walter had other things on his mind: the American shirt and collar company in the City where he was the stock keeper was doing badly (and would soon close). The last straw had been the ruining of almost all the collars in the warehouse. By some oversight, these hadn't been stamped 'Made in the USA', and the error was rectified so hurriedly that the ink hadn't dried when they were repacked; almost all of them had had to be destroyed. Months short of his twenty-first birthday, Walter was wondering about his future.

The newsreel of the Sidney Street siege played night after night in the Palace Theatre to catcalls and boos for the Home Secretary and shouts of 'Shoot him!' from the gallery. If Walter was there he may have joined in: 'I had heard a good deal about him, much of which was inspired by his outspoken manner, which many people resented and to a degree disliked. This resentment influenced me and, without any real reason, I did not like him!' – a less-than-surprising judgement of the grandson of a duke made by the son of a working-class insurance agent from Brixton.

Walter was to come into contact with Churchill on three subsequent occasions. The first was in 1915, when, as a junior detective, he replaced someone on his day off. On that occasion he accompanied his charge to a canvas enclosure erected on Horse Guards Parade, where 'small mounds of earth had been constructed and a number of toy vehicles fitted with caterpillar tracks lay here and there on the ground. With deep interest, Winston watched while the toys were sent trundling over the mounds. He asked for small obstacles to be put in their way, and he smiled his pleasure when the little cars easily climbed them.

Excitedly he said: "We can put a gun on vehicles like that."' It was a moment that Walter later 'realised was an historic one': he had seen in miniature what Churchill was to call 'a landship' – the tank.[4] Shortly after this, Walter was posted to Southampton, the only English port not wholly taken up with military traffic, where a unit of Yard detectives processed the 5,000 people arriving and departing by sea every week, on the lookout for subversives and spies. The next encounter was on Armistice Day 1918 when, having just delivered a suspected spy to the Yard, Walter just happened to be one of the crowd in Whitehall, where he saw Churchill make a brief address – standing up in a car with tears streaming down his face – before he returned to Southampton and in the small hours careered around the town on his motor-cycle combination 'with three of my colleagues piled into my sidecar, smothered in bunting'.

In Southampton he again ran into Churchill, who was now overseeing the demobilisation of the troops who'd been fighting in France.

The war over, troops were returning home from the Continent and being replaced by other men who had seen no fighting. A large number of these new men, billeted in a camp in the town, refused to go overseas, and Winston, coming in on a ship from France and hearing of their attitude, demanded to be taken to see them. When he stood up to talk to them, the mutinous soldiers booed, but as he spoke they quietened. He pointed out that they were needed for an essential job – to act as an army of occupation. Most seemed satisfied with his explanation, but a few continued to murmur. Angry now, Winston let fly: 'You will go whether you like it or not,' he shouted, 'and if necessary at the point of the bayonets of the men who have been fighting.' There was no further trouble. Soon afterwards the troops sailed.

Walter had little sympathy with the troops: 'duty' was one of his guiding tenets, and as far as he was concerned it was the troops' duty to go. Later he would find out that duty meant as much to Churchill. They had more in common than he might have believed.

*   *   *

The two weeks passed very slowly. In the mornings Churchill was at the Colonial Office, in the afternoons at the House of Commons. When sometimes he went home to dinner, Walter hoped to finish for the day. 'What an illusion. We returned to the House until any time between 11 p.m. and 2 a.m. On some occasions he would go there at 3 p.m. and stay until the early hours. This meant waiting indefinitely, for I never knew exactly when he would leave. Of course, it was very seldom that he could give me a time, for anything may arise in the House which may be for him to deal with in connection with his ministerial duties.' To him, Churchill appeared 'unapproachable, just saying, "Good morning and good night, Thompson". What really annoyed me was the fact that he would automatically say good night when it was nearly always in the morning.'

Walter considered Churchill to be 'difficult, almost priggish, lacking in consideration . . . a thoughtless and self-centred individual', and he longed for his time to be up; when it was, 'I marched into my chief's office at Scotland Yard and said: "I'd like very much to be relieved of this protection duty, sir." I tried to make it sound more like a demand than a request. The chief looked up. He was smiling. "You don't want it then, Thompson?" he said. "No, sir." His smile grew a bit sadistic. "Whether you want it or not, it's yours," he said. "Winston's asked for you to be with him permanently."' Walter was speechless. He was convinced that Churchill couldn't stand him. More pointedly, he realised that guarding such a hyperactive man meant that 'For the first time in my life I had to be prepared to sacrifice even my private life to my job, and there seemed to be no way out, other than resigning from the force'.

He trudged to Sussex Square for an interview with Churchill. 'I felt quite gloomy as I entered the house, where his secretary told me that the great man would see me for a few minutes. Winston was pacing up and down the study, almost ludicrously preoccupied. The frenzied concentration was almost burlesque. Had Walt Disney created Mickey Mouse in those days, I would have been tempted to believe that his gait was the inspiration for the famous cartoons.' Walter's feelings about Churchill at that moment are pretty evident, but he was immediately thrown by the 'charming intimacy' of the greeting he received, which 'was coupled with a human and a very refreshing smile'. After listening to Walter tell him that 'I would endeavour to carry out my duties with as little annoyance to him as possible', Churchill thanked him, added, 'I have no doubt that we'll get on well together', and 'resumed his walking, oblivious to the secretary or me'.

On the doorstep once again, Walter no longer knew what he thought.

Churchill had only recently been given the Colonial Office by Lloyd George – a hot potato of a portfolio with responsibility not only for Ireland but also for the colonies and protectorates that Britain had acquired as an outcome of the war, those in the Middle East involving the Arabian Peninsula, Mesopotamia (the whole of today's Iraq), Egypt and Palestine. The region was a powder keg of unrest; in Egypt, independence was being demanded and there had been several bloody insurrections; in Palestine, where the British had promised the setting up of a permanent Jewish homeland, Arab–Jewish hatred and rival ambitions seethed. The Middle East was one of the most dangerous places in the world – and within weeks Walter found himself going there at Churchill's side. Churchill was to chair a conference in Cairo to sort out how the new territories were to be governed. He was also wearing his other hat as Minister of Air, intending to assess whether squadrons of the RAF, not yet two years in existence, could police Egypt (as it was in Mesopotamia), which was in open revolt against the British, saving the huge expense of standing garrisons that could be released for service elsewhere. To carry out his dual role, Churchill brought with him Lord Trenchard, Chief of the Air Staff, and, as his chief adviser on Arab matters, T. E. Lawrence – Lawrence of Arabia. Trenchard struck Walter as one of the coldest and least forthcoming personalities he'd ever encountered (a good match for the Sphinx, it later occurred to him), but he was taken with Lawrence, enjoying the 'amusing, cynical asides' that peppered his conversation, though he found it hard to credit that this 'shy, untidy and even awkward little man was indeed the "Uncrowned King of Arabia"'.[5]

Walter, who'd got his first passport to accompany Lloyd George to peace talks in Belgium, was unhappy about a trip that would keep him away until April, leaving his wife Kate alone with their three small sons and the daughter born only months earlier. And he soon found himself at odds with Churchill. He was smoking his old briar pipe in the corridor of the train from Paris to Marseilles, where Mrs Churchill (who was holidaying on the Riviera) was to join the party for the sea trip to Alexandria, when Churchill's private secretary came out of the compartment 'and through the open door Winston saw what I was at. He called out sharply: "Put that beastly thing out. If you must smoke in the early morning, smoke a cigarette, and a Turkish one."' A heavy pipe smoker who didn't like cigarettes, especially Turkish ones, Walter thought that pretty rich coming from someone who smoked 'perfectly foul cigars – and always put on a cigar immediately after breakfast'.

What exactly he expected Egypt to be like, he certainly didn't anticipate what greeted them as the liner docked in Alexandria. 'Heat and a swarm of flies hit us as we tied up . . . a huge crowd of tarbooshed Egyptians and Arabs collected on the dock, and the sight of Winston and his party coming down the gangway made them yell with fury.' Lawrence had said that 'the Arab masses were dangerous and inflammable', but 'even Winston was taken aback as the clamour rose to a veritable crescendo of fury'. Worried, Walter 'stuck to his man' as the party were hustled into the waiting air-force cars. By the time he'd shielded the Churchills through another menacing crowd at the hotel, he 'was certain that most of Alexandria was against us'.

His day didn't improve. On a visit to an RAF camp, one of a number that Churchill would visit during the trip, the seat that as a bodyguard he should have occupied in the front of Churchill's vehicle was taken by a senior RAF officer who rudely ordered him to the car behind. 'But as I had no real experience in such matters and as the tour concerned the RAF, I did not quite know how far his authority exceeded my own.' Mrs Churchill heard an intruder in the room next to hers where the boxes of official documents were locked and Walter had to crash down the door, 'only in time to see an Arab clambering for dear life towards the roof'. Nothing had been touched; but the upshot was that Churchill ordered Walter to remain in the small, stuffy room through the night. Sleep was impossible on the hastily found camp bed on which he lay with his revolver under his pillow. 'Not being used to the heat, I was in a pretty bad temper, so it was as well nobody else tried to break in: he would have caught a packet.' It wasn't just the heat keeping him awake: now the local police were taking seriously a rumour that in the morning a mob would attack the cars on the route to the station, where the party were to board the royal train to Cairo, which King Fuad had put at their disposal.

In the event, the party got to the train without trouble. Walter arranged for them to leave the hotel by the back door and drive through the backstreets. Trouble, however, greeted them almost as soon as the train, its engine as well as its carriages gleaming white, steamed out. As it slowed at a level crossing, 'every window on one side was smashed to smithereens'. Walter remained standing in the doorway of the royal saloon while Lawrence went to the end of the carriage as

a huge mass of ugly-looking Egyptians fought for a hold on the outside window ledges . . . All the while Winston sat totally unperturbed in the corner, calmly smoking a cigar. I was close behind, holding his dispatch box, when a stone whizzed through the broken window and hurtled between us. Winston turned to me and said, 'Thompson, you'd better give the case to Archie [Sir Archibald Sinclair, his parliamentary secretary]. You might be wanting both your hands soon.'

As it happened, he didn't: the train gathered speed. But five miles outside Cairo it suddenly stopped, making Walter go tense until two British staff officers came aboard to ask the party to transfer to waiting cars to avoid another demonstration from a large and hostile crowd waiting at the terminus.

At the outset of the trip, Lawrence had warned Walter 'that Churchill's life would be at risk from the instant we were on Arab soil'. Now Sir Thomas Russell – Russell Pasha, founder of the Camel Corps and head of the Egyptian police – added to his worries when he drew him aside at the hotel and told him: 'Churchill is in great danger. Never, on any account, let him out of your sight. Trust nobody, black or white. Guard him as you would your own life – even in the sanctuary of his own bedchamber.' Going to Churchill's room, Walter found him sitting at a table, writing. Churchill told him to stop worrying and freshen up for dinner. First taking the precaution of having a word with the manager to make sure the staff were alert, Walter went to his own room. A short while later, while he was washing, the doorkeeper knocked to say Churchill had suddenly left on foot and on his own.

His heart in his mouth, Walter pulled on his clothes and made a quick recce in the teeming street, but without luck. Back in the hotel, someone thought Churchill had got fed up waiting for the High Commissioner, Field Marshal Allenby, and gone to meet him. Ascertaining where Allenby lived, Walter dashed there just as Churchill emerged, without a care in the world, smiling a greeting that his bodyguard didn't feel like returning. He'd endured a stressful couple of days, had a bad night – and the man he was supposed to protect had let him down. 'In a burst of wrath I said: "Look, sir, we can't have this. How can I possibly look after you if you treat me like this? You're making my job quite impossible."'

Though his outburst, while respectful, was 'definitely Scotland Yard at its most official', Walter thought he might have gone too far and Churchill's reaction took him by surprise. 'He was softness itself in his reply: "In future I will do all I can to help you, Thompson. We're just beginning to understand each other."' Afterwards, when he looked back on this, 'my first experience of anything approaching intimacy with him', Walter concluded it was Churchill's way of saying, 'I'm sorry, Thompson, but you can never expect me to be like a sheep in the herd. You will just have to try to keep up with me.'

The remaining hours of the day were uneventful, if not for the hotel's houseboy. This 'mountainous individual', a Nubian eunuch, had earlier taken half an hour to bring Walter hot shaving water; he'd arrived just ahead of the doorkeeper with the news that 'Churchill had slipped my lead'. Now that Churchill was safely back, Walter found the manager to complain about the service and was advised that, if satisfaction wasn't forthcoming, a good kick was the remedy. Walter ordered more shaving water. Another half-hour elapsed before the Nubian made his appearance, placed the steaming shaving mug on the dressing table and turned to go. Just as 'the most protuberant part of the eunuch's anatomy disappeared through the door', Walter vented his frustrations by taking the manager's advice, noting with satisfaction that the houseboy 'shot down the passage, his feet flip-flopping at a tremendous rate and his voice uttering screams worthy of a pig in its death agony'.

Walter lost his room again, Russell Pasha advising him to sleep in the small one that interconnected those of the Churchills. He did, but was very embarrassed. 'Either one would pass through my room to the other at all times during the night and, of course, trained to sleep with both ears open and one eye shut, I woke on each occasion.'

Before leaving Sussex Square, Churchill had asked Walter to take charge of his painting equipment on the trip and, 'not seeing any harm in this', had said he'd do his best.[6] He'd already regretted it: in Marseilles, where Churchill got him to set up his easel while waiting for the liner to sail, he'd covered his suit in paint (Churchill replaced it in Cairo). Now Churchill wanted to paint the pyramids, and Walter had come to the conclusion that 'painting was no mere enthusiasm for him – it was a disease –

and before any time at all had passed I had become worn out at the thought of the menial lugging of his damned boxes'. It concerned him that 'draped with the painting kit, the box that opened up to make the easel and palette slung over my shoulder by a strap, a long leather case like a golf bag containing the poles for the table, an attaché case containing the tubes of paint and the rest, as well as a stool and an umbrella', he would have no chance to reach for his revolver if he needed to. But he was amused at the pyramids by the bunch of British soldiers who stood behind Churchill making comments ('Love a duck, guv'nor, you don't half use some paint. Lucky for you you ain't a house-painter with my old foreman. You wouldn't half cop it') and their embarrassed astonishment when he turned grinning to them ('Gawd, it's Winston!').

He was less amused when he found out that Churchill and some of the party planned an outing to the tombs at Saqqara – on camels.

The cavalcade of sheiks and other dignitaries who accompa-nied them on horseback made a colourful sight, but Walter was too occupied trying to hold on to his beast as 'my very spine and ribs clattered together'. But it was Churchill who fell off. Walter had 'a near heart attack' as the Arabs swung their rearing horses round, putting the prone figure, it seemed to him, in danger of being trampled, and then clamoured in what he took to be menacing tones. In fact, he discovered, 'they were imploring the great man to mount on one of their steeds and not to hazard himself again upon a "ship of the desert"'. Churchill, unhurt, dusted himself off, growled, 'I started on a camel and I'll finish on a camel', and remounted. At least Lawrence saw the funny side. 'Your animal knew he was going to have the honour of carrying you, Winston. So he blew himself out as a demonstra-tion of his pride on this occasion. Then, because of your riding style, he decided his rider could not have been the great man of whom he had heard, but merely a very common person who should be got rid of as speedily as possible. So he just let out the air, the saddle girth loosened – and off you came!'

Churchill not only finished the two-and-a-half-hour ride to the tombs, but he insisted on making the trip back the same way, accompanied only by Lawrence and his reluctant bodyguard, while the rest of the group gratefully went by car. When, finally, the journey was completed and Walter painfully lowered himself into the car in which his two companions were waiting, Churchill delivered 'the unkindest cut of all, leaning forward and chuckling: "You're very sprightly today, Thompson. I haven't seen you jump about like that for a long while."' Over the next few days Walter got fed up with hearing how sprightly he was.

When Churchill was involved in the conference negotiations, Walter relaxed: security was in the hands of Russell Pasha's efficient men. Anywhere in the open, however, was Walter's responsibility – a responsibility that was taken away from him, for the second time, when Churchill paid a courtesy call on King Fuad at the Abdin Palace. Allenby, like the air-force officer on the earlier occasion, requisitioned Walter's seat in Churchill's car. Faced with the authority of the national hero who had defeated the Turks during the First World War (and who had, in fact, recognised Lawrence's charisma and given 'the excitable and scruffy officer' arms and money to keep alive the Arab revolt that supported the British Expeditionary Force), Walter had no option but to follow in the car behind. Again he was put out that he wasn't being allowed to do his job, but at least he acknowledged that in telling him 'I'll do my best to guard your precious master', Allenby had at least been genial.

Just as the front car reached the palace and Walter was thinking how comfortingly like Buckingham Palace it was, a huge mob

overflowed the square, howling and gesticulating. Churchill and
Allenby got through the gates before the sentries clanged them
to, leaving the second car on the wrong side of them. Stones
began to fly, with which 'the sentries vanished from their posts
like greased lightning'. The headlights and windscreen were
smashed, and as the crowd swarmed over the running boards,
some wielding sticks, the ugliest incident of the trip developed.
Walter's companion, an RAF sergeant, shouted: 'Don't show
your gun, Mr Thompson, just use your fists.' Six feet tall in his
shoes, a little over thirteen stone and with a powerful upper body
developed through weight training, wrestling and jujitsu, Walter
needed no second bidding: 'This was really right up my street.'
In his late teens he'd been a sparring partner to a number of
professional boxers in the gyms of south London; as a copper on
the beat he'd more than once put his massive fists to good use.
Now he took such a toll of the attackers, assisted by the sergeant
armed with a spanner, that they withdrew, palace officials came
out to speak to those who remained, and Churchill emerged to
drive back to the hotel before another angry crowd gathered
there in yet another demonstration.

*   *   *

On the eve of the party's departure to Jerusalem, with a scheduled stop at Gaza, Sir Herbert Samuel, British High
Commissioner in Palestine, arrived with unsettling news: a plot
'to blow him [Churchill] to bits by a bomb or to shoot him
somewhere en route'. The information was vague, but Sir Herbert
had brought with him two police officers from the Palestine force
to provide extra protection. Russell Pasha now had different
advice for Walter, telling him the party were moving 'into a
climate of unclassifiable fanaticism' and he was to shoot on sight
if danger threatened. If that was the case, Walter thought when
he caught up with Sir Herbert's policemen aboard the train, they

weren't going to be much use, 'the oddest-looking couple . . . one as thin as a lath and as tall as a hop pole, the other a roly-poly tub'. Their nicknames, he discovered, 'were Mutt and Jeff'.[7]

The following morning Walter awoke to see they were passing through desert, with nothing between the railway track and the horizon. Before he'd finished dressing he received a summons from Churchill, whom he found lying in bed, saying he wanted a bath. So did Walter. 'So did everybody on this hot, grubby journey. But there was no bathroom on the train. There was no bath for miles.' Churchill sent him forward to look and, 'more or less to humour him', Walter went – and in the baggage car discovered a hip bath, 'a tall-backed, old-fashioned, tin-plate affair of the kind used in front of bedroom fireplaces before a bath-room became standard home equipment'. Churchill had evidently seen it or had it brought. Walter returned to say he'd found the bath but to ask where the water was. 'You're slipping, Thompson,' Winston said, his grin infuriatingly wide. 'When you first came to me I thought you were a man of intelligence. Now I doubt it.' He instructed Walter to have the driver stop and draw water from the engine.

Winston got out of bed. He put on a brightly coloured dressing gown, seized a towel and led the way along the tracks to the front, where the steaming bathtub lay on the dusty desert. He smiled up at the engine crew, stripped naked, and fitted himself into the bath. As Archimedes predicted, most of the water spilled over and was swallowed up by the parched earth. But he got a bath of sorts, dried himself, waved to the crew and sauntered, pink and clean, back to his compartment

– leaving his bodyguard agape at his eccentricity.

When the train stopped at Gaza, where Churchill was to receive an address of welcome and speak to a number of tribal chiefs, 'Mutt and Jeff, hitherto closeted in their compartment, showed the first signs of activity in combating the "peril" of which they alone had (or had not) precise details ... the pair rushed into Churchill's compartment and took up positions at windows at each end of it. Both looked most important' – but they didn't, he noted, get off with everyone else but stayed where they were, taking photographs. Had the policemen not arrived with Sir Herbert, Walter 'might have considered them impostors'. The crowd was vast, about 2,000 strong, and tumultuous, but, as Lawrence seemed to consider the situation peaceful and friendly, Walter wasn't worried. He might have been had Lawrence told him that among the cries of 'Cheers for Great Britain' and 'Cheers for the Minister' were others of greater intensity: 'Down with the Jews' and 'Cut their throats'.

He did worry when it came time to leave the hall where the meeting was held: the crowd had been waiting two hours, shouting and swaying, and had grown restive; the police were using their lead-loaded staves, and fighting was taking place. Some of the mounted police were unhorsed and sought protection on the porch; the rest drew their sabres, riding their horses straight into the crowd, attempting to force a passage,

but they might as well have tried to ride down a brick wall: people simply seized the horses' bridles and pushed the riders backwards. 'What is this?' Churchill asked Lawrence. 'A demonstration for or against?' 'I think they only want to look at you,' Lawrence replied. 'But how long are they going to keep us here?' Winston wanted to know. 'The longer we wait, the more I shall deteriorate.'

It was then that Walter witnessed the great prestige Lawrence of Arabia commanded. Lawrence merely held up his hand, said a few words and stepped back behind Churchill. Instantly the throng fell silent and parted ('as if the Red Sea had once more parted to allow the passage of the fleeing Israelites,' Walter recorded, his admiration leading him into a rare bit of purple prose); 'many threw themselves on their faces with arms outstretched towards him. As Winston saw this, he turned to me and said, "They worship him."'

Escorted by what appeared to Walter as 'Gaza in its entirety', the entourage returned to the track. In amazement Walter saw Mutt and Jeff still leaning out of the windows taking photographs. When the journey continued, the pair kept themselves to themselves, but whenever the train slowed down they rushed to the windows of Churchill's compartment, finally annoying him so much he told Walter to keep them out, which he did with infinite pleasure, telling them that if they didn't he'd 'scatter them along the track and take a picture of myself doing so for their families back home'. Some way out of Jerusalem, the train stopped dead because a crowd was blocking the line with their bodies. Again Lawrence quickly assessed the situation as peaceful, quietly addressed the crowd, and again Walter 'had the sensation that those brown hawk-faced men outside were worshipping him'. They only wanted to present 'Shershill' with a scroll (dealing, Walter thought, with the problem of Jewish influence in Palestine), which they duly did.

In Jerusalem itself, which the previous year had passed from British military to British civil administration, a capital city for the first time since the Crusades, Lawrence frequently appeared in Arab dress, and the reception he received was no less remarkable: people rushed to him, some once more prostrating themselves. Lawrence was almost ever present, ahead of them in the narrow streets that resonated with noise and teemed with a mixture of races: 'Arab women wearing yashmaks, European women of fashion, Palestinian men in burnouses or Western suits and tarbooshes, Bedouins in keffiyehs, white-turbaned Muslim mullahs, Greek priests, tourists' (Walter even spotted a Scandinavian in plus-fours), all jostling with water carriers, street vendors and shop owners trying to entice the passers-by. Ever curious, Churchill kept darting away, up alleys, into bazaars. It was an impossible situation for a bodyguard, and Walter groaned. 'By now I was almost convinced that I would never get this man back home alive.'

During this leg of the Middle East visit, Churchill held private talks, treading a delicate line between Arab and Jewish factions, hoping to encourage Jewish settlement while allaying Arab fears.[8] He also fitted in some sightseeing. At a new Jewish settlement between Jericho and Jaffa, Walter was struck by how healthy the people, mostly young, looked, 'which contrasted vividly with the anaemic, undersized inhabitants of the East End of London . . . Yet quite a number of [them] undoubtedly originated from Whitechapel and other East End districts.' Indeed, many shook his hand, 'delighted at seeing a "real, live London bobby" in their midst'.

Government House, where the Churchill party stayed, was built on the Mount of Olives for Kaiser Wilhelm and would have been his 'Eastern palace' had the First World War had a different outcome. Walter was intrigued to see the German eagle carved over the main gateway and two rooms inside with 'The Kaiser's Bedroom' and 'The Kaiserin's Bedroom' picked out in gold above the doors. On a rise in the grounds was a small, finely carved structure with a built-in seat called the 'Chair of Imperial Contemplation', which faced a panoramic view of the landscape. Here one day, out of Churchill's sight, Walter sat down ('My countrymen had helped to deprive the Kaiser of his view, and I felt it was my right and privilege to sit there in his place'), lit his pipe and did some contemplation of his own. The Middle East had proved to be a baptism of fire for him as Churchill's guard. There had been very real warnings of attempts on Churchill's life; there had been unexpected dangers caused by the volatility of the people. All in all, the trip had been a jumble of high drama and low comedy (not to mention the boring dinners that Walter hated) and, he admitted, for all his experience at the Yard, even with six commendations to his name, there had been times when he was out of his depth. He had, however, warmed to the 'Old Man', as he was now beginning to think of Churchill. He had watched him closely, 'not only from the point of view of his security but to get to known the "man"'. His Yard training had involved the study of faces, and he found Churchill's face a map of changing moods. He hadn't entirely altered his first opinion – Churchill *was* self-centred, he made the world revolve around him – but Walter had found that much of Churchill's behaviour 'was little more than a rough shield to cover a sensitive, sentimental and humorous interior'. He had watched Churchill during the visits to the holy places, particularly the Church of the Holy Sepulchre and Bethlehem, noting 'how visibly moved he was; in each case he just stood not saying a word and left in a similar manner' – something that Walter, with his Methodist background, appreciated. 'The truth was,' he concluded, 'that he was one of those dynamic persons whose original ways would need getting used to.'

But if he was to be effective in his role at Churchill's side, he resolved, he wasn't going to be pushed around as he'd been in the Middle East. When it came to Churchill's safety, no one's authority exceeded his own.

CHAPTER 2

'If They Want Trouble, They Can Have It'

Walter had enjoyed his seven years in Special Branch, keeping tabs on the suffragettes, trailing anarchists just before the First World War (there were hundreds in London) and arresting aliens and enemy agents once it broke out. But a bodyguard for only a few months (six weeks of them away in the Middle East), he was finding the routine work hard to settle into. He no longer had the freedom he was used to, and too much of his time for his liking was spent in the Colonial Office or the House of Commons hanging around.

While he'd been away with Churchill, the Sinn Fein threat had racked up: on the eve of the Cairo Conference, Eamon de Valera, President of the Irish Parliament, had secured support for a formal declaration of war with England. On their return, as part of his responsibility in dealing with the situation but also in making a fresh start with Churchill, Walter began sharing the sleepovers at Sussex Square with his detective constable. Churchill was pleased, showing Walter all over the house, including the room he would now 'Box and Cox' with his junior officer. This was on the second floor between the front and back staircase from which anyone moving on either could be heard. Churchill also showed Walter his own room, where a high-backed chair stood between the door and the bed, a loaded Colt .45 on the seat. Grinning, Churchill raised the chair's tapestry to reveal that the back was reinforced with a steel plate. 'You guard me from below,' he said. 'Nobody will have a walkover with us both on the lookout.'

When a newspaper ran a story about 'Winston's new shadow', accompanied by his silhouette, Walter admitted to a glow of pride. He was even more pleased to find out from talking to members of Churchill's staff that the Old Man disliked subservience: 'If you were a yes man he did not want you.' Well, Walter certainly wasn't that – even if he had given up his pipe. But that was a matter of common sense and good manners, as he was now sleeping in Churchill's home – and the cigarettes he now smoked were Virginian!

The pair still had what politely might be called differences of opinion. At such moments Churchill's head came forward and down, making Walter feel 'a foot taller than he was' as Churchill adopted his 'rumpled slump'. Sometimes these conversations were to do with the sudden decisions Churchill made without telling Walter, which could compromise his security, but mostly with his 'insane' working hours, which necessitated his bodyguard being with him. Churchill didn't seem to appreciate that 'even members of the Special Branch of Scotland Yard have a private life – at least the rules recognise time off and wives of members expect to see their husbands from time to time'. Even when

Walter did get off and 'might get into some work clothes to dig in my garden and was partway to the tool shed', he'd receive a call from the Yard saying that Churchill wanted him to accompany him here or meet him there. What irritated Walter most was that this seemed to happen almost every time he went to football. A left half who when younger had been thought good enough for the professional game with Clapton (later Leyton) Orient, and then had been scouted by Arsenal – and while stationed in Southampton trained at the town football ground and took part in a friendly[1] – he no longer had time to play. But he liked to watch Tottenham Hotspur; only now he couldn't see a game start 'with any belief that I'd see it through to the end'.

*   *   *

Walter seemed destined to become a policeman, although at first he took dead-end jobs as a post office telegraph messenger, office boy, telephonist and then stock keeper. But the thirty pages of an autobiography he began and abandoned reveal that between the ages of twelve and fourteen he 'gave serious thought to the subject of right and wrong generally' and their relationship to justice. And, he wrote, 'I would stand out to the bitter end in support of my principles'.

One day at Hackford Road Board School (now Durand Primary) in Stockwell, south London, the boy sitting next to him was jigging the desk with his knee, which made Walter's writing waver. Walter told him to stop and the boy struck him – and told the teacher it was the other way round. Ordered to fetch the cane and the book in which punishments were recorded, Walter, 'seething with the unfairness of it', refused. He was sent to the headmaster and still refused to be caned ('though I was used to it. Discipline in "the big boys' school" was severe: six good strokes for talking in the classroom, in which there were upwards of fifty pupils'). Every morning and afternoon for two weeks he refused, and only agreed to accept the punishment when the head told his parents that otherwise he'd have to be expelled. 'But justice in this matter was not complete from my point of view,' he wrote. 'Fights out of school hours were not the concern of the schoolteachers, so I very severely dealt with the boy who had caused the trouble.'

Walter had already shown an inclination to use his fists in the pursuit of justice. His first pair of woollen gloves had been stolen from his desk, and he kept a lookout in the playground. When he saw a boy 'whom I disliked very much' wearing them, 'I ripped them off his hands and with that I hit him on the chin and knocked him clean out'. Before he left school, his sense of righteousness made him 'take up the cudgels on behalf of other boys'.

At fourteen Walter started work at the post office in St James's Street off Pall Mall, and two incidents made him 'fully aware of the dishonesty and lawbreaking' that happened in the outside world: a fellow messenger filched a postal order from a pile of registered envelopes that Walter was responsible for sealing ('had he not been made to leave the firm I should have most certainly dealt with him myself'); and the new cycle he'd saved hard to buy – and had padlocked to railings – was stolen. 'I am sure that these occurrences were creating in my mind a resistance to persons breaking the law,' Walter wrote. 'I was now always on the alert.' At eighteen he apprehended a man stealing a cycle and held him until the police came and took him away; he confronted a drunk in Brixton marketplace waving a revolver and marched him to the police station; and then he went to the help of an officer struggling with two men, one of whom tried to attack him with a plank. Walter grappled him to the ground and held on until the policeman's whistle summoned reinforcements. The police presented him with a silver watch.

24

But even when the shirt and collar company shut down and put him out of work at nearly twenty-one, he still didn't consider the police: the money was £1.1s.6d. a week ('with uniform'), and, now engaged to Kate Beale, the only child of a cabinetmaker, whom he'd first seen through the office window in the shipping company where she worked, he thought that inadequate. The police sergeant who lived next door to Kate's parents in Leyton impressed on him the opportunities in the force if he got qualifications, and Walter went to night school to study French and shorthand, which, the sergeant said, were not only assets in the Met but might even get him to Scotland Yard. Walter became a special constable in Leyton but still prevaricated – until at the Siege of Sidney Street, in which policemen died and 'feeling angry at this attack . . . on the law officers of the country', Walter decided to apply.

PC 549 Thompson, attached to Paddington Green station, patrolled the beat until the spring of 1913, when the government, nervous about increasing activity by the suffragettes in their pursuit of the vote, decided to expand Special Branch; the suffragettes had moved from disrupting political meetings and acts of public disorder to outright violence, such as damaging the property of those who opposed them and burning down buildings, including churches. When the evening detail paraded at Paddington Green, they were informed there were thirteen vacancies, for which a written exam was to be held at the Yard the next day. 'Curiously enough the words "There are thirteen vacancies", spoken by the senior officer', gave Walter a momentary feeling of hope: 'I was one of a family of thirteen, and that number had always been my lucky one.' But with only two years' service behind him, he didn't even consider it worth putting in an application. As the parade was dismissed, he heard a whispered: 'Thompson won't go in for it; he hasn't got sufficient education.'

The man who'd spoken was a one-time schoolteacher who 'held the certificates of that craft [and] was always chipping me about education', but Walter didn't let it rile him. Mentally, he agreed. His basic education had been poor. He'd had 'no difficulty in learning whatever I was taught', but from the age of eight or nine he'd had to work to help the family finances, as did the other children and his mother Rebecca. She had a little kiosk selling sweets in a local park in Kennington; he had a part-time job at Mr Blick's drapery shop, paying three shillings a week (of which he was allowed to keep three pence). Every morning he ran the three miles there before school to take down two dozen big wooden shutters and store them in the cellar, clean the windows and polish the brasses, went back at lunchtime to deliver parcels, and back again after school for more errands and, late in the evening, to put the shutters up. The work was hard even for a strong small boy, and he frequently fell asleep in class. He'd left Hackford Road with not much to show for it.

He was out on patrol when a trivial incident occurred in Bayswater Road around midnight that made him change his mind about applying for the Yard: a horse and cart came plodding in the direction of Covent Garden market with the driver fast asleep. Walter stepped into the road and brought the horse to a halt, at which the driver woke up. 'Fancy you noticing,' the man bantered. 'You ought to be a detective.' In fact, lots of drivers fell asleep at night, and the police were under instructions to be on the lookout because of the potential risk to them by motor-cars, although the roads were deserted and 'the horses knew the way so well they would have reached their destination even if the driver were dead'. Walter, however, took the remark as a kind of omen. When he came off duty he put in an application and a few hours later turned up at the Yard, where he found seventy other police hopefuls from across London. He sat the papers, which he thought simple enough, and a week later he found out that his trust in his lucky number wasn't misplaced.

If the suffragettes were instrumental in Walter's rapid promotion, he didn't always thank them: 'hour upon hour I used to loiter' outside the Kingsway headquarters of the movement that 'had set all England by the ears', often having to tail its members. 'Once you start . . . you have to go on until the quarry is safely ensconced for the night, so it can be a heartbreakingly unexciting business.' He got to know all the leaders, including Emmeline Pankhurst and her daughters Sylvia and Christabel, very well. Once, he was one of the officers who arrested Mrs Pankhurst at a nursing home in Notting Hill, where she'd been taken after a hunger strike in Holloway. Then and on other occasions he found enforcing the 'Cat and Mouse Act' distasteful.[2] More to his taste was the time he 'was ordered to follow a certain enterprising young suffragette whose activities were then earning her some celebrity. She realised that she was being followed, and as it began to pour with rain she looked round at me in an enquiring manner.' Walter shared his umbrella all the way to her home: 'I quite enjoyed that excessively moist day!'

The political extremists of every kind who flocked to Britain just before the First World War made a lot of work for the Yard, which had to prepare dossiers for their countries of origin. Anarchists of this period 'were the strangest of human phenomenon', Walter thought, as he rubbed shoulders with them in their clubs, where, to fit in, he went unshaven and shabby. His French was frequently useful. He trailed assorted oddities all over London, sitting in so many cinemas he 'was cured of ever becoming a "movie fan"'. Often he wore disguises. On one stakeout he and his colleague had 'a number of spare hats, caps, mackintoshes and jackets in a nearby shop [and], to the infinite astonishment of the customers, did a quick-change act behind the counter'.

As a junior officer, Walter had nothing to do with keeping surveillance on suspected foreign agents, but he took part in the great round-up of them on the August bank holiday of 1914 when war was declared. In the twelve hours from midnight, nearly 500 suspects across Britain were taken to prisons or internment camps. Subsequently, like most of Special Branch, he helped in collecting evidence in the Lody, Rosen and Müller spy cases. All three men were executed. Carl Kuperferle, whom Walter arrested at Victoria Station, would also have faced a firing squad at the Tower, but he hanged himself in Brixton Prison.

Spies, Walter found when he was posted to Southampton docks, continued trying to get in and out of the country, 'showing either consummate impudence or complete folly'. Two Frenchmen arrived from Holland claiming to have escaped from the Germans after months of internment and were passed through to rejoin their regiments. About a year later the pair arrived again with the same story – startling, but not impossible: it wasn't unknown for prisoners of war to escape twice. But when they turned up a third time, spinning the same yarn, they were handed to 'our more tempestuous Gallic colleagues to ascertain the truth of this remarkable trilogy'. Both men were executed.

Walter was on duty the night of the only Zeppelin raid on Southampton, which the passengers about to board the evening Channel packet saw through the open end of the huge baggage shed. The anti-aircraft guns opened up, several bombs dropped and the sound of the Zeppelin's motors faded in the direction of Portsmouth – at which point Walter was jabbed in the ribs with an umbrella 'by a sour-faced old lady who spluttered: "Most disgraceful. I shall complain to Mr Lloyd George about this. Why weren't we let on to the ship?"'

In January 1920 Walter was ordered back to London. He was sorry to leave Southampton, where the docks in which he worked were only minutes away on his motorbike, the hours were pretty regular and the family was settled – his two youngest sons were born there. Now, however, promoted to detective sergeant, he was to begin his life as a bodyguard.

*   *   *

Whatever the state of their relationship, in June 1920 something happened that made Walter forget his disagreements with Churchill and brought them close in a way that was to last. He was sleeping at Sussex Square when 'I heard Winston coming down the stairs in considerable haste, and as I reached the door of my room he was tucking his nightshirt into his trousers and I could see tears in his eyes'. His mother, Churchill said, was dying. Without putting on any more clothes, he ran to her house, two hundred yards away, talking disjointedly. The previous month Lady Randolph had tripped coming downstairs in very high heels and had so badly broken her leg that it had to be amputated. Gangrene set in. Now her leg was bleeding profusely, and she was not expected to survive.

> I noticed at this time more so than at any other the lisp as he spoke. This was always more noticeable when he spoke in a hurry or if he was very tired. I immediately said that if I were the same blood group I would willingly give my blood. He turned to me and put his arm around my shoulder and said: 'Thompson, I shall never forget this even if it is too late, as I am afraid it is.' Doctors arrived and, although my blood group was the same, it was too late.

Churchill was to be further battered by grief two months later: Marigold, his fourth child, died of septicaemia at the age of three while on holiday at Westgate-on-Sea in Kent. Churchill dashed from the Commons and went straight into the house, leaving Walter in the garden. 'A few minutes later he came out, with tears rolling down his cheeks. We walked up and down together for what seemed hours, never speaking a word. Then he was called back in. He was inside for half an hour, then he came out, calmer now, and told me she had died.' Churchill invited Walter in to view the little body – 'beautiful, like a piece of marble sculpture' – before taking refuge in the home of friends in Scotland, finding solace in his painting. He wrote to Clementine: 'I went out and painted a beautiful river in the afternoon light with crimson and golden hills in the background. Alas, I keep feeling the hurt of the Duckadilly [Marigold's pet name].' One of the things about Churchill that Walter was to comment on time and again was his resilience in the face of adversity, even personal tragedy.

Between the two deaths Churchill was instrumental in instigating a truce in Ireland, having moved from a position of believing that the IRA had to be militarily defeated to a position of believing that it wasn't possible without virtually laying waste to the country – in two and a half years over 1,300 people, including 550 troops and police, had been killed. An Irish peace delegation came to London. Walter saw IRA leader Michael Collins coming out of 10 Downing Street and found it hard to stomach that 'the gunman' was negotiating with the government while 'at that moment every soldier and policeman in Ireland was looking for him'. There were hurdles to be overcome in the north as well as the south. When Sir James Craig, the leader of Unionist Northern Ireland, stood in the way of giving the south independence, Churchill used subterfuge, in which Walter was complicit, to bring him and Collins together to thrash out some sort of understanding.

He invited Collins and Craig to go secretly to the Colonial Office. He told me to arrange for them to arrive at exactly the same time, but to enter by different doors. I brought this about by having a word with the Special Branch officers who were guarding the two men while they were in London. Collins came through the main entrance; Sir James entered through a door leading from the yard to the Foreign Office. An official showed Sir James into an empty room and left him there alone. A few minutes later Winston brought Collins to the same room. Immediately he was inside, Winston stepped back and locked the door. The dour Ulsterman and the rebel lad from Cork stood face to face for the first time. Half an hour later the door was unlocked and the two emerged. They were not exactly arm in arm; but a truce was proclaimed.

Two weeks later Collins and his colleague Arthur Griffiths met a committee of the British Cabinet. During these talks, Collins reproached Churchill for putting a price on his head, 'saying bitterly that he had been hunted day and night like an animal, with a £5,000 reward for his capture, dead or alive. "What are you grumbling about?" Winston said and from the wall of his office took down a framed notice issued by the Boers during the South African War, offering a reward for Winston Churchill. "You're lucky," Winston said. "They only offered £25 for me."'

The House moved into the autumn recess and Churchill went to stay at the Duke of Westminster's Highland home at Loch More. While he was there, Lloyd George called a Cabinet meeting on the subject of the Irish Question, and as most MPs were holidaying in Scotland or the north of England he arranged for it to take place in Inverness. Churchill and his bodyguard set off in a ramshackle hired car to negotiate the 120 miles of narrow country lanes turned into a quagmire by recent heavy rain. They were making good progress to reach Inverness for dinner when one of those cartoonish episodes that seemed to punctuate the high purpose of Churchill's life unfolded. There was a loud crack as they descended a steep hill – the brake linkage had snapped. The car was saved from going into a loch only because it sank to its front axles in the soft mud at the edge.

After an hour of slogging effort to extricate themselves, Walter and Churchill were plastered with mud. 'Each time we raised the car, it slid down again. Only after a huge effort, with stones rammed in below the jacks, did we manage to get the wheels on a bit of firm ground. Then the driver pointed out one fact that had not occurred to Winston or myself. With the brakes out of action, we could not use the car anyway.' It was a long wait for any vehicle to appear: a postman in a red Royal Mail van who refused to stop, although, slowing, he agreed to send a car back. To save time, Churchill stripped to his underwear by the side of the road, changing out of his muddy morning suit into his evening suit, which became equally muddy in the process. Only his silk socks and evening shoes, which he put on in the back of the old Ford that eventually rattled up, remained clean. He alighted at Inverness looking 'exactly like a Cabinet Minister from the ankles down. But above the ankles he looked very much more like a tramp.'

On 6 December 1921 the Irish Treaty was signed. The six predominantly Protestant counties of Ulster would remain part of the UK, retaining the separate Home Rule that Parliament had granted the previous year; the other twenty-six counties would be granted independence as the Irish Free State within the Empire, but still with allegiance to the Crown. Collins put his name to it, fearing all-out war but knowing that militants would see it as a betrayal. 'I have just signed my own death warrant,' he told Churchill. He was right on both counts. Bloody civil war ensued, former comrades in arms turning into bitter enemies. In April 1922, after Republicans occupied the Dublin Law Courts and other strongholds across the country, Churchill began to provide the Free State with arms and ammunition. At the end of June, having failed to dislodge the militants from the Law Courts by negotiation, Collins, now the commander-in-chief of the Irish army, tried to drive them out, using cannon borrowed from the departing British garrison. By the time the Republicans surrendered, having mined the building and set fire to it, thirty of them had been killed; later, seventy-seven were executed by Free State firing squads – and Collins was ambushed and shot dead.

In the middle of this opening engagement of the Irish civil war, Field Marshal Sir Henry Wilson, commander of the British army in Ireland in 1914 and then Chief of the Imperial General Staff, was assassinated on the steps of his London home, returning from Liverpool Street Station, where he'd unveiled a memorial to Britain's war dead.

Walter, who'd been sitting in the little room at the Commons set aside for Yard bodyguards, was stretching his legs when he glanced idly at a chattering teleprinter to read the news of Wilson's murder. He hurried to see Churchill, 'tucked up as safe as could be' working in his private room. Churchill had already heard. More: an IRA man had been picked up carrying a list of prominent Englishmen marked for death and Churchill's name led it. Taking Churchill's official car, Walter 'sped down Constitution Hill to Hyde Park Corner, through Hyde Park and along Bayswater Road to Sussex Square. Armed police were already at the front and the back of the building. I searched the house from top to bottom.' Walter's chiefs at Special Branch put an armour-plated Rolls-Royce at the Minister's disposal. That night, Churchill decided to sleep in the attic, telling his wife Clementine that his bedroom would be the first place an assassin would look, and got Walter to bring up his steel-backed chair and his Colt.

For the next few weeks Walter slept on the premises every night, and Churchill 'lived like a man in a fortress'. But it got on Churchill's nerves, and he had to be stopped on a number of occasions from trying to go out for a stroll. One day when he left the Colonial Office he refused to use the Rolls and walked through the streets to the House, not heeding Walter's implorations. '"You can look after my back, Thompson," I was told. "I'll attend to the front." My hand was never far away from my revolver.'

To make a would-be assassin's task more difficult, Walter tried to vary the daily route to the Commons, not getting much cooperation from Churchill, who insisted on driving through Hyde Park – which covered half the distance. One morning, entering the park from Bayswater Road, Walter

saw two men standing a little way back from the pathway. As I watched, one of them gave a signal, and looking ahead I saw the signal being acknowledged by a third man standing among a clump of trees. As I drew my gun, I saw that Churchill had seen the men and read the same significance into their presence. 'If they want trouble, they can have it,' he said. But it was not part of my duty to pander to his desire for a hand-to-hand scrap in Hyde Park. I leaned over and shouted in the chauffeur's ear: 'Step on it. Drive like the devil!'

and he pushed Churchill down in the back, shielding him with his body and holding him down until they were past. Sitting up,

Churchill bellowed: 'Don't ever do that again!' Well, Walter had decided that nobody's authority exceeded his own when it came to Churchill's safety – even Churchill's.

There were lighter moments even in such tense times. During the summer following the Anglo-Irish Treaty negotiations, Churchill took his family to Frinton-on-Sea in Essex, a favourite resort of wealthy Britons. 'In the circumstances, this holiday had its dangers, and three other Special Branch officers came along to help me with the night and day guard duties,' Walter wrote.

Sitting in the sun did not suit Winston, and one day he announced that he was going to build a sandcastle – 'the biggest and best ever'. He rolled up his trousers and took off his boots and socks, and we detectives smiled in anticipation of seeing the boss do some hard digging. We smiled too soon. I, for one, should have known that Churchill's way of doing any job was to set himself at the head of a hard-working team. While one man kept watch, I and one other were pressed into helping . . . [with] a gigantic system of mud-pie towers, surrounded by a vast system of moats which satisfyingly filled with seawater as the tide rolled in.

The children stood on the highest tower to watch the sea flood in. Tired from his labours, Winston sat on a wooden breakwater and put on one sock and one brown suede button boot. At that point he stopped to watch the children's antics, putting both feet on the sand. The next wave flowed over boot and sock. Winston looked down at his submerged feet. 'Well, Thompson,' he said. 'We must treat them both alike.' He put on the other sock, then the other boot, and plunged his foot back into the water. Then he sloshed towards the shore, saying, 'We must be thorough in these things, Thompson.'

*   *   *

Churchill often resolved not to be reckless, but it never lasted. He appeared to have no permanent sense of personal safety, and the desire to see for himself almost always got the better of him – as at the Sidney Street siege, the photographs of which prompted Arthur Balfour to ask in the House: 'I understand what the photographer was doing, but why the Home Secretary?' (Churchill called Balfour's comments 'not altogether unjust'.)

Churchill's impetuousness was in evidence from his childhood when he would leap from chair to chair and fall, hurting himself. On holiday in Bournemouth playing chase, he was trapped by his brother John and a cousin on a little bridge over a deep cleft in the cliff. Rather than be caught, he jumped for the branch of a tree below and fell thirty feet, rendering himself unconscious for three days and rupturing a kidney. As a young man, when a night-time fire broke out at a country house, he commandeered a fireman's helmet and got on the roof, shouting down orders.

He longed to confront danger. Commissioned in the 4th Hussars, he pulled strings to get to a small war in Cuba as a non-combatant, attached to the personal entourage of the Spanish general, riding only fifty yards behind the forward company. A few bullets whistled through a hut in which he slept; outside his tent, a bullet meant for him barely missed his head and killed a horse. He was exhilarated. When again at twenty-three he pulled strings to join Kitchener's Sudan expedition, he took part in the last great cavalry charge in British military history at Omdurman. Unable to use a sabre – on the way to the first of two campaigns in India he had permanently damaged his shoulder against a wharf in Bombay in his impatience to disembark from a skiff – his Mauser pistol almost certainly saved him from being killed.

In all, he took part in five campaigns, the last, sensationally, in South Africa against the Boers who attacked the British armoured train on which he was travelling. Here, he was only a newspaper war correspondent, but he took command, uncoupled the locomotive, got all the wounded on board and conveyed them to safety. Going back to try to free the rest of the train, he was taken prisoner. Escaping from detention, he walked 300 miles to freedom.

In South Africa, in one of those coincidences that knitted Churchill's and Walter's lives together, Walter's oldest brother, serving with the Scots Guards, shook his hand.

Churchill's impulsiveness didn't diminish with the years. When, as First Lord of the Admiralty in the First World War, he was driving to the Loch Ewe anchorage of the fleet, he spotted a searchlight on the roof of a large private house, thought it might belong to someone passing information to the enemy about fleet movements and went there at the head of an armed party; had the house been used for the purpose he suspected, the reception he received would not have been the puzzled one he got from the former Tory MP who used the searchlight at night to spot deer. When he was dismissed from his post after the failure of the Gallipoli campaign (which earned him the description of 'the butcher of Gallipoli'[3]), he took leave of the Commons, joined the army, crossed to Flanders and commanded a battalion in the trenches, a course of action that no other ex-Minister would have contemplated. A shell demolished his dugout after he'd just left it. He constantly went out under fire to inspect the defences, writing to Clementine: 'This is fun.'

Guarding the adventure-seeking Churchill was sometimes anything but fun. But that was also true of Lloyd George, as Walter had found out. The two shared many traits: the same terrible restlessness, the almost inhuman capacity for work, the ability to do without sleep yet to fall asleep almost at will (not for nothing were Lloyd George as Chancellor of the Exchequer and Churchill as President of the Board of Trade known as 'the radical twins'). And the same recklessness. When Walter was with Lloyd George at the Belgium peace talks in Brussels and Spa, he'd suddenly decided to cross over into Germany – in an open car. Walter had suffered acute anxiety. 'Those recognisable flowing locks . . . LG was about as popular a figure to the Germans as Wilhelm had been during the "hang-the-Kaiser" campaign. I had visions of an infuriated populace hanging him from the nearest lamppost.' But where Sinn Fein was concerned, Lloyd George was merely contemptuous of the threat, whereas Churchill was confrontational. Walter had even heard him tell his wife he was ready to 'fight it out'.

*   *   *

When Lloyd George fell in October 1922, Churchill fell with him. The coalition broke up, and the Conservative Bonar Law became PM, dissolved Parliament and went to the country. Churchill, a Liberal, resigned his secretaryships, prepared to fight his old seat in Dundee – and finished up in a nursing home with acute appendicitis.

Walter was sitting outside his nursing home room hours after Churchill had come out of the operating theatre and

> was unable to believe my ears when I heard him shouting my name as if he were at his desk. He wanted my newspaper! Then he wanted his secretary. Then he wanted several secretaries. He kept sending people to telephone people, insisting they answer little questions written to them on slips of paper; insisting that they come to the nursing home right away. When

his doctors told him he was sick, he told them he knew it and that was why they had been called in.

When Churchill wanted to rush off to Dundee to begin electioneering, the doctors refused to let him go. In fact, he was too ill to travel until six days before polling. Clementine, who'd recently given birth to their daughter Mary, went to Dundee in his stead and received a hostile reception. 'The idea against you seems to be that you are a "War Monger",' she wrote. 'But I am exhibiting you as a Cherub Peace Maker with little fluffy wings round your chubby face.' She warned: 'If you bring Sergeant Thompson, tell him to conceal himself tactfully as it would not do if the populace thought you were afraid of them.'

Churchill still had his stitches in ('I shall wear them in remembrance of you,' he told his doctors) and Walter helped to put him on a stretcher into the special carriage attached to the Scottish express. He got off it with the aid of a stick, but was so weak that Walter had to carry him from street level to his hotel room, up platforms at public meetings and up stairs in assembly halls. It was no mean feat of strength: Churchill was not the seventeen stones he would weigh during the Second World War, but he was still a heavy man.

The security risk in Scotland was minimal, but there was great antagonism, and Walter was shocked, at a large meeting in the Cairn Hall, when the chairman's announcement that the candidate, with the audience's permission, would speak while sitting was greeted with a crescendo of jeers: '"Stand up, Churchill, stand up, Churchill!" His face tight with pain and fatigue, he tried to rise and half did so, then slumped down again, and then made it to his feet and stayed standing for a full hour. He would not give up. But the strain was too much, and on our return to the hotel he had to go straight to bed.' As it turned out, his 'bleakly brave' performance was to little avail. He lost – to a Prohibitionist, of all things, in what Walter considered 'the most drunken of cities, at least for its size, that I have ever seen in the British Isles'. Met by reporters in London, Churchill quipped that he was now without a seat, without a party, without an office and without an appendix. But just as he wasn't without his sense of humour, he wasn't without his bodyguard. The authorities still believed that as a signatory of the Irish Treaty Churchill remained a Sinn Fein target – and Churchill became the first out-of-office Minister to retain his personal protection.

Walter thought Churchill wasn't sorry to give up his responsibilities: 'Illness had vitiated his boundless vigour and he needed to recuperate.' He even gave Walter two days off (promising he wouldn't leave the house) – but almost at once had his secretary ring to say they were leaving for Cannes in a few hours. His guard 'was in no way surprised' at another sudden Churchill decision, but he felt guilty, knowing that this holiday would be protracted (in fact, it lasted five months). So Kate again was stuck with the children on her own. At least he'd moved the family to Westcliff-on-Sea to be near his parents, who were now living there, as was his older married sister, Emily.

In Cannes Walter stayed in a cottage opposite Churchill's rented villa, sharing it with the chauffeur and his wife, who was Clementine's maid. Churchill wrote (he'd begun *The World Crisis*, his history of the First World War), swam in the sea and painted. Walter, still complaining but resigned, lugged the equipment and sat watching him on this or that rock or promontory, enjoying the peace and beauty of the Côte d'Azur. On one of their excursions, at the villa of Churchill's cousin, previously the Duchess of Marlborough but now married to the millionaire balloonist Jacques Balsan, Walter innocently got drunk for the only time in his life. Their hosts had provided an excellent but soporific meal – and while Churchill painted on the shoulder of a slope, Balsan placed a bottle of white wine in an ice bucket at Walter's side. 'Wholly unacquainted with wine either as to flavour or efficacy', he sipped for two hours. When Churchill had done for the day and Walter stood, he was perplexed to find 'The sun seemed in the wrong part of the sky and the whole stretch of water was aslant'. Folding up the easel, he got paint all over himself. He hoped the Old Man didn't notice his condition: 'Perhaps he thought it was sunstroke.'

As he grew stronger, Churchill did away with the stick and discovered the casinos in Cannes and Monte Carlo, which he visited frequently, losing more often than he won but winning enough to pay the rent on the villa.

Nearly every night, after dinner, he went to the casino. I waited in the car until he came out, usually in the early morning. After a while he began to send the car back and walk the return journey, puffing and panting up the steep hill to the villa. I took no exception to this, for we both needed the exercise, and it was really very pleasant to breathe in the mimosa's perfume.

Churchill 'was still receiving a regular supply of threatening letters from Ireland', and one night as they went up the hill he suddenly asked if Walter had his revolver; taken by surprise, Walter hesitated before saying yes. The hesitation made Churchill demand to see it and Walter showed him. Some weeks later, asked the same question, Walter answered affirmatively and Churchill said no more. Following Churchill up a narrow part of the road, Walter patted his gun pocket and found nothing there – putting on a fresh jacket to go out, he'd forgotten to transfer the weapon. 'This incident was a useful corrective to the carefree attitude that the Cannes way of life engenders,' he told himself. 'I never again forgot the revolver.'

Apart from the chauffeur, Churchill had no male staff in Cannes and Walter usually saw him to his room, where he scattered his clothes in all directions (for Walter to pick up and fold for the maid to attend to in the morning), put on a silk vest, brushed his wispy hair and, as soon as he was in bed, checked that the pillow was his – it travelled everywhere with him – before pulling on the black satin eyemask he took from under it and without which he never slept, even in a car. Walter was on hand in the mornings, too, as Churchill, after his bath, bathed his eyes, sprayed his throat and 'put on his face a fluid called larola, which kept his complexion very fair; suntans were not fashionable on the Côte d'Azur in 1923'. It amused him that Churchill sometimes forgot to don one of the gaudy dressing gowns he loved and, 'deep in thought, strolled naked from room to room. When one of the female servants working in the house complained to Mrs Churchill about this, Winston was astonished; he had no recollection of doing any such thing.'

With unemployment at the staggering figure of 1.3 million, talk of a general election was in the air and Churchill found it necessary to make a quick trip to London. On the way, he told Walter uncomfortably that it was unlikely he'd be returning with him when he went back to collect his family: Scotland Yard, he thought, would want to discontinue his protection and, Walter could tell, 'he was feeling guilty at having a bodyguard provided at the taxpayers' expense at a time when he was unable to serve the country in return'. For days he put off calling the head of the Criminal Investigation Department, doing so, finally, only at Walter's insistence. 'I was in the room while he spoke with Sir Wyndam [Childs] . . . After a few minutes' conversation, a smile came over his face as he turned to me and said: "Thompson, you are returning with me."'

CHAPTER 3

Chartwell and Fisticuffs

Attempting to stem unemployment, the Conservative Prime Minister Stanley Baldwin raised tariff barriers against imports, the very issue on which Churchill had deserted the party for the Liberals nineteen years earlier. In the general election of 1923 he stood in Leicester on a free trade ticket and lost to a Labour man. The first Labour government came to power. Churchill was still writing at a prodigious rate his four-volume history of the war but, barred from the political fray, Walter thought he was 'like a fish out of water' and 'a kicker of wastepaper baskets, with an unbelievably ungoverned bundle of bad temper. It [was] better to stay away from him at such time, as his family sought to do, and any such of his retainers as could take the day off, or find an emergency miles or countries away.'

Fortunately a new venture had arrived to channel his energies: while still Colonial Secretary he'd bought Chartwell Manor.

Until now, Churchill hadn't been well off financially, as some of his clothing proclaimed, to Walter's distress: 'seeing him at close quarters, as I did, I saw his unwillingness to spend money on himself. His striped trousers were threadbare at the knee.' Walter himself was always immaculately turned out, his suits pressed, his shoes brought to a polish with a deer bone. But Churchill had had three windfalls: he came into a great deal of money on the deaths of his mother and his great-grandmother, Lady Londonderry, and when a distant cousin died in a train accident he inherited an estate in Ulster worth £4,000 a year in rents and revenues (perhaps £60,000 today). He was also now earning large sums from newspaper and magazine articles.

Together, Churchill and his bodyguard scouted the Home Counties, alighting on Chartwell on the same summer day that Churchill's last child, Mary, was born. They found it three or four miles from the little town of Westerham, overlooking the Weald of Kent. Churchill's official biographer, Martin Gilbert, interviewed the estate agent, H. Norman Harding, who showed them the property, taking them there in Churchill's car. Getting in, he remarked: 'It's the darkest car I have ever been in,' to which Churchill replied, 'Well, you see, it is armoured, and the windows are bullet resisting and I have a loaded revolver.'

And he produced it; and in front, sitting by the chauffeur, was a gentleman, who, he informed me, was Detective Sergeant Thompson, and Mr Churchill said, 'He also has a revolver.' He then turned round, slid back a small shutter, and said: 'You see that car behind us?' As far as I remember there were three men in it. 'That car will accompany us ten miles out of town, and on our return will pick us up again and escort us back to the Colonial Office or to my home.' He then went on to say: 'I have a number of threatening letters each week, some telling me the actual time and method of my death, and I don't like it.'

It was less than two months since Sir Henry Wilson's assassination.

Churchill was full of plans for Chartwell on that first visit, telling Walter 'there were many parcels of land not attached to the original grounds that he wanted to have' (in time he got what he wanted, expanding his 80 acres to 500, including the adjoining farm). As to the house, which was in poor repair, it had to be largely rebuilt and considerably extended. It took almost two years before the family could move in. In the meantime, Churchill leased Hosey Rigg nearby, where Lewis Carroll had written *Alice in Wonderland*.

*   *   *

He was still trying to get back into Parliament. He put himself up in Leicester when a seat fell vacant and lost, then in Westminster, in a constituency embracing the Abbey and the Houses of Parliament but also some of London's worst slums and roughest districts, including Soho. He was moving back towards the Conservatives, telling his bodyguard: 'I feel that the present Conservative Party is more liberal in its outlook than the old Liberal Party ever was,' though he wasn't yet calling himself a Conservative, instead standing as an 'Independent Anti-Socialist'.

Churchill attacked socialism, fascism and communism and his hustings were good sport for anyone spoiling for a fight. They attracted attacks from strong-arm thugs with knuckle-dusters and clubs; they also attracted the help of Commander Oliver Locker-Thompson, 'England's most colourful hater of communism', who turned up with a group of protectors armed with mallets. Walter took to standing on a box to keep an eye on the crowd and got into so many mêlées he lost twenty pounds in weight.

On the last evening of electioneering, Churchill left a meeting near Long Acre on the way to another, and Walter had to use a truncheon to force a way to the car for him, his brother John and Brendan Bracken, the red-headed MP for North Paddington who was always Churchill's stalwart supporter. The mob swarmed after them – and the driver turned into a dead end. It was rather like the Abdin Palace over again. As the driver sought room to turn, 'his goggles gone and his windshield smashed to powder', Walter 'sprang to the running board and knocked down so many who tried to manhandle the occupants of the car that I grew tired'. Churchill 'was determined to do his bit . . . and I was the recipient of his fists on the back of my neck'. Walter couldn't prevent Bracken from being stabbed twice, 'to the bone in hip and thigh'. Once an ambulance came for the unfortunate Bracken, it was on to another meeting in a hall in Berwick Street – and Walter got a punch right on the jawbone, delivered by 'a strong man with his full shoulder'. He staggered but didn't go down (actually admiring the punch) and laid out his attacker. For days he himself 'had a bit of a swelling . . . and a pair of green-yellow eyes'.

When the votes were counted at Caxton Hall, Churchill, who'd 'been rolled about by the mob a good bit', at first seemed to have triumphed. But when a re-count was demanded, Churchill found he'd failed – by forty-seven votes – his third defeat in a row. On the way home, Walter didn't know what to say, except he was sorry. As they passed the Parliament buildings, Churchill 'saluted them with a long wave. "You know, Thompson, they really can't run that thing without me. I've lost again, so nobody will be thinking to shoot me tonight. We'll rest tonight."'

Within the space of twelve months there was another general election. Churchill stood in Epping (the name later changed to Woodford), this time as a 'Constitutionalist' but with the backing of the Conservatives, to whom he returned the following year, nonchalantly remarking that 'Anyone can rat [change parties], but it takes a certain ingenuity to re-rat'. The Tories formed the government. And Churchill was back, with a whacking majority, Baldwin making him Chancellor of the Exchequer, the office that had once been his father's. Churchill, who, Walter had observed, 'was only silent when he painted', was lost for words when he found out. Perhaps, Walter thought, Churchill, 'considered by his father to be too dull for anything but the army', had found 'approval in his father's ghost'. Many people, Walter recorded,

> were puzzled by Baldwin's appointing Winston Chancellor. Some said that Baldwin was a quiet, pipe-smoking person who needed a 'strong man' at his elbow. Others said that Baldwin was a wily old fox who, committed to a return to the gold standard to satisfy the bankers, wanted somebody to take the blame when this policy led to unemployment . . . Either view could have been right.

As Chancellor, Churchill moved from Chartwell to 11 Downing Street. The appointment meant upheaval for Walter, too. With the Old Man back in office, his workload was going to be heavy, and he couldn't afford to be two hours away on the Kent coast. He brought Kate and the children back from Westcliff to Sydenham.

Churchill's first Budget was on 28 April 1925. As Walter helped him on with an ankle-length blue melton fur-lined overcoat with an astrakhan collar, he 'thought I recognised the garment. I asked him if it was the one I had seen at the Sidney Street siege. "Ah, so you were there, too, Thompson," he said, before saying, "Yes, it's the same coat. It has had a new fur lining, a new outside and a new astrakhan collar." He held out his arms and looked fondly at the sleeve. "But it's the same coat"' – an explanation that nowadays may put viewers of *Only Fools and Horses* in mind of Trigg's broom.

'As happy as a sandboy, his top hat extra glossy', Churchill emerged into Downing Street, where a large crowd waited, with Clementine, his sixteen-year-old daughter Diana and his son Randolph, then fourteen, at his side. Walter, who usually carried Churchill's documents on the walk to the House, offered to carry the dispatch case. 'No, no, Thompson!' Churchill told him, his baby face wreathed in smiles. 'There's only one proper person to guard this little box, and that person is me!'

The Budget received scathing criticism from many quarters: Churchill did return Britain to the gold standard, rejecting the counsel of John Maynard Keynes, who said markets abroad wouldn't be able to afford British exports. George Bernard Shaw was a Churchill critic. 'In a letter he invited Winston to attend the first night of his play. "I am enclosing two tickets," Shaw wrote, "one for you and one for a friend, if you have one." Winston replied, regretting that he would be unable to go on the first night – "But I shall certainly attend on the second night – if you have one."'

Keynes proved to be right, not just about Britain's overseas fortunes but in his prediction of deflation and calls for lower wages. A Royal Commission on the coal-mining industry recommended just such a reduction; the mine owners, unable to compete with the German, Polish and Belgian coalfields, additionally wanted longer hours. Walter had just checked the security at Downing Street and was off home when the Yard told him that the miners' night shifts had downed tools and walked out, and that the Trades Union Congress was bringing out every major industry.

Often, coming in to work from Sydenham on his big ten-horse-power BSA combination, Walter picked up some of his colleagues. Next day, with no trains or underground, buses or trams,

the roads were black with people waiting to get lifts to town. In a jiffy I had a pillion rider and three in my sidecar. All offered to pay their normal fares towards the costs of my petrol but, of course, I refused . . . It was the same every day. Later, when I overhauled and cleaned the machine I found a quantity of coins on the floor of the sidecar that my passengers surreptitiously dropped en route.

Churchill was vociferous in calling the strike an attempt to hold the nation to ransom and in demands for a military response. Extra men were assigned to his family's protection while he involved himself in maintaining food supplies and essential services with the use of troops, special constables and volunteers, 'rushing from place to place, giving orders, cajoling, reprimanding, organising, getting things done at top speed'.

Printers were among the strikers, so there were no newspapers. The Prime Minister badly needed to counter the *British Worker* news-sheet that the strikers were bringing out and jumped at the offer of the militantly independent editor of the *Morning Post* to use his plant and the help of those of his staff willing to work. Baldwin gave the job to Churchill ('who loved his papers more than his food,' Walter said).

When he first visited the *Post*, on the corner of Aldwych, Walter was horrified: 'it was a worse security risk than a country bazaar' – anyone could enter without a pass and go wherever they wanted. Churchill, 'determined to run everything' and deeply absorbed, ignored his bodyguard's repeated worries, 'singing abominable melodies through his nose'. Walter instituted a system of passes. Then the union stopped the workers. Churchill called Lord Beaverbrook, the proprietor of the *Daily Express*, who at once sent his night superintendent. 'This man could not be touched by union control and sat down by himself and all alone played the linotype machine like an organ, while Churchill stood at his shoulder. It was only two pages, but it was a start.'

Churchill got the Automobile Association to carry out distribution. He rang a submarine base at Devonport and had some of their expert mechanics sent over. He rang trade schools and university printing departments to recruit more helpers. 'We had,' said Walter, 'a lot of very well-educated men running all manner of toys all over the building.' When the building was attacked, Churchill drummed up police reinforcements and a company of Irish Guards. In a few days his *British Gazette* was up to eight pages and its first printrun of a few thousand rose to two and a quarter million.

Even when an agitator got into the building and threw a steel bar into the press, which gave forth 'an unearthly metallic screaming and ground to a halt', Churchill wasn't stymied. He 'lighted a cigar as he regarded the dying giant' – and rang the Royal Navy dockyard at Chatham; 'the mangled unit of the machinery was isolated from the body of the main assembly, hoisted by block and tackle and set in a truck.' It was returned the same afternoon 'all shined up, wrapped in bunting and with a Union Jack sticking out of her top'.

Every day Churchill was at the *Post*'s offices until 2.30 a.m., then back at his desk in the Treasury by 7.30. Walter, with him for all but the four or so hours he slept, was so tired that 'once I went sound asleep while standing up, leaning against a doorjamb, just listening to the sound of those damn presses, and toppled over with great embarrassment into a pile of paper boxes'.

The indefatigable Churchill held talks with union leaders and still found time to attend the House in the afternoons, where the Opposition called his newspaper 'trash' and a 'rag'. To one attack 'Winston replied: "If you ever let loose another General Strike on us, we shall let loose another *British Gazette* on you." After this debate, Winston and I walked back to Downing Street. He was laughing to himself. "I expect this is the last newspaper I shall have the pleasure of editing. But it was not the first. I edited a school journal called *The Critic*. Unfortunately there was only one issue."' Walter particularly liked Churchill's later reply when the Opposition criticised his editorials as propagandist and inflammatory: 'I decline utterly to be impartial as between the fire brigade and the fire!'

For most of the nine days that the General Strike lasted, Baldwin was on holiday in Aix-les-Bains taking the waters. His return coincided with its end, but instead of praising his Chancellor, 'who broke the strike and made the settlement',[1] Baldwin took the credit. Walter, in the public gallery of the Commons, felt Churchill's 'shock of ingratitude'. Looking down on Baldwin, 'With the evidence of many days of the sunshine of southern France on his face, while Churchill looked dead and ashen and almost useless', he resolved that if the Yard ever assigned him to Baldwin he would refuse.

Hurt and depressed, Churchill went to spend a weekend near Dieppe at the home of his friend the Duke of Westminster, something he often did. At Dover Walter got a jolt: a group of Sinn Feiners were on the dockside, one of whom he personally had experience of and three others he recognised from photographs. Not that he needed this knowledge, because the ten or a dozen men were wearing Sinn Fein badges and 'being ostentatious in their anti-British calumniations'. Seeing Walter and his charge, they went aboard and into the steamer's saloon. Walter escorted Churchill to his cabin, stepped back ashore and called the Yard. A sergeant who was on Customs duty at the port was detailed to travel on the steamer in disguise.

Ostentatiously Walter 'passed through the saloon looking like Scotland Yard in every dart of the eye . . . Some of the ship's officers came with me to embellish the appearance of our "security tour". I meaninglessly inspected passports and pocketbooks, opened a valise or two, and asked one of the officers to show me his gun (though I had to loan him a Webley). In less than a full minute the Irish knew I was the man to follow, for where I would be there would be Churchill also.'

Walter and Churchill were first off the boat at Calais; lifted out of the doldrums and 'extra lively and simply delighted' by the possibility of danger, Churchill ate in a local restaurant by the station where the Dieppe train was standing. When the Paris train came in, with Churchill locked in the restaurant lavatory, Walter boarded it 'with a large supply of hand luggage, two of the bags bearing Churchill's name. The train pulled out – and all the Irish were riding with me. I examined tickets, peered into bags that were none of my business, followed conductors ... I was particularly impressive in the dining car.' At the Gare St-Lazare Walter and baggage were taken by other Yard men, who appeared as French baggage clerks and office staff, into the manager's office, 'where I was momentarily invisible. I went quickly through a side door and directly into the back of a goods van, dropping the tarpaulin flap, and was driven to the Gare du Nord, where I boarded a train for Dieppe.'

Churchill had been at the duke's estate for hours, picked up by one of the duke's chauffeurs and guarded by the Yard man who'd gone aboard at Dover. As Walter related his travels, Churchill, 'dressed in hunting pink and velvet cap, said, "Maybe they were more interested in you than in me", and charged away with the weekend party on a boar hunt'.

In the late 1920s Churchill had a sneaking admiration for Benito Mussolini, who'd made himself the dictator of Italy. For all its violence, Churchill saw fascism as a bulwark against communism and socialism. Having spent a week during summer recess 1927 with the Mediterranean fleet on exercise off Greece, Churchill took the opportunity of a face-to-face meeting, landing at Brindisi with Walter and taking a night train to Rome. First he paid a visit to the Italian King, Victor Emmanuel, who met him courteously at the palace entrance and after lunch just as courteously saw him out. 'Winston's visit to the arrogant Mussolini was very different,' Walter was to say. 'According to the Italian press, they spent an hour in "cordial conversation". The little I saw of the meeting seemed far from cordial.' Churchill 'had a cigar going' as he and his bodyguard came to the door of Il Duce's office and was told by an official that he couldn't enter while smoking. Walter wondered 'what Winston would do and was surprised when he simply dropped the cigar on the floor and ground it out with his foot. Then he entered. Mussolini remained seated at his large desk at the far end, making no attempt to greet his guest.' The room was immensely long, 'the idea being,' Walter supposed, 'that a visitor had a long clattering walk along marble floors before he reached the dictator – by which time he was supposed to be over-awed and malleable . . . [but] Winston reached into his pocket, took a new cigar from his case, pierced it and applied a light to it. When the cigar had a powerful head of smoke, he began the long walk.'[2]

Churchill's admiration for Mussolini's strong-arm rule was to wane over the years and 'the waning began during this visit to Rome'.

*　　*　　*

Once he'd acquired Chartwell, Churchill set about improving it, adding a new wing at the back, providing a dining room at ground level, a sitting room on the floor above, and a bedroom for Clementine on the floor above that. While the architect and the builders toiled, Churchill set to in the grounds with a whole army of gardeners, diggers and planters – and Walter. A bell installed on the roof rang a different number of times if Churchill or his bodyguard were wanted at the house.

Churchill found plenty to do, planting fruit trees, hundreds of strawberry runners and asparagus, creating an azalea glade and a water garden, reshaping and re-laying the lawns. 'Having nothing to do but watch over him', Walter joined in: 'it gave me a proper kind of exercise I had been missing while jumping about the Houses of Parliament, election meetings and the innumerable colleges and universities that were for ever offering him a new degree or an invitation to make a graduation speech.' Walter was 'head lawn mower and it was fun to use my arms again – I have tremendous arm power'.

Churchill 'loved to stand on his porches and shout at us, giving wild and encouraging instructions', but he got stuck in himself, to Walter's satisfaction: 'Winston had areas of fat that could not be worn with comfort . . . and which melted away when a gratifying hardness came back to him', and he was happy to take his turn to go up to the house to collect the things for the tea breaks. This Churchill, dressed in one-piece overalls that he called his rompers, like a small child's playsuit – 'in embryo Winston's famous wartime siren suit' – a cigar protruding from beneath a variety of headgear, might have been a character from Lewis Carroll.

All his life Churchill was fascinated by the possibilities of changing the course of water, as he'd told his bodyguard on the banks of the Jordan, imagining the energy of that river harnessed and 'turned into electricity [which] will indeed make this desert blossom'. Until now, Walter humorously observed, Churchill 'had only been able to gratify this urge on visits to the seaside'. Now, in the grounds of Chartwell, where he had a lake, fed by many streams, and two small ponds, 'he began devising ways of using the constant flow of water to provide more pools'.

Churchill got a team of men from Westerham to build a dam across the top end of the lake where the water entered, causing a new lake to form as the water built up behind it. This allowed the first lake to empty for the first time in twenty-five years and the accumulation of mud to be removed. The plan was to take this away in little trucks running on rails across the lake bed. But the rails couldn't be laid until the mud had dried and, 'as usual, Winston was impatient for action. Day after day he patted the surface of the mud with his foot to test its viscosity. Finally, for no reason beyond his eagerness to get on with the job, he pronounced the mud dry enough.' He called for a plank, which Walter duly fetched from the builders' material by the house and laid out towards the centre of the lake. With Walter's

policeman's weight on the firmly based end holding the plank steady, gingerly Winston began edging along it.

It turned out he was wrong about the mud being dry. I could have told him, but he liked to find things out for himself. When he was halfway along, well away from dry land, the plank began to wobble. He waved his arms wildly . . . the plank tilted, and over he went. He managed to keep one foot up on the plank, but the other, together with one arm as high as the shoulder, plopped into the stinking slime, sending up an appalling smell.

Walter pulled him out with a lot more slime covering him now than it had on the road to Inverness. Walter fell about laughing. Churchill wasn't prepared to see the joke and demanded slippers and dressing gown. When Walter came back from the house with these, 'I could not see him at first. Then, hearing splashing sounds from the new lake, I climbed up past the dam. Winston was in the water, rolling over and over like a porpoise, once more his usual clean, pink self.'

The next time Churchill took a header into the mud, Walter went with him – the locking shank on one of the skips that the workmen hauled back and forth along the rails hadn't been fastened and it suddenly tilted, the contents knocking them both on their backs. Churchill found the situation as funny as Walter.

Even when he was Chancellor, Churchill squeezed out time at weekends to carry on with his building work. A large leak developed in the new bitumen foundations of the top lake, and to trace it he and his bodyguard shifted a lot of muddy soil with shovels. One day Walter's overalls

became so wet that I had to take them off and give up work. Unwilling to ruin my suit, I stood off at some distance, contenting myself for the moment with unadulterated guard duty. Winston plodded on alone, digging and tunnelling like a badger.

The bell on the house signalled me to go and pick up a message for him. I went and got it, then looked to find where he had burrowed to. Walking round the lake, I stepped over an opening. From below came an angry shout of 'Damn you!' I had found him. I looked into the opening and said: 'Were you speaking to me, sir?' 'Sorry, Thompson,' he said. 'I didn't know it was you.' I decided to push him a little. 'Whether it was me or not,' I said, 'there was no need to speak like that.' His contrite manner disappeared. 'What would you have said if you'd had clods of earth dropped on your head?'

Churchill was never still. If he wasn't writing in his office ('my factory'), he was playing polo (a special strap allowed him to use his damaged arm) or 'looking for more ways of getting water to do his bidding'. He decided to enlarge a small pond at the side of the house, the inflow to pass under a walk made of large paving stones, the outflow to pass over a waterfall into a swimming pool being built at a lower level. The majority of the work was carried out by the men he employed, but Churchill chose to enlarge the pool himself, using bricks and rock to edge it. 'Naturally, Winston was the craftsman, I the labourer. I mixed immense quantities of mortar, but there was never enough to keep up with Winston's capacity for using it. Typically, where others would have applied the mortar with a trowel, Winston used a shovel.'

The job gave him a taste for bricklaying, the press heard, and the bricklayers' union invited him to become a member, only to withdraw the invitation weeks later under internal protest that he wasn't a craftsman. Churchill, furious, his subscription already paid, refused to return his card and next day employed a local builder to put up another cottage in the grounds, announcing that under guidance he would help. He was busy for some time after this with other responsibilities, and the cottage was at bedroom level when one day he appeared, rompered, gloved and smoking a cigar, to begin his apprenticeship.

'Come along, Thompson,' he said. 'We are going to do some bricklaying.' 'You are,' I replied, 'but I'm not.' 'Why not?' he asked. 'Because I'm not a member of a union and I don't want to be.' 'All right,' he said, 'you can come along and watch.'

We went over to the half-built cottage. We climbed a long ladder and I helped him across the temporary flooring. The builder came over and showed Winston where to begin: he was to build a central wall that was to run from the outside wall to the centre of the building, forming a divider between two rooms.

Winston worked busily all morning, until the wall was waist high. Then the bell rang from the house and he left for his lunch. As soon as he had gone, the builder came over to me, a worried look on his face. 'Look at his wall,' he said. 'If he puts one more layer of bricks on it, it'll topple over.' I looked at the wall. From the bottom up, each layer of bricks was progressively more out of line so that the wall came upwards in a gentle curve. I hated to have to tell him. I considered that on the subject of bricklaying his feelings had been hurt enough. But obviously the wall could not be left in this dangerous state. 'Pull it down,' I said, 'and rebuild it while he's at lunch.' 'I'm not pulling it down,' he said. So I did.

Knowing that Churchill would be a couple of hours, Walter had the wall redone ('But don't make it too straight, or he's sure to notice. Just make it good enough for safety'). Eventually

Churchill's head appeared at the top of the ladder. The builder and his men tried to look unconcerned as he took me by the arm and drew me to the centre of the floor, where we stood looking at the wall from its end . . . He leaned out and looked along one side of the wall. Then he walked round behind my back and looked along the opposite side. Then he asked me to move aside so that he could stand directly behind the end of the wall and take a sighting along the top.

He held both arms stretched in front of him. The builder and I exchanged worried looks. 'Look at that, Thompson,' Winston said. 'My first effort – and straight as a die!' A clap of laughter exploded from the builder. Winston turned, a look of great surprise on his face. 'What's the matter?' he asked. 'I've got a pain,' the builder said.[3]

These Chartwell years were the happiest of Walter's early married life. In the first full summer he brought down the family on the motorcycle (his eldest son Harold, then eight, behind him, Kate in the massive sidecar holding Grace, not quite three, Fred, six, and Harvey, four, sitting between her feet). That year they stayed in Westerham; in the second summer Walter found a cottage to rent at the end of the road leading to the manor, and his family spent even more time in the grounds. For Harold, these were 'two wonderful summers, fishing on one side of the lake, swimming on the other, though that stopped – Churchill let a scout troop camp by the lake and one of the lads got drowned'. He remembers the loud laughter and teasing that went on among the Churchill family, though the Thompson children had little to do with them, and Churchill's kindness: 'He was good to us in those school holidays. We also went to a wonderful Christmas party, with a massive Christmas tree, wonderful food and a present for everybody.' To this day the friendly banter between his father and Churchill, 'the fondness between them' as they worked together, occasionally sharing a cigar, stays with him. 'I can see Dad now, mixing up cement and handing Churchill the bricks. Churchill didn't do much on the labour side of the job at all.' His father, as he remembers it, 'had no alternative but to always be with Churchill, always. I mean, he was on duty all the time, even when he was supposed to be taking leave – Churchill was so difficult with anybody other than Dad it was hard to find someone else to take over.'

It was at Chartwell four or five years later that something happened that bound Walter even more closely to Churchill, as his offer to give blood to Lady Randolph had bound Churchill to Walter.

One day I was in the garden with Winston when a servant called me to the telephone. When I came back, he immediately saw I was worried and asked me what was wrong. I told him that a school doctor had examined Grace, then eight, and said that her middle ear was gone and that she would be deaf for life. Winston looked appalled, then, typically, surged into action. 'We'll see about this, Thompson,' he said and went straight to the telephone to call a specialist in Harley Street. The specialist saw my daughter. Grace had her tonsils and adenoids removed and retained her hearing. Winston paid all her medical bills.

Five times in five years, guarding his little box, Churchill made the walk from Downing Street to the Commons, with Walter in attendance, then lost office when Labour returned briefly to power, again under Ramsay MacDonald ('The Boneless Wonder' Churchill called him – 'a cruel appellation' even Walter thought). His time at the Treasury wasn't regarded as a success; he'd been bored by humdrum financial matters and been rigidly orthodox – there'd been nothing of the imaginative radical about Chancellor Churchill. Briefly he was Tory Shadow Chancellor. But, again, he fell. The issues were protective tariffs, his old *bête noire*, and Home Rule for India – dominion status putting her on a level with Canada, South Africa, Australia and New Zealand. Churchill, an imperialist to the tips of his fingers, was appalled; the British Raj was the jewel in the imperial crown. India, he told Parliament, was 'a geographical term. It is no more a united nation than the Equator.' Hostility towards him in his own party forced his resignation; he became a leading member of the India Defence League. Wryly Walter observed that the Old Man no sooner lost one set of enemies than he acquired another. Churchill was now a political pariah, out of joint with the times, a Member of Parliament, and a hard-working one, who delivered some of the great speeches of his life, but who was 'condemned, though he did not then know it, to more than ten years in the political wilderness'.

Walter was withdrawn by the Yard once Churchill was no longer a government Minister and went off to other duties, keeping an eye on the activities of extreme political bodies (and, despite himself, having a sneaking admiration for Oswald Mosley). After nearly nine years with Churchill he felt strange and 'lost for a while . . . A policeman is not an automaton. My equilibrium was certainly destroyed at first.'

CHAPTER 4

Guilt in New York

In December 1931 Churchill, who'd just started a lecture tour in the United States, took a taxi from the Waldorf Astoria in New York to have dinner at the Fifth Avenue home of the financier Bernard Baruch. He found he didn't have the address with him but was confident he'd recognise the building. The cab cruised around for an hour without success, and an increasingly exasperated Churchill got out on the Central Park side of the avenue to search on foot. Crossing to the other side, he made two mistakes: the traffic lights – new to him, as they hadn't yet been introduced back home – were against him, and he forgot that Americans drive on the right. He glanced left, stepped out and was struck by a car that dragged him several yards.

Covered in blood, Churchill was taken by a cab to the nearby Lenox Hill hospital, where he staggered into the casualty department. Asked if he wanted free or private treatment, he replied, 'I can pay. I'm a British statesman' – and collapsed.

While these events played out, Walter, who'd accompanied Churchill on the trip by special arrangement with Scotland Yard, was in bed at the hotel, having previously spent twenty-six hours without sleep. He was awoken by Mrs Churchill banging on his door to tell him what had happened. Walter was beside himself with remorse. Churchill hadn't slipped Walter's leash: Walter had let him off it, though unwillingly. 'Why did you bring me to leave me behind on the first day?' he'd asked, bleary-eyed. 'I can't control you by remote control.' They 'both became rather heated, until [Churchill] finally said, "You will be no use to me tomorrow when I make my speech unless you have some rest – it is important for you to be fully awake there."' There'd been other occasions when Churchill had got stubborn about going somewhere unescorted and Walter had let him, 'but followed him without his knowledge, shadowing him from a distance'. This time, he reasoned, Churchill, delivered door to door, could come to no harm.

He and Mrs Churchill rushed to the hospital. Walter 'could not forgive myself. During all the years I had guarded the man I had never let him out of my sight on the roadway . . . [he] lack[ed] enough in the road sense needed to stay alive in his own country.'

It was only later that Churchill pointed out that the accident occurred on the thirteenth. Thirteen may have been Walter's lucky number, but as he knew, having seen the Old Man refuse to take a compartment or cabin with that number, it was Churchill's unlucky one.

*　　*　　*

Churchill had taken the lecture tour because he needed the money.

Despite the large sums he had inherited, and the £20,000 he'd made from *The World Crisis*, he was strapped for cash and, since losing his ministerial post, had no regular income – ordinary Members of Parliament at the time were unpaid. Chartwell, with at least eight indoor staff, three gardeners, an estate bailiff, a chauffeur and two secretaries, was expensive to maintain. And Churchill was extravagant; as his friend the barrister F. E. Smith (later Lord Birkenhead) said: 'Winston is a man of simple tastes; he is always prepared to put up with the best of everything.' Clementine Churchill was for ever budgeting, except, that is, where her wardrobe (which made her one of the best-dressed women in London) was concerned. More significantly, however, in the stock market crash of 1929 Churchill had lost about half a million pounds at today's prices. Indeed, he would have been bankrupted but for Baruch. Then also in America on a lecture tour that took him into Canada, Churchill happened to be in the visitors' gallery of the Wall Street exchange on the very day that share prices went into freefall. In tears, he speculated heavily, plunging deeper and deeper into the red. He feared himself totally ruined – and would have been, except that Baruch, a friend since 1917 when he was in charge of munitions production in the US and Churchill was Minister of Munitions, had left instructions to buy every time Churchill sold and to sell every time Churchill bought.[1]

On the earlier tour, when he'd taken advantage of his growing reputation as an author and the fame of his escape from the Boers, Churchill had made enough money to bankroll his early years in politics. This time, with a new book (*My Early Life*) to promote, the negotiated fee for a forty-lecture engagement was £10,000 – the annual cost of running Chartwell – with another £8,000 agreed with the *Daily Mail* for a series on the American situation.

Walter was back at Churchill's side because of his continued attacks on the idea of Indian independence, which he believed would diminish Britain's industrial and commercial power; he'd also expressed the view that India was unfit to exercise self-government – deeply insulting to those educated Indians who were part of the British administrative machine in the subcontinent, many of whom had trained in Britain. Indian anger came to a head after Mahatma Gandhi (who'd studied law in London and who was the prime opponent of British rule) came to a round-table conference wearing his native loincloth and cloak and went to tea with the King and Queen in them. Churchill described him 'as a seditious lawyer, now posing as a fakir of a type well known in the East, striding half naked up the steps of the vice-regal palace . . . to parley on equal terms with the representatives of the King-Emperor'. It was unsurprising that there was talk of assassination from different Indian groups and individuals – and a number of the American cities that Churchill would be lecturing in had large Indian populations, many of them students at the universities.

On 13 November 1931 Churchill wrote to Sir Ernley Blackwell, legal assistant to the Under-Secretary of State at the Home Office (specifically mentioning the Ghada Party as having issued threats on his life), asking for Walter's temporary return. 'He is a very trustworthy man and knows my ways, and I am used to him,' his letter said.

'Churchill and I were all smiles when we met at his London home,' Walter recorded.

'I'm more than glad you're coming with me, Thompson,' he said. I drove with him to the House of Commons. On the way, he said: 'You'll need some extra clothes. Buy a suit and a dinner jacket. I shall pay for them.' I thanked him and told him I had just bought a new dinner jacket. 'All right, Thompson,' he said. 'Let me have the bill for that as well as for the suit.' He must have been very sure that I would agree to go with him. He had booked my passage ten days earlier, together with those for himself, his wife and his daughter Diana.

Walter was relieved to get out of the Old Man's little open two-seat Wolseley. 'To sit beside Winston driving a car was to take your life in your hands. [He] was for ever just missing things and denting cars – his own and others. People shouldn't be in his way, was his theory. Time after time I had to reach over and literally tug the steering wheel almost out of his small, white hands.' Walter, in fact, his son Harold thinks, was the person who taught Churchill to drive – or tried to. On one occasion, when they were coming from Chartwell to the Commons, Churchill found that a policeman on point duty 'was directing traffic towards a newly established one-way system, which had only just been put into operation. The officer waved frantically, for well he might, for Winston drove the car in exactly the opposite direction . . . "I hold a police pass which entitles me to break any line of traffic to get where I want to go," he said.' On another occasion, a diversion in Croydon forced Churchill down a narrow side street just as a bus turned into it from the opposite direction, taking up most of the width. Yet again a policeman signalled to him, this time to stop, and was ignored: Churchill mounted the pavement and rounded the bus.

Without whys and wherefores the policeman started to tell Winston what he thought of him, using very strong words. After a moment Winston looked into the policeman's face and said quietly: 'If I have done wrong, constable, you have your remedy.' Then, with considerable force: 'But I will not have you talk to me like that. Take his number, Thompson.' Only then did the policeman realise whom he'd been ticking off. Churchill drove for half an hour in complete silence before suddenly saying: 'He was right. I deserved all I got. I should have stopped. Forget all about it, Thompson.'

Time and again Walter noted that Churchill was prepared to admit he was wrong – 'eventually'.

Whenever he could, Churchill travelled on a British ship; 'to his great disgust' he'd discovered that, 'of all ships afloat', the only one that would get him to the States in time for the start of his itinerary was a German one, the *Europa*. Going aboard, 'he cursed and swore and banged his cane about . . . In all truth, we had gorgeous accommodation, superb food . . . and service of a kind I'd never seen.' And there was a shooting range on the ship. '"You must get some practice, Thompson," Winston said. We spent some time on the range. In the ten years I had known him I had never seen him fire his Colt .45. I got a surprise. His marksmanship was deadly.'

In the early hours of the day they docked, Walter was up cleaning his and Churchill's revolvers when 'There was a great pounding on my stateroom door. Outside it was pitch dark . . . I ripped the door open and stood there half dressed, amazed, and loaded down with guns. Forty people stood right in front of me, about ten of them women.' It was his introduction to the American press.

Walter was used to British reporters, 'who are always willing to work with you', but found this group, who'd come out on a launch to interview Churchill, a handful 'impervious to any kind of semi-civil persuasion. One found a steward's jacket and cap and slipped into my cabin to look about or pick up information . . . I just picked him up under the arms, planted him hard outside

and slammed the door. Later I had to use more forceful methods.'
Eventually he gathered them all into the smoking saloon for their
interview and 'I thought we had finished with them. Actually,
we had scarcely begun.'

Churchill's welcome ashore astounded Walter: 'A half-dozen
celebrities and city officials . . . and several hundred police . . . In
a whirling parade [we] rocked up Broadway with enough sirens
to waken the dead.' Because heavy seas had made them a full day
late, within two hours they were on a train for Churchill's first
engagement in Worcester, Massachusetts, then back to New York
on an overnight sleeper. Churchill had a sleeping compartment
and, after seeing him to bed, Walter 'climbed to my own – a top
one in a compartment with many double-tier bunks'. He was
unable to sleep, though: the heat was unbearable.

Back at the Waldorf, Churchill began dictating his next lecture
to the stenographer he'd employed, and Walter hoped to get some
shuteye. But 'there was no staff but me to deal with the jangle
of telephone calls from newspapermen and photographers.
Somehow I fought them off, even the cameraman who got a foot
in the door of our thirty-ninth-floor apartment.'

It was late in the evening when Churchill suddenly decided
he was going to see Bernard Baruch.

*   *   *

Walter and Mrs Churchill found her husband 'smothered in band-
ages waiting to go into the operating theatre'. His injuries were
serious but not life threatening: a deep wound to the head (he
carried the scar to the grave), severe lacerations to his face, chest
and thighs, a badly strained back and two cracked ribs. 'They
nearly got me that time,' Churchill joked.

The press tried to get to him in their own way: 'reporters hid
in the laundry bins, in the wards, and came in wheeling loads of
things, unordered. Some would come in white jackets. All the

chambermaids were suspect . . . One woman reporter really tried hard to get round our security by offering a substantial bribe to a ward maid to allow her to take her place for two hours.' Walter was kept busy 'propelling people away from Churchill's door'. Meanwhile, the London papers had been alerted, and Walter, having satisfied himself that the hospital security system was effective, tried to get some sleep at the Waldorf but soon had the news editor of the London *Evening Standard*[2] on the line demanding to talk to Mrs Churchill or Diana. 'I told them they could speak to "a member of Mr Churchill's staff" (me).' After some angry exchanges and yet more calls, Walter was aroused yet again, by which time the paper had discovered who he was – the consequence of which was that questions were asked in the Commons as to why an out-of-office Minister was enjoying personal protection 'on government pay', which wasn't true, as Churchill was paying Walter's expenses. Other papers joined the chase and soon Walter, who 'was really acting as [Churchill's] secretary and having a hard time of it, was unpopular with the press of two continents'.

Now the US newshounds, 'indecently adhesive', turned 'the hue and cry' on the man they knew was from Scotland Yard. 'They wanted my picture, to know what I thought of the American police, how we worked at the Yard, why I was in America, my suggestions for dealing with gangsters . . . I was hard put to it to defend myself from the yelping pack.' Within a few days, Churchill agreed to speak over the telephone to the BBC, and again the hospital corridors swarmed with press wanting to listen to the broadcast. Walter ensured they got nowhere. He was pleased that 'no one got a scoop [but] Winston got the scoop himself, by writing the story of his accident, describing his exact sensations at the moment of impact and afterwards, which he sold to *Collier's* for about three thousand American dollars'.[3]

Churchill (who received a get-well phone call from King George) had numerous visitors he was glad to see. There were two in particular, other than his wife and daughter – though Walter mistook one of them for a reporter or perhaps someone more sinister. Spotting a figure going into the washroom near Churchill's room, he burst in after him, tackled him to the floor and handcuffed him, before finding out it was the driver who'd knocked Churchill down, looking for a vase for the flowers he'd brought. The conscience-stricken Mario Constasino, a young out-of-work truck driver, had been calling at the hospital every day. 'Touched by this, Winston later invited him to the hotel. He asked if the publicity had hindered Constasino's efforts to find work and wanted him to accept a cheque as compensation. Constasino declined. Winston gave him a copy of one of his books, *The Unknown War*, and exonerated him from blame.' Churchill also exonerated the depressed Walter, who still held himself culpable for the accident, and squared the matter with the Yard. 'It was not your fault. I told you not to come,' he said to comfort Walter.

The other visitor was Baruch, who was sitting with Churchill one day when Walter arrived. Asked by Churchill to show Baruch the information he'd gathered on the Indian threat in London at the India Office and the Yard, Walter hesitated. 'I had been instructed not to show the information to anyone in the United States, otherwise it would get out. I reminded Winston of this, but, although he was far from well, that famous grin came over his face as he said: "Yes, that's quite right, Thompson. Here are my keys. Open my box and give Mr Baruch my copy. You will have then obeyed your instructions." Mr Baruch studied the documents and then turned to me and said: "I will take these to the President."'

Churchill returned to the Waldorf in a wheelchair eight days after the accident, giving the press their photo opportunity. A nurse came in daily to massage his back until the family left for the Bahamas to let him recuperate. He was very weak; Walter again had to lift and carry him. They left (on a British ship) on New Year's Eve, and once outside the three-mile limit the passengers, mostly Americans who'd had twelve years of Prohibition, did a considerable amount of drinking. 'Time lags on all sea voyages; perhaps that is the reason for the continuance of celebrations until we reached Nassau harbour three days later,' Walter wrote with some irony. In Nassau he and Churchill 'caught a glimpse of a rum runner loading up preparatory to running the gauntlet of the Customs vessels that patrol the shores of America' and later found him a very civilised fellow. 'He told me if either myself or Winston wanted a drink at any time in New York to just ask any policeman where the nearest speakeasy was to be found.' He gave Walter a phone number – which on return to New York he used. 'In less than ten minutes the man had come with the goods. Very excellent whiskies, too, and uncut. It would not have been possible to fool Winston about fine whisky or champagne.'

In the Bahamas, Churchill was able to use a secure local club, where he lay in the sun, freeing Walter to go swimming and even 'to snatch my first game of football for years . . . The local side certainly played good football.' The Old Man's recovery was slow; he was suffering from aftershock, depression and an inability to concentrate; he didn't even feel like painting. Once, leaving the hotel, there came a moment that Walter thought he would never see – Churchill showed fear, triggered by his accident. 'A Ford car driven by a West Indian came very fast round the corner, missing us both by inches. Winston cringed against the wall, terrified . . . Sweat poured down his face and darkened his cream-coloured shirt. It was shock, almost malarial in its symptoms.' A physically tough man unafraid of almost anything, Walter seemed the last person to have personal experience of irrational fear, but he did – for years, after being struck by lightning, he was afraid of thunderstorms. His accident had happened during the war at the Southampton football ground, where he kept his motorbike in a shed at the side of the main stand. He was tinkering with it when a ball of lightning knocked him off his feet, laid him up for two weeks and left him so dreading an approaching thunderstorm that he got 'a severe headache and a compulsion to hide away in a secluded corner'. He'd rid himself of the phobia by going out into a big storm[4] – in Cannes, as it happened, when he was there with Churchill. Now, holding Churchill's arm, he urged him to confront his fear, saying: 'Sir, that won't do. You must overcome that.' Churchill made every effort to pull himself together. 'You are right, Thompson,' he said. 'It will not occur again.' Nor did it: 'in all the years I stood at his side did Winston again show fear – though he has confessed that he often felt it.'

*   *   *

Once they'd returned to New York, Walter got round to something he would have done earlier if circumstances had been different: he went to police headquarters, taking his and Churchill's revolvers, to find out what authorisation was needed to carry them, only to be told that no one was permitted to carry firearms in the United States. He was incredulous. '"But we have to have something to protect ourselves," I protested. "Only this morning I read about five people in Chicago being shot with machine guns." The police chief was remarkably sanguine. "We can't give you official permission, but if you have to use weapons just let us know and we will square it for you." "What an amazing people," Churchill said when I told him.'

Half the original lectures had been salvaged and rearranged, and the schedule was hectic. The Churchills and Walter criss-crossed the country: Hartford, Connecticut; Springfield, Massachusetts; St Louis; Chicago; Cleveland; Toledo; Detroit; Chicago again; Rochester; Washington; Nashville; New Orleans; Cincinnati; Grand Rapids; Indianapolis; Ann Arbor; Atlanta; Boston – with other lectures in New York at the beginning and end, and in Chicago, a second time. 'It was a case of alighting from the train, motoring to the meeting, speaking and motoring back in time to catch the train that would get us to the next meeting.' Churchill's themes were the world economic crisis and the need for greater ties between the United States and the British Empire, and his audiences were never less than 3,000 and sometimes over 8,000. The tour, Walter concluded, 'was a veritable Churchill triumph' – especially after a farewell dinner in New York. Taking questions after it, he was asked: 'What would you do if we nominated you to run for the Presidency?' There was a moment of astonished silence, then Winston smiled. 'Gentlemen,' he replied, 'there is a deal of difference between nomination and election. But if my father had been American-born instead of my mother, I would have got there on my own.' America loved him for that.

The tour was disquieting, nonetheless: Churchill received about 700 threatening letters, which Walter 'turned over to the police of whatever city we were in'. Mostly, he considered that the cooperation they got from the police was 'magnificent. At any meeting when I saw Indians I would ask the local police either to remove them or have someone sit beside them.' Whatever Bernard Baruch had said to the President about Indian militants (there were, Walter believed, about 600 in the US altogether), detectives were highly visible in various spots around every venue Churchill spoke at. But 'at one city four local detectives attached to us . . . managed to smuggle a cask of beer into their bedroom. When we left in the evening for a lecture our local guardians were missing. Next morning I found the four of them sprawled, dead drunk, on their beds.'

Detroit and Chicago, Walter's information indicated, would be the main trouble spots, and so it proved to be. In Detroit there were demonstrations and placards, 'our car was twice stoned and filth was dumped in our hotel' and an Indian tried to approach Churchill in the venue, with what intent Walter didn't know but didn't wait to find out, bustling him away at the point of his gun. A more serious incident happened in Chicago. At the end of the lecture ('perhaps in Orchestra Hall'), when Churchill was standing with a group in the auditorium near the glass entrance doors,

> a very correctly dressed Indian suddenly hurried in and made straight for Winston in a determined way, keeping one hand in his pocket . . . I pulled my gun and advanced on him, where-upon he spun like a top and crashed into the glass door behind, striking it with such force that he passed clear through the shattered frame and right into the arms of two detectives standing between the supporting columns of the forecourt. All of us got cut up a bit. The Indian's companion fled down the street.

Three and a half months after the tour restarted, the Churchill family left America but there was one final alarm hours before they did. 'The Secret Service sent me an urgent message: a few of those not rounded up by them had declared "Winston will not get out of the USA alive".' It was possibly a threat of more wind than fury, but it made sense not to take chances. The Churchills and Walter made an early back-door exit from the hotel to board the *Majestic*.

*   *   *

Walter returned to ordinary protection duty, now assigned to Jimmy Thomas, who was in Churchill's old job as Dominion Secretary and was a potential target for Irish extremists because of the trade war that had broken out between Ireland and Britain.[5] 'That,' Thomas told him when he reported to him, 'is a lot of bloody nonsense. It's a waste of my time, your time and the nation's money.' A one-time engine driver and general secretary of the National Union of Railwaymen, Thomas was regarded as the most vulgar man in government. Walter liked him for his breezy good nature, his jokes and because he was a football fan – and because he reminded him of Churchill, 'rough-hewn ... but from the same quarry'; he was sorry when Thomas was forced out of politics for leaking Budget details, leading to insider trading (Walter couldn't help but be amused that on the golf course Thomas dropped more than a heavy hint to his companions that import tax on tea would be raised by bellowing, 'Tee up!'). Thereafter Walter shadowed Prince Charles of Sweden, who married a commoner in Great Britain against the wishes of his grandfather, King Gustav; he was part of the security team at the wedding of the Duke of Kent to Princess Marina of Greece; again at the Jubilee celebrations in 1935 (with the Saudi Crown Prince in his charge); and again at the funeral of King George, when he had Prince Paul of Yugoslavia in his care, a passionate golfer who played 'in patent-leather shoes, fawn gloves, stiff collar, formal suit and derby hat'.

He was in sight of having done his twenty-five years and his retirement when he was promoted to detective inspector. The promotion was long overdue. On the American lecture tour, Churchill had asked Walter why he was still only a DS; Walter told him what, in all likelihood, he should have told him a lot earlier: 'that working for him had kept me down to the rank of detective sergeant while others with less service were now promoted, because I had been with him instead of doing normal police work.' This simply hadn't occurred to Churchill, who on at least three occasions when his bodyguard had been with him full time had refused Yard requests to have Walter back. Upset by the realisation, as soon as he was home Churchill asked the Commissioner of the Metropolitan Police – none other than the dour Trenchard – to lunch. As Churchill later relayed to Walter, 'Trenchard said that while Thompson was a very good man, he would have a swarm of bees round his head if he were to promote men who were away from the Yard on special duties'. Even with Churchill continuing to write to Trenchard, Walter's elevation in rank took over two years to come through. It made only a small difference to his pension, which was £207.7d. per annum.

Walter 'took leave of my colleagues, had the customary farewell dinner, received the homage of my brother officers [and] made the proper acknowledgements for the customary watch' – and went looking for a job. Churchill gave him a glowing general reference, adding at the bottom of the typed letter in his own hand: 'He is an altogether exceptional man and I should be ready to give further information if necessary.' When Walter decided to join the Motor Trade Association in Birmingham, inspecting garages to ensure car manufacturers' fixed prices weren't being undercut, and they wrote to Churchill, he replied in similar terms but added: 'Besides that, he has sometimes lived in the same house with me, on and off, for very long periods. You could not possibly have a more trustworthy man, or one more intelligent and capable. I think you are very fortunate to have obtained his services, and you would go far to find his equal.' Unfortunately Walter found the work dissatisfying. Restless, he came back to London, working for the association for a while but soon set up his own private detective agency. Mostly he dealt with divorce cases, and Harold, in and out of jobs as a motor mechanic, went with him from time to time: 'There was an awful lot of standing around.' Failing to make a go of that, Walter bought the lease on a large provisions-cum-sub-post office in Anerley Road, Norwood, alongside the Crystal Palace and then on a smaller grocery store in Thornton Heath. He also bought a van and Harold made the deliveries.

For his part, Churchill refused to be becalmed in his wilderness years. He planted ever more trees and shrubs at Chartwell, fed his golden orfe, his ducks and black swans, bred exotic butterflies, travelled, painted, wrote (his four-volume *Marlborough* was out and he was completing *A History of the English-Speaking Peoples*), and with his friends and connections talked politics for hours after lunch, or after dinner, or both, to the exasperation of his wife. But he did more: he warned of the threat of war that Hitler posed to Europe;[6] that Germany was building up her oil reserves to feed her armour and air force and was bringing her divisions up to strength. In speech after speech he warned of the unpreparedness of the British army; that the 30,000 factories geared to the war effort by 1918 were now run down to barely a dozen. Neither Parliament nor the country wanted to listen: Baldwin and then Chamberlain pursued a policy of appeasement (although on Churchill's advice twenty radar stations were installed from the south coast to Scotland) and in Parliament he was subjected to sneers and snubs. ('I don't know what to make of him,' one Tory MP told Lady Astor. 'How about a nice rug?')

Walter was still in touch, sometimes corresponding, sometimes paying social visits (once to deliver budgerigars for Mary, bred by his sons), on occasion to discuss 'business errands' that the Old Man asked him to carry out.[7] When the Yard was worried about 'alien immigration', Walter sent Churchill newspaper cuttings and went to Chartwell to give him details. The book he'd laboured on about his years at the Yard, most of it devoted to his adventures with Churchill, was published, with Churchill providing a foreword. Walter sent him a copy just before Christmas 1938; Churchill wrote back to say 'It seems to me that it has been widely noticed in the Press' and how much he appreciated 'the charming inscription'. The following April, Walter 'visited for several hours' and 'We went over the grounds that we had all laboured so hard to beautify', with Churchill 'keen to know from me what the "man in the street" was saying. "There will be war, Thompson," he suddenly said. "I cannot see any other way out now ... We shall be at war within six months."'[8] Driving home to south London in the second-hand Clyno tourer[9] that had eventually replaced the motorcycle, Walter found 'the thought of war sickening'. His three sons were of service age. Indeed, the youngest, Harvey, was an RAF regular, serving in Rhodesia. At least Freddie was in a reserved occupation – he'd followed Walter into the police. As for himself, he was on the Met reserve list; if war came, he'd be a policeman again, back in uniform doing he knew not what.

CHAPTER 5

High Risks for France

MEET ME CROYDON AERODROME 4.30 P.M. WEDNESDAY STOP
CHURCHILL

'It was a strange order for a grocer' was Walter's laconic thought.
The date was 22 August 1939, three days before Britain signed
an agreement guaranteeing to come to Poland's aid if Hitler
invaded.

The following afternoon Walter dutifully went to Croydon
and waited for the flight from France to land, 'very impatient to
know the reason for this sudden call'. Even when Churchill
'bounded out looking fit and full of energy, as usual', he didn't
find out. 'Hello, Thompson, nice to see you. Put the baggage in
your car and follow us' was all he got – the usual fine line
between request and rudeness that Churchill never seemed to
know he so often crossed. Walter was used to it: 'I might never
have been away from him.' At Chartwell, he 'had a warm feeling

inside when [Churchill] approached me and put one arm over my shoulder, and we walked into the sitting room together'.

Churchill, with his wife and Mary, had been staying with the Balsans and was about to visit the Duke of Windsor in the south of France at the Château de la Croe at Cap d'Antibes when information was passed to him from French intelligence that the Germans might attempt to assassinate him there, possibly by parachuting in snipers.[1] Large numbers of organised Nazis were already in England, he told Walter, and (as he wrote in *The Gathering Storm*), 'it would only have been in accord with their procedure in other friendly countries that the outbreak of war should be preceded by a sharp prelude of sabotage and murder'. When Walter 'asked if he had plans for meeting this dark prospect, he turned most cordially to me and said: "Yes, I have one very good idea, and it's you, Thompson. I would like you to come back to me. I can look after myself in the daytime, but I need you to take care of me at night."' Without hesitation Walter agreed to Churchill's offer of £5 a week ('it was a request from a friend'). The next evening, when his shops shut, he arrived to start work. As he was no longer a policeman and was therefore weaponless, he was to borrow Churchill's Colt.

Told to collect it from the Old Man's secretary, he went to Kathleen Hill's office but found that she'd gone off duty and he didn't know the secretary who was there – Mary Shearburn, May to her friends, had been taken on as Mrs Hill's new number two after Walter's last visit. When he asked for the revolver, which was in a drawer of her desk, she refused to hand it over. As she told him later: 'You *looked* all right . . . But I didn't suppose that a Nazi assassin would come in wearing a brown shirt and singing the "Horst Wessel Song".' In fact, she was tired and cross; she'd just got back from France, where Churchill's sudden decision to return to England had stranded her there with seventeen pieces of luggage, his painting equipment and the problem of finding her own way home from a country where she didn't speak much of the language.

Walter was put out by her attitude. 'I told her what I wanted and immediately she wanted to know who I was. This was a most unusual position for me, as I was used to asking the questions. I produced the telegram which she had sent from France to me. She was not prepared to accept it as identification. However, on showing her my Scotland Yard official driving licence she was satisfied and gave me the automatic.' Armed with the Colt, which six months earlier Churchill had had fitted with a new trigger and cross-pin as well as having the barrel re-jointed, Walter went on patrol in the house and grounds of Chartwell. He saw the funny side of being in 'the quiet of the Kentish country-side in peacetime ready to pounce upon a would-be Nazi murderer'.

He was back the next two nights. Then a state of emergency was declared. Army, navy and air-force reservists were recalled to their units, and Walter was ordered to report to Marlborough Street police station. 'When I got back to the shop at Norwood, the telephone was ringing. I picked up the receiver. It was the Old Man himself. "What are you going to do now, Thompson?" he asked. I told him. "You don't want to bother about that," he said. "I have already been through to the Commissioner. You will now come to me officially."' Walter picked up a Webley at the Yard, handed back the Colt – and told Harold: 'The shops will have to go.'

'It was a shame; they were good businesses,' Harold says. 'We had a number of staff at the Anerley shop – an ex-post-mistress as well as two assistants and a man who dealt with the butter and bacon. Dad and I worked Boff's, the other shop, with another chap. Dad cured his own hams there. For a while

I carried on while we ran things down, but then I joined Civil Defence in Sydenham for a bit – we were mainly concerned with people being injured and that sort of thing. Dad agreed that our van should go to the unit, and it was fitted out with safety equipment.'

A little later Harold joined up as an RAF fitter.

Still busy with his *History of the English-Speaking Peoples*, Churchill had just gone to bed in the early hours of 1 September when German bombers struck at Warsaw: the invasion of Poland had begun. Two days later Britain was at war. 'There was tenseness all round us as Winston, his wife and the staff waited [at the London flat in Morpeth Mansions near Westminster Abbey] for eleven o'clock. There was absolute silence, as though everything had stopped for the Prime Minister's broadcast.' Chamberlain's voice had hardly died away when 'the sudden screech of the air-raid sirens was heard. "You have to hand it to Hitler," Winston said. "The war is less than a half-hour old and already he has bombers over London." He was in no hurry to leave for the air-raid shelter and looked up at the sky . . . at last his wife and I prevailed upon him . . . Down we went . . . the Old Man with a bottle of brandy under his arm.'

They made their way to the shelter, located in the basement of an adjoining building and already nearly full. Churchill complained there was no telephone or portable wireless (the Germans, he said, would have much better organised air-raid shelters). Another tenant, a German as it happened, said he had a portable radio in his flat – and Churchill sent him off to fetch it. When at last the all clear sounded, 'Winston was out like a flash and up to the top of the building, where he gazed around the sky for aircraft'. The episode had been a false alarm. Subsequently Churchill instructed his secretaries that 'on hearing future alarms, they were to take first-aid equipment to the shelter, together with whisky, ice and soda water for him – and "sherry for the ladies"'.

The next day Chamberlain called Churchill to 10 Downing Street, and Walter sat outside in the car with Clementine, who was nervous; she'd seen her husband ignored for so many years. With war looming, the only crumb that had come his way was on a committee examining Britain's air defences – 'What a paltry way to use a man of Winston's brains!' was Walter's view of it. Just as Clementine said, 'I hope they don't give him a silly little job', Winston stepped out of the most famous door in Britain. He was smiling as he took the few steps to the car. 'It's the Admiralty,' he said. 'That's a lot better than I thought.' In the evening Churchill's delighted chuckles turned to tears: the *Athenia*, an unarmed ocean liner carrying over a thousand passengers, most of them European refugees heading for asylum in the US, was torpedoed by a German U-boat; the 112 dead included 28 Americans. 'It was,' observed Walter, 'a sad initiation to Winston's naval duties.'

For Walter it was like the old days: here, there, a flurry of activity. The Churchills continued living at Morpeth Mansions (where Mrs Hill and May Shearburn made up beds for themselves on the dining room floor) while two flats in Admiralty House were quickly knocked into one for them. Part of the outside of the building was being repaired at this time and, back and forth setting up in the library overlooking Horse Guards Parade the kind of map room he'd had during the First World War, Churchill now and then watched the workmen, 'but at last he could not resist the urge to help. "Let me have a go!" he said and laid some bricks, much to their amusement' – the old days indeed.

Something that wasn't like the old days was that Churchill announced he was giving up driving. 'And he never did drive again – to my great relief.' Churchill's Daimler (which Walter thought 'hearse-like – how I disliked that car') was laid up in favour of an official Humber 'fitted with a gong for getting priority through traffic, and with double mirrors in the front so that I, as well as the driver, could see what vehicles were following. Later, when Winston became Prime Minister, we had another police car as a following escort, and I used a prearranged code of signals through the mirror to instruct the following car when to cut out or hold off overtaking traffic.'

Under press scrutiny as he now was, Churchill asked the newspapers to make no reference to his bodyguard for some months or to print photographs of them together. The *Daily Express* considered a four-month silence sufficient, printing a paragraph, accompanied by Walter's silhouette, under the heading WINSTON FINDS HIS SHADOW AGAIN. In his notes, Walter commented: 'Much to my amusement I am described in this paragraph as looking like a schoolmaster. Not sure whether the implication is that I have to act the schoolmaster to Mr Churchill.' A German radio broadcast in English swiftly responded 'that all the Thompsons in England would not prevent them from assassinating Churchill when they were ready'.

They were now plagued by photographers, and Walter was under instruction to see that the backgrounds against which Churchill was snapped couldn't be identified. As one day they walked from the Admiralty to the back garden gate of Number 10, a photographer tried to take Churchill's picture. Walter stopped him, only to be overruled by the Old Man. 'That night, in several of London's papers, I was exasperated to find many smiling poses of the First Lord in the garden of Number 10, with myself, an angry scowl on my face, in the immediate background. The caption saved me a light reprimand at headquarters: OVER THE PROTEST OF SCOTLAND YARD, OUR FIRST LORD RETURNS FROM FRANCE AND SMILES AT PRESS CAMERA.'

*   *   *

Twenty years earlier, Churchill had left the Admiralty with the navy spick and span. Now, wanting to know what kind of navy he'd been given back, he set out on a tour of inspection. He was quickly incensed. Standards had slipped; so had maintenance – everywhere he saw tarnished brasses and sagging coils of rope. In September he went to Scapa Flow in the Orkneys, sea anchorage of the home fleet, and found what a report he'd commissioned had already told him: that the defences there wouldn't be ready until spring of the following year. There were few anti-aircraft guns, the base's entrance wasn't properly netted and the steel webs of the boom were rusted and broken. As they passed through the boom, Walter asked Churchill 'whether there was any possibility of a U-boat following us in before the boom closed. He answered me: "I hope they will not be able to do so. According to the powers that be . . . the possibility is very remote."' The visit, Walter noted with some understatement, 'left a very bad impression on the First Lord's mind [and] before leaving he expressed himself on this point in no uncertain manner'. By the time the train reached Euston from Inverness, the aircraft carrier *Courageous* was sunk in the Channel. By the end of September, Britain had lost twenty-seven merchantmen.

A month after Churchill visited Scapa Flow, a U-boat did penetrate the anchorage and sank the battleship *Royal Oak*, with the loss of 833 men. Churchill returned, 'wept over the wreckage', then issued orders for new nets and booms, and more block ships (ships sunk to bar entrance channels), anti-aircraft guns, balloons and searchlights. And he ordered the fleet out of the base to Greenock until the work was done. When it was, he went back again and found it more to his liking, but he still detected something that had been overlooked.

About the huge anchorage there were mock-ups of warships as big as the other ships and so true to the illusion of the real thing that they could fool a bomber at a thousand feet. Yet Winston pointed to one . . . and told a warrant officer that it would certainly be spotted by German pilots as a dummy, and that they would not waste a bomb on her. 'But it hasn't even been spotted by our own reconnaissance,' he was told. 'Then they need spectacles!' 'How so, sir?' 'No gulls about her!' he snapped. 'You will always find gulls above a living ship. But not around a dummy, unless you drop refuse from it too. Keep refuse in the water day and night, bow and stern of all these dummies! Feed the gulls and fool the Germans!'

At the beginning of November Churchill, with Walter in attendance, flew to France to review the naval situation; he wanted the French to get on with the production of anti-submarine craft to protect Allied convoys. While there, he called in to see the Duke of Windsor in Paris, then visited the château headquarters of the British Expeditionary Force at Amiens, close to the front lines. An air-raid warning went off and 'a proper mix-up in the sky between German and Allied planes' developed. 'It fascinated Winston. He lay down in the grass the better to see it. He was therefore overlooked by the orderlies whose duty it was to shoo us all inside. I shook him by the shoulder and yanked him to his feet. "Keep your head down, you fool!" he shouted at me, pushing me off. "Do you want us to miss everything?" And he plunged into a hedge, parted the foliage and went on watching the show.'

The Germans had smothered the shallow waters of British harbours and rivers with a new type of mine that caused Churchill considerable worry. Dropped by parachute, these mines sank to the bottom but rose by magnetic attraction when a ship passed over. A number of merchantmen fell victim, and the Admiralty were at a loss for a counter-measure. At the end of November, however, a mine dropped over the Thames Estuary drifted on to the mud and was recovered. 'On a visit to Portsmouth dock-yard shortly afterwards, Winston was able to examine the clever mechanism . . . Shortly after, I suggested that wooden boats, towing metal at a distance, could cause the mines to rise and explode. He listened and in his most charming manner said: "Thank you for thinking about it, but I understand the navy have now thought out a means to defeat them."' The method was simple but ingenious: ships were demagnetised by girdling them with an electric coil – degaussing. Walter accompanied Churchill back to Portsmouth for a demonstration. 'Absolute secrecy was to be observed over this find,' he noted, 'but unfortunately details were published in American journals, and the information had to be released here through official channels.'

Churchill was again back in France in the early days of 1940 for a three-day exploration of the eighty-seven miles of the Maginot Line, seeing strong points along the Rhine, ingenious new anti-tank obstacles, underground railroads and heavy-artillery sites should Hitler attack through Switzerland. Walter, looking forward to accompanying the Old Man on his inspection, 'for like everybody else I had read in the newspapers at home of the wonder of this new technique of defence and of the impossibility of the German army now being able to overrun France', didn't get there. At the last minute Churchill made him stay at the hotel in Metz 'to guard a model of a new invention he had brought from England . . . an automatic entrenching machine which cut a deep, straight trench and threw up a parapet at the same time; and [which] if trench warfare had developed on the lines of the First World War would have saved many lives'. Walter 'tried to point out that my place was with him.

Winston was, however, somewhat impatient that morning. He cut me off abruptly, and I was left behind.' On his return, Churchill tried to pacify his put-out bodyguard. '"Never mind, Thompson," he said. "There will be many more chances for you to see the Maginot Line." That was one of the few of his prophecies that did not come true . . .' Convinced that the French were complacent about the Line's impregnability, Churchill discussed the threat of parachute troops and the weakness of the Belgian flank, the power of the new weapon, armour in strength, and told them bluntly that Marshal Pétain's view that the Ardennes was impassable was 'very unwise'. The French, as he told Walter on the way home, 'laughed politely', just as they'd done in 1915 when he'd explained his theory of landships.

Big things, little things: at Croydon airport on his return, he found 'that the buildings and concrete aprons had not been camouflaged, that airport authorities were "obstructing" the digging of trenches for pilots and crews during [anticipated] air raids, and that construction of underground shelters was proceeding far too slowly'. He stopped to issue orders about these matters, too.

He was to and fro across the Channel in February 1940, on the destroyer *Codrington* with Chamberlain, for a meeting of the Supreme War Council in Paris, a meeting that the French Prime Minister, Daladier, described as the finest he had attended and had a photograph taken of the statesmen present. Later, Churchill asked Walter if he'd got into the photograph. Told no ('being to Winston's right and between him and the only exposed corridor'), he replied: 'Pity. I am certain that the people in that group will never meet again in similar circumstances, and the same group will never meet intact under any circumstances.' On the homecoming trip, 'several mines were seen to be floating in the

Metropolitan Police Constable 549, attached to Paddington Green station: the twenty-one-year-old Walter Thompson

Home Secretary Winston Churchill at the Sidney Street siege in 1911 where members of a gang of armed Latvian robbers were holed up. Churchill was heavily criticised for taking personal control. 'I should have done better to have remained quietly in my office,' he later wrote. 'On the other hand, it was imposssible to get into one's car and drive away…'

Reluctant bodyguard. When first assigned to Churchill in 1921, Walter found him 'difficult and priggish' – and thought the assignment would last only two weeks, not a total of fifteen years!

A visit to the pyramids during a break in the Middle East Cairo conference in 1921. Churchill fell off his camel – but Walter could barely walk for days afterwards. On Churchill's right is his wife Clementine; on his left, Gertrude Bell, the archaeologist and traveller who was one of his advisors, T. E. Lawrence and the saddle-sore Walter

Ever alert: Walter (front left) keeps an eye out during electioneering at Epping, which returned Churchill to Parliament after losing his seat: 'I have rarely seen Winston as pleased as at that moment when he came back to Westerham... Winston Churchill, MP once again,' Walter wrote

Right hand on revolver in his pocket, Walter accompanies Chancellor Churchill on his walk from Downing Street to the House of Commons, 1928

Churchill eventually learnt to be a competent bricklayer working in the grounds of his home at Chartwell. Right: a crack shot with any weapon, Churchill, seen here firing the new, cheap Sten submachinegun, took on the American generals Eisenhower and Bradley at target practice with the US carbine and, Walter wrote, 'showed up well against them'

Arriving back from Paris, 1940, Walter carries Churchill's steel helmet as well as his own – something he finally refused to do

Walter admired May Shearburn's skill at being able to take down Churchill's 'curiously sibilant pronunciation' on her silent typewriter aboard a fast-moving train

Historic moment in World War Two: Roosevelt and Churchill meet for the first time, aboard the American warship *Augusta*, in Newfoundland, 1941. Walter, back left, for some reason is wearing naval headgear

In peacetime Walter, here with his much younger American counterparts, would have been considered too old to be a serving protection officer

More historic moments: Churchill leaving his villa to attend the Casablanca summit, with Roosevelt, in January 1943, Walter, as ever, in attendance (back right)

Roosevelt and Churchill at the Cairo summit in November that year, with Chinese nationalist leader Chiang Kai-shek on their right and Madame Chiang Kai-shek, admired by Walter, on their left

Channel, and Winston suggested they be blown up. One was fired at and some wreckage came to the surface, including the door of a lavatory. This amused Winston, who, with an impish grin on his face, said: "They must have thought I was aboard – the door has my initials on it."'

Back in England, Walter was immediately called over to the Yard to hear concerns about potential enemy aliens in England. Many Germans had been interned at the outbreak of war, but others that the Yard considered suspect were still free – 'the dockets concerning them having been marked up for "No Action"'. Walter spoke to Churchill, who asked for the files. Shortly after, Walter was standing inside Number 10 waiting for Churchill to come out of a Cabinet meeting when Chamberlain emerged first and was asked by a civil servant if there was anything new. Chamberlain 'looked very tired and grave, but said with some spirit: "He's just come back from Paris and is of the opinion that the Germans will reach there. Of course they will not – the French will stop them." He added, shaking his head: "I do not know what has come over Churchill. He telephoned direct to Scotland Yard to carry out more internments. Some of these people I am sure are our friends."'[2]

The same month Churchill authorised the destroyer *Cossack* to pursue the *Altmark*, a German supply ship for the pocket battleship *Admiral Graf Spee*, into Norwegian waters, to rescue 300 British seamen known to be prisoners aboard her. Churchill was 'more than delighted with the news'. The Norwegians, however, protested at the breach of their neutrality and allowed the *Altmark* to return to German waters. Churchill was scathing of the neutral states – Belgium refused to allow British troops to move forward to fill the 200-mile gap between the Maginot Line and the North Sea, and Norway wouldn't allow its coastline to be mined. When Norway, with three other neutrals – Holland,

Denmark and Switzerland – protested at his call to join the Allies, he commented: 'Each hopes that if it feeds the crocodile enough, the crocodile will eat him last.' He wanted to saturate the Rhine with fluvial mines floating just below the surface, to paralyse all movement on the river, but he needed French agreement – a stretch of the Rhine being inside French territory – which wasn't forthcoming: the French feared that German retaliation 'would fall on France'.

Chamberlain's hope was that Hitler would step back from all-out war or that he would overreach himself. Despite what was happening at sea, the feared air attacks failed to materialise: the barrage balloons floated peacefully in the skies through the winter of 1939 and into the spring of 1940. People began to call the war the phoney war. On 4 April Chamberlain announced in a speech that Hitler had 'missed the bus'. Five days later the Germans invaded Denmark and Norway and the next day began the offensive on Holland, Belgium and Luxembourg, towards France and the Channel. 'The Maginot Line?' Walter wrote. 'They walked round its two ends.'

There were suddenly two new Prime Ministers. In France, 'the heavy and slow Deladier was succeeded by the dapper little Reynaud . . . who was referred to in various German newspapers as "the French Churchill", which Winston liked'. And, at last, on the day that Hitler invaded the Low Countries, Churchill succeeded Chamberlain. And not before time, in Walter's opinion: 'The changeover to a wartime economy was proceeding in a leisurely and gentlemanly fashion. Apart from where the hand of Churchill was evident, the direction of the war lacked both urgency and purpose.' Churchill went to the Palace without saying why he was going, although Walter knew it was for the King to ask him to form a government. Their ride back to Admiralty House was made 'in complete silence', but when he alighted from the car Churchill said: 'You know why I have been to Buckingham Palace, Thompson?'

'Yes, sir,' I answered, and congratulated him. He looked pleased, but he was tense and strained. I went on: 'I am very pleased that you have at last become Prime Minister, sir, but I wish that the position had come your way in better times, for you have undertaken an enormous task.' Gravely he replied: 'God alone knows how great it is. All I hope is that it is not too late. I am very much afraid it is, but we can only do our best.' Tears came into his eyes, and as he turned away he muttered something to himself. Then he set his jaw, and with a look of determination, mastering all emotion, he entered the side door of the Admiralty and began to climb the stairs.

Churchill was sixty-six and, Walter thought, 'he looked it, too. He walked with a conspicuous stoop . . . most of his hair had gone . . . his cheeks were pouchy'; and in his moment of triumph Walter saw his uncertainty. But 'never again at any time' was such a moment repeated. 'It was always: "We shall win, Thompson. We shall win."'

Churchill's first broadcast as Prime Minister was given on 19 May, six days after he told Parliament: 'I have nothing to offer but blood, toil, tears and sweat.' Now he spoke to his audience of the coalition he'd put together: 'We have differed and quarrelled in the past, but now one bond unites us all: to wage war until victory is won and never to surrender ourselves to servitude and shame, whatever the cost and the agony may be . . . the long night of barbarism will descend . . . unless we conquer, as conquer we must, as conquer we shall . . .'

*   *   *

May Shearburn had typed Churchill's address as he dictated it and, she told Walter, she was 'thrilled to see the story evolving under my fingers'. She'd been delighted four months earlier when she'd typed Churchill's clarion call, delivered in Manchester's Free Trade Hall, for a million women to help the war effort;[3] but she was so overwhelmed by Churchill's first broadcast that 'I could hardly control my voice when he ordered "Read that back"'. Often a speech would go through three drafts before Churchill was satisfied, and then it had to be typed again, as Walter recorded, 'into what he called "speech form". Paragraphs, sentences and even phrases are broken up into the exact periods in which they will be delivered. The result looks rather like blank verse.' Dictating a speech, then correcting, retyping, revising and retyping it yet again and possibly again was several days' work. For May, the most memorable words she ever typed as they came from Churchill's lips were those from his tribute to the RAF after they'd won the Battle of Britain:

> Never in the field of human conflict
> Was so much owed
> By so many
> To so few

*   *   *

Walter was sometimes in the room when Churchill was dictating a speech (he doesn't say which, or where), and he was fascinated. He wrote of Churchill's general method:

He not only composed but he acted every line. He would start off with a good flow, pausing only at the end of the typed page to snap out, 'How many [words]?' and he expects his secretary to reply without hesitation. The inspiration would dry up for a little while. Winston would pace up and down, muttering words and phrases to himself. Sometimes he would appear to be dictating, but really he is rehearsing. When the flow started again, he would rap out the words, emphasising a climax with a violent gesture. Now and again he would throw up his arms. Suddenly his voice would break at the emotion he put into his words and tears would pour down his cheeks. His arms would be thrown out to the side. As he continued, he would come to a part, which was meant to be humorous, and he would chuckle. At other times he might stamp the floor in emphasis of a phrase. He lived every moment.

Churchill had begun writing in longhand, but long before the war he had moved to dictating his books, articles, addresses and correspondence. Kathleen Hill and May worked the mornings together, taking everything in shorthand turn and turn about; then Mrs Hill worked the rest of the day, with May coming back for the late shift, which ended whenever Churchill went to bed, virtually never before 2 or 3 a.m. 'On one such occasion,' Walter wrote, 'Winston announced that he would go to bed, and added benevolently: "I shall want a fair copy of that – but don't stay up to do it. I'll have it at eight o'clock in the morning." With thirty pages of typescript to do and five hours in which to do it, there was obviously only one thing to do.' May suggested getting a noiseless typewriter and dictating straight on to it, which would save everybody time. At first Churchill would have none of it, anticipating that however silent the machine might be he would still be disturbed by its clack-clack, but grudgingly he agreed to give it a try – and was delighted at being able to see the results so quickly. Soon he had silent typewriters everywhere, including one to take on journeys; he even had a special box made for it. Shorthand was relegated to dictation in the car.

Getting Churchill down directly on to a typewriter, 'on a train travelling at speed, was sometimes very difficult,' Walter, often present, thought. The task usually fell to May, as the older Mrs Hill didn't enjoy travelling, and Walter admired her skill at catching the

curiously sibilant pronunciation of some of Winston's words ... Sometimes he would be in patient mood and would give a repetition of the words his secretary missed. At other times a desperate guess was a far safer gambit than the risk of an interruption. In full flow he would become irritable at any hold-up and could hardly wait for the changing of the paper and the carbons at the end of each page. He would snap: 'Come on, come on, what are you waiting for?' And if the flimsies [the carbon-paper copies] crackled as they were put into the machine he would grumble: 'Don't fidget with that paper.'

Once, in the early days of the war, he was dictating in a train a memorandum concerning the German warships *Scharnhorst* and *Gneisenau* [and] his secretary just didn't know how to spell them. She cast an imploring look at Admiral Sir Dudley Pound [now the First Sea Lord] sitting in the next seat. He smiled and she omitted the names from her typing and went on taking down what Winston was saying. A few seconds later [Pound] slipped her a piece of paper on which he had spelled the names of the two ships. 'What's going on?' Winston growled. The truth came out, and so did some scathing Churchillian comments on her spelling ability. 'And if there are two ways of spelling a word, you'll choose the wrong one,' he added as a general rider.

There were times when Walter wondered how May put up with it: not just the insults or the hours but what she called Churchill's 'genius for not recognising other people's problems'. But Walter knew the answer. May, like himself and 'so many others', was in thrall to Churchill's 'sheer personality'. Whatever else, the unpredictable Churchill, 'angry and inconsiderate' one minute, 'full of impish kindness' the next, wasn't dull to be around.

*   *   *

The month of May 1940 was disastrous. Holland fell. Reynaud notified Churchill that France was defeated; Churchill at once flew with Walter to Paris, coming back satisfied he'd kept the French in the game – 'for the time being', Walter cautiously noted. Churchill stayed in London long enough to put his friend Lord Beaverbrook ('as volatile a character as Churchill . . . I had seen Churchill leave Beaverbrook's house smiling, as if the two men had agreed, [yet] on other occasions angry and muttering to himself, as if there had been an almighty clash over the dinner table') in charge of aircraft production. Then, after the rout of the French 9th Army, he was back in France to shore up French morale once more, while discovering the devastating fact that the army had never been at the strength officially claimed: large numbers apparently mobilised included railway workers, postmen and municipal employees who were still at home doing their jobs.

Belgium surrendered. The German mechanised divisions smashed into northern France and trapped the British army, which retreated, principally to Dunkirk's beaches. Once more Churchill was in the air, the embodiment of pugnacity; he had

the pilot fly so low over Calais that they could see the hand-to-
hand fighting. He was over the Channel during the evacuation
of Dunkirk in a small civilian aircraft – 'refusing an air escort so
that the fighters could help to cover it' – as the RAF tried to
keep the German dive-bombers away from the makeshift fleet of
rescue ships. As the last vessels left the beaches, he flew on 3 June
to France (with his deputy, Clement Attlee, and Generals Dill
and Ismay), this time with an escort of Hurricanes. German
fighters in the skies north of Paris forced a wide detour, first to
Jersey, then across the French coast west of St-Malo, Walter seeing
from the plane 'the struggling masses of humanity – refugees with
their worldly possessions in carts, prams and even on their backs
– hurrying away from the fighting line'.

At the British Embassy in Paris that evening, Churchill asked
his bodyguard to guess the number of men who'd been rescued
from Dunkirk. 'I could see that his face was a little more cheerful,
so I suggested: "Fifty thousand, sir?" His answer was, "Do you
know, Thompson, I thought we should be lucky if we got away
safely twenty thousand, but now, thank God, ninety thousand
are already back in England, and we hope for many more to
come."'[4] On the homeward journey, Churchill 'wanted the pilot
of our aircraft to go near to the Dunkirk beaches – however, he
kept rigidly to our course'.

May Shearburn's fingers were soon busy on her silent typewriter as Churchill dictated the speech that helped turn the
disaster of Dunkirk into a kind of victory: 'We shall go on to
the end ... We shall fight on the beaches, we shall fight on the
landing grounds, we shall fight in the fields and in the streets ...
We shall never surrender.'[5]

Things now moved swiftly. The Germans took French town
after town and were almost in control of the Channel ports, but
still Churchill went back to France on 10 June to encourage the

French to defend Paris – which the government was evacuating as he prepared to fly. All was confusion on the day that Italy declared war on the Allies, 'stabbing France in the back', one of Walter's notes records. Churchill tracked the French Cabinet to the town of Briare on the River Loire, where the meeting was held in a château in the country. Walter 'was struck by the fact that Marshal Pétain sat in a side room . . . and at times walked in the grounds during the discussions'. Two days later Le Havre was in flames 8,000 feet below them as they flew home – only to return to France the next day. With the French Cabinet preparing to give in, Churchill felt he had to stiffen their resolve. He went with Foreign Secretary Lord Halifax and Beaverbrook, despite bad weather and the increasing dangers of flying, and not even knowing where the Cabinet were to be found: 'Flying blind in both senses of the word,' as Walter put it. 'Incredible! The Prime Minister of Great Britain high in the air, trying to discover the whereabouts of our principal ally . . . a terrible fantasy.' And Churchill had gone despite the date, too, the thirteenth – 'the day he usually avoided'. But before leaving England he'd asked Walter for his revolver (which he rarely carried but which Walter always had with him). 'One never knows,' he said. 'I do not intend to be taken alive.'

They finally located the French at Tours. Reynaud talked about taking his government to North Africa and continuing the fight from there, but 'it was evident, despite all Winston's eloquence and persuasion', that the majority view was that France was finished. Reynaud asked Churchill to release France from her obligation not to negotiate for an armistice. Churchill refused and outlined plans for a rearguard action, giving time for the bulk of the French army to withdraw to North Africa and join with the powerful French navy stationed there to carry on the struggle. Saying goodbye to the French Prime Minister, Walter saw 'tears were pouring down his face'. In the courtyard the duchess Hélène de Portes, Reynaud's mistress, who supported a treaty with Germany, tried to physically attack him. 'She came out in a fury of hatred . . . She came forward with a determination to do him some harm. I caught her and silenced her hysterics. She had no gun, though we found a knife on her person. I have never been so rough with a woman since the suffragettes in World War One.'

On the return flight over the Channel without a fighter escort, their plane suddenly dived down towards the sea: 'a German Heinkel had swept in near us and was attacking some French fishing boats. The steep dive into the sea mist was what saved him from seeing us, a civilian plane not armed except for Winston's Colt and my own automatic. We continued to fly over the wave tops until we reached the coast of England. Some German pilot will never know how near he was to winning an Iron Cross – First Class.'

Churchill hadn't yet given up. He telegraphed Roosevelt – but America wouldn't enter the war to help save France. Through the British Ambassador he offered the French joint nationhood with Britain and had his hopes raised that that would prevent capitulation when a message came through asking him to come to Bordeaux. Churchill decided he would go – by submarine. Walter

hurried with him to Waterloo Station to catch a train to Portsmouth. He was eager to set off – the trip in a submarine was a tremendous lure for this man of adventure, as much as anything – and we arrived early at the station. We took our seats in his special compartment, and waited. Just before the train was due to leave, a messenger arrived from Number 10.

He had a sealed envelope. Churchill quickly read the contents. Then he seemed to droop, and the note fell from his hand on to the seat. It was a message to tell him that Marshal Pétain [Reynaud had resigned] had decided to capitulate. We left the train almost immediately. He was very shaken and sat in the car back to Westminster with a pale, distraught face. He said only one thing to me. 'I never thought they would do this. Never. But nothing is changed, nothing is changed, Thompson.'

Churchill laid the catastrophe before the House of Commons in another speech that May Shearburn had typed at her silent typewriter as it was being dictated to her and had turned into 'speech form' only hours before. It ended with a typical Churchillian flourish: 'Let us therefore brace ourselves to our duties, and so bear ourselves that if the British Empire and its Commonwealth last for a thousand years, men will say: "This was their finest hour."'

A week later Churchill was back in the House to announce that British warships had shelled the main French fleet in the port of Mers el Kebir near Oran in Algeria. As part of the armistice agreement, the French should have handed over to the British 400 interned German pilots shot down by the RAF; the Pétain government, however, had refused to honour this (wringing from Churchill the growled comment: 'Then we will have to shoot them down again'). Dreading the French navy falling into German hands, Churchill had ordered the many French ships already in British ports (like Alexandria) to be seized, and sent Admiral Somerville's naval force, which was in the Mediterranean, to offer Vice-Admiral Gensoul in Algeria four options: sail to Britain and fight; hand over to the British navy;

sail to a French West Indies port and accept demilitarisation; or scuttle his vessels in Mers el Kebir harbour. Loyal to Pétain's Vichy government, Gensoul refused all options. Somerville launched an attack; two cruisers were sunk, two badly damaged and 1,300 sailors killed. 'An unutterable grief and pity,' Walter wrote, noting the incident as a measure of the ruthlessness that Churchill could show. Walter expected 'repeated attempts on Winston's life' as a result of it (though these, in fact, didn't materialise). He could hardly believe 'all the staggering blows [that] had struck Churchill when he had not yet been Prime Minister for eight weeks'.

CHAPTER 6

Exhaustion on the Home Front

Once the RAF began beating the Luftwaffe from the skies over the Channel in the late summer of 1940, Hitler rescinded an order forbidding attacks on civilian targets and tried to batter Britain into submission. At the beginning of September 7,300 bombers and 600 escorting fighters raided London in daylight, Fighter Command for once failing to intercept. After that, the British response inflicted such heavy losses on the Luftwaffe (1,800 aircraft and over 2,500 aircrew, compared with Fighter Command's losses of 1,100 aircraft and 550 aircrew) that by the end of October daylight raids had virtually ceased. German bombers were now directed against the cities at night, up to 400 aircraft appearing over London after dark to drop hundreds of tons of high-explosive bombs and tens of thousands of incendiaries.

Beneath this blitzkrieg ('lightning war'), Churchill at first stubbornly remained in occupation of his prime ministerial dwelling, sleeping in his bedroom on the top floor 'and no efforts on my part or that of anyone else would deter him', Walter groaned. Churchill did make the concession of having a small dining room set up in the basement, with the ceiling strengthened, but Walter considered the old building on its shallow foundations 'a death trap'. An air-raid shelter[1] had been put under ground in the garden, 'but only on a few occasions did he make use of it'. He did on the night King George dined with him, after a raid became very heavy. 'Within a few minutes of being inside it, he turned to His Majesty, saying: "I must go out and see how things are going."' The King asked him not to, 'but he was already on the move and out into the garden. He did this several times, just peeping out from the door. Then he really decided to go out, and as he went away from the door without his steel helmet I clapped it on his head. With an absent-minded gesture he flung it off. I reminded him that everyone was expected to wear their steel helmet in the open during an air raid. He looked at me in silence for a moment, then grinned and put it back on his head.'

Not long afterwards, when he was again dining in the basement, a bomb fell close enough to make Number 10 shudder; Churchill 'left his guests, stalked into the kitchen and ordered the staff to go to the shelter immediately [but] then returned to the table'. It wasn't until another bomb dropped on the Treasury behind, 'wrecking the kitchen' of Number 10 and jagging a large crack in the east wall, that he reluctantly led the way to the shelter.

Churchill finally conceded that he should move to a safer place than Number 10 and agreed to go into a suite of offices and living accommodation underneath 'the very powerfully built government building' at Storey's Gate, two blocks south of Downing

Street at the park end of the Board of Trade building. As work was being carried out to reinforce the below-ground levels with a fifteen-foot-thick slab of steel and concrete, he was persuaded to use the abandoned Down Street tube station[2] just off Piccadilly, where the Railway Executive had offices. But he disliked being so far under ground and the roar of passing trains, and after dinner he sometimes obstinately went back to Number 10 to sleep, and was certainly back there by daylight, in either case even when a raid was still on. Walter worried so much that at least once when the Old Man returned to his own bed he slept just inside the front door of Number 10, the only way he could be sure that his charge couldn't try to leave without him knowing.

When completed, the Annexe, as it became known, provided the Churchills with a flat on the ground floor, above the protection of the vast slab that covered the Cabinet War Room, his office and those of his Ministers and Chiefs of Staff and, in a level below this, reached by spiral stairs, a series of low-ceilinged tiny bedrooms and a large dormitory for the seventy or so marines who guarded the Annexe and the nearby Air Ministry.[3] Clementine and her husband had bedrooms down here, too, for when the air raids were particularly heavy. She used hers; he rarely did, if ever, preferring to sleep in the flat, where there were steel shutters over the windows and where, he said, he felt perfectly safe.

One evening Clementine called Walter to her sitting room and told him that the Air Ministry had phoned her to say a bad raid was expected and suggesting that she and Winston should sleep in the sub-basement.

'I have asked Mr Churchill if he will go down, and, much to my surprise, he has told me that he will,' she explained. 'But you know, Inspector Thompson, that if he can wriggle out of this promise to me he will do so. Will you see that he goes down and carries out my wishes?' I promised to do my best. So when I made my usual report to him about the approach of enemy bombers . . . he gathered up his papers and we marched down to the basement room. I was mystified by the docility with which he went downstairs. I just could not believe that he would do this. However, down he went; he undressed and got into bed. After putting his clothes in order, I went to leave, reaching to turn off the light. 'Leave it on, Thompson,' he said. 'Then, sir,' I replied, 'you will have to get out of bed to turn it off.' Sharply he said: 'Leave it alone.' I looked at him and I noticed the grin on his face – despite his tone. I went to my own room, but did not undress. I waited: I felt he was up to something. My bell rang, and I went to his bedroom to find him up with his dressing gown and slippers on. 'Well, Thompson,' he said cheerfully, 'pick up my clothes. I have kept my promise to Mrs Churchill. I came downstairs to bed, but now I am going upstairs to sleep.'

While he was prepared to hold evening meetings in the Annexe with his Cabinet or the Chiefs of Staff, or to broadcast on the BBC from there, he refused to work anywhere other than Downing Street during the day: the drab warren of the Annexe, where the Cabinet War Room was ribbed with girders, the bedrooms were furnished with monastic austerity and everyone worked in perpetual artificial light, got on his nerves. It meant that his office files had to be duplicated on both sites and staff were for ever scurrying to and fro; and they were expected to remain in Downing Street if a daylight raid occurred. Against the advice of everyone around him, Churchill held daytime Cabinet meetings there and had his appointments arranged there.

May Shearburn arrived for work from the Annexe one morning and found that Number 10 had suffered more blast damage during the night from a direct hit on another building. A big beam had come down at an angle across the bed in what had been her room. 'You'd have been all right, Miss Shearburn,' Winston remarked gaily on his tour of inspection. 'The bed is still there!'

Despite the blackout imposed on the declaration of war, Churchill insisted on taking his constitutionals in St James's Park. On Walter's first outing with him in the pitch dark, 'I walked into a tree and was only just in time to prevent him doing the same thing. I suggested a torch, and the thought occurred to me that perhaps I could get one fixed to a walking stick, and it would then serve a dual purpose. He had a stick with a crooked handle, which I took to a leather shop, where they made a leather fitting to hold a torch – and this he used right through the war.' Once the Blitz began, however, whenever there was a raid 'he wanted to be out watching it – what he called "the conduct of the war in person"'. Churchill's 'total disregard for danger as he walked the streets when bombs were falling' made Walter constantly beg him to take cover, in return getting 'a very firm and direct reply: "I have asked the people of this country to carry on in their homes, in the streets, in the factories, everywhere. If you think I am going to hide in an air-raid shelter, not for you or anyone else will I do it."'

Churchill usually returned from Downing Street to the Annexe by car, but 'he loved to walk if there was an air raid'. Walter noted that he 'would never leave Downing Street until the guns had started up, then he would walk through the barrages around St James's Park to the Annexe'. One evening he told his bodyguard 'to send the drivers away to their meals and he would walk [but] I did not expect him to walk around St James's Park by way of The Mall, where many incendiaries had been dropped. My plea to him not to do so fell on deaf ears.' They had just stepped into the Annexe when there was a tremendous explosion behind them and Churchill went back to have a look. 'The pavement where we had been walking twenty seconds earlier was now a crater [a thousand-pounder had hit, Walter found out]. As we went to the edge, the water main burst and we were drenched. I hoped this would teach him a lesson, but it did not. Hardly a month went by when we could not have been wiped off the earth.'

That night, as Walter waited outside the dining room, Churchill came out on his way to his office, 'took hold of my arm and, in a way, pulled me towards him. "Thompson," he said, "when you came to me in 1939 I told you something unusual – do you remember?"' Walter said he did, and repeated, 'You said, "I have something to do." "Those are the words I wanted, Thompson," Winston said. "Because now we have come to the second phase. There is somebody looking after me besides you, Thompson." "Do you mean Sergeant Davies?" I asked. His finger went heavenwards in a characteristic gesture. "No, Thompson, I have a mission to perform and That Person will see that it is performed."'

Churchill didn't confine his surveillance of air raids to what the bombers dropped in his immediate vicinity: he wanted to see the ack-ack and gun batteries hitting back. In the middle of heavy raids he visited gun sites around London, often for hours. Walter knew 'trying to dissuade him was useless' but he tried, and they often exchanged blunt words, though Walter knew when 'that tone meant no further argument – I knew how far I could go'. Churchill had an armoured car but refused to use it. 'I will travel in the same type of car as anyone else in the country,' he said. 'I will not have any privileges. I will take the same chance as anyone else.'

One night just before Churchill was intending to go out, Walter

decided to take a chance. I told his driver to go and get the armoured car. 'He won't ride in it – you know that, Inspector,' he said. I told him to bring it and I would be responsible. To make sure he got into [it], I had all other cars removed from the front of the building, and sent my police car with my colleague to await us en route. Of course, Winston told me in no uncertain terms what he thought of the armoured car, but being so busy telling me off he forgot to ask where the police car was – it always had to follow his.

The first stop was Richmond Park, but at Hammersmith the aerial activity was so intense that Walter turned to question whether they should continue. 'Winston anticipated me by saying: "Carry on."' When they got to the park, Churchill observed that the accompanying staff officers were travelling in ordinary vehicles and angrily told Walter: 'Change the drivers over. Send that sardine tin back and don't bring it out again or you and I will part company.' When they moved on to another gun site at Caterham he and Walter went in one of the staff cars.

Churchill's bad mood changed when he saw a German bomber brought down and he became affable; and he did something curious as they were about to return to London. 'During my years with him, Winston had always travelled in the seat on the nearside of the car, sitting behind me, and he never opened or shut a car door. On this occasion I went ahead of him as he left the guns and opened the nearside door for him. To my surprise, when he reached the offside, he stopped, looked at me, then opened that door, got in and shut it.' They'd gone only a short distance, 'as usual travelling fast', when a bomb exploded close by. 'It lifted all four wheels from the road surface and we ran on two wheels for many yards before rocking back. Our speed probably prevented the car from turning over on its nearside. Winston was not disturbed in the slightest. "It must have been my beef on this side that pulled the car down."'

Talking to Churchill about the incident back at the Annexe, Walter asked him why he'd got into the car on the side he never did. Churchill told him: 'I saw you with the door open, but when I reached the other side something seemed to say "stop", and it appeared to me that I was to get in the other side, which I did.' Again Churchill's finger went heavenwards. 'That mission has to be carried out, Thompson.'

The most dangerous of Churchill's escapades during the Blitz, Walter thought, was watching air raids from the high, exposed roof of the Annexe. As soon as the sirens sounded, Churchill was reaching for his field glasses. At first Walter told him no liftman was on duty to take him up and got the reply 'You can take me' – leaving him to arrange to have the keys (there were six locked rooms to pass through) and the nightly password to get by the sentries. And up Churchill would go, wearing 'his thick blue siren suit[4] and his air-force overcoat' (and his tin hat when he remembered), fascinated by the drone of the planes, the arcs of the ack-ack tracers, the fingering searchlights; he counted the fires and the explosions, which 'he would time by the flashes and calculated the intervals to judge their distance – five seconds per mile'. As Churchill's enthusiasm remained unabated, Walter 'on my own authority had sandbags put around the sides of the roof and a form of covering above'. At least then Churchill 'could be persuaded to take cover when he heard the shell splinters splattering down on the leads'.

An incident of the kind Walter feared eventually happened –

but at ground level. Churchill was standing at the Annexe entrance, with one of the double doors open to see 'the fireworks', talking to Sir John Anderson, now a member of the War Cabinet, about improving the use of searchlights, when Walter

> heard something whistling through the air. 'Something is coming this way,' I shouted. The words were hardly out of my mouth before an ack-ack shell hit the railings opposite and exploded. I grabbed the Prime Minister and with all my strength hurled him behind the closed door. Winston's immediate reaction to having been so violently handled was one of indignation. He glared at me. 'Don't do that,' he shouted . . . and poked his jaw right into my face. I have quite a bit of jaw myself and poked it right back. 'See there!' I shouted.

Churchill looked. Behind him, Cyril Davies, Walter's colleague, had been wounded. A man taller than Walter, he'd taken a lump of shrapnel the size of a penny in the upper thigh; the much shorter Churchill would have taken it in the abdomen. Without a word, Churchill 'walked back into the Annexe and never again referred to the matter'.

*　　*　　*

After Dunkirk, Churchill was on the move around the country, often in his special train (his own carriage with bedroom, bathroom, lounge and office; dining car divided between him and any VIPs and the staff; a twelve-compartment sleeping coach). He went to almost every stretch of the coast where an enemy landing was possible. His first call was Harwich, as Hitler's invasion barges began to cluster across the Channel from the Cinque Ports in anticipation of Britain being bombed into surrender. During the Blitz he visited sixty towns and ports where large areas were devastated in the onslaught. At Coventry 'his control was nearly shattered' by the sight of the razed cathedral.

While at the huge defence headquarters inside the cliffs of Dover – a town shelled across the narrowest part of the Channel – he watched a dogfight in which two German planes came down in the sea (the Luftwaffe were still making hit-and-run daylight raids). 'Within a matter of seconds, three small RAF sea rescue launches put to sea to pick up the pilots who had baled out . . . Contrary to our methods of sea rescue work of baled-out pilots, the Germans used rafts supplied with food and first-aid material, a pilot having to reach the raft by his own effort, although German rescue planes, painted white with Red Cross markings on them, patrolled up and down.' Walter was incensed, later, when he saw that a German rescue plane that had come into British possession 'was fitted with radio and was in actual fact acting as a reconnaissance aircraft . . . the logbook found intact'.

On the drive from Dover to Ramsgate they saw a fighter plane spiral in flames into a field about half a mile away. '"I hope to God it is not a British plane," Winston said and demanded the driver take us as close as he could get. He jumped out and proceeded on foot . . . an unnecessary risk as the Germans did a great deal of strafing.' The downed craft was the enemy's, and the pilot was in the hands of some ARP men. 'Winston, who was visibly affected by the whole scene, said: "Well, anyway, he is safe – even if he is a German."' They were touring Ramsgate when the alert sounded and the mayor took them into one of the chalk shelters, Churchill lighting a cigar as he moved towards the entrance. 'One of the men waiting to go in was an opportunist. He asked for the cigar [and] when Winston handed it to him gave up all thought of taking shelter and sat in the opening smoking it. I suppose he thought that he could shelter from bombing at any time round "Hell Fire Corner" but that the chance of smoking a good cigar did not often come his way.'

Keeping himself safe in the general way of things never entered Churchill's consciousness. Visiting Plymouth, which had already taken a severe pasting, his arrival coincided with another raid, and his train was stopped in the mouth of a tunnel 'while ahead in the darkness we could see flares and bombs dropping'. After a while 'Winston started to ask, "Why are we remaining here?" He was told that it was a precaution until the raid had finished, but he wanted to go on just the same. Only after the repeated pointing out of the danger did he decide to wait.' If personal safety wasn't on his mind, his bath was, Blitz or no Blitz. When he reached the hotel where they were to stay, he found that it had been partially destroyed the previous night; nevertheless, 'within minutes of arriving Winston asked for a bath. The manager informed him that the supply of hot water to the rooms had been destroyed but that he would do his best. He certainly did . . . the staff and some of the guests formed a chain to pass pails, cans and jugs of hot water from the kitchen to his bedroom.'

Everywhere he went, Churchill stomped through the rubble, chewing his cigar and giving his V for victory sign, comforting, encouraging. 'Sometimes, surrounded by the intense devastation of a whole block or cluster of homes and shops, he would stand and talk, chatting with survivors, listening to their recounting of what had happened to them.' In Plymouth he spoke with an elderly woman in a very distressed state who 'suddenly turned away with the remark: "I cannot waste time talking to you. I have to clean my house up."' Or what was left of it: Churchill followed her to see 'not only the front door in pieces, but every window blown out and the furniture badly damaged'. In Bristol, where people were still being rescued from their destroyed homes by the ARP, 'Winston went down on his knees to clutch a woman who, still conscious, was being dug out. They remained like this for some minutes until she was released . . . For a moment they looked at one another – Winston with his coat and trousers spattered with mud, the woman covered from head to foot in dust. Then, with a tremor in her voice, she thanked him and was taken away by friends. "There goes greatness," Winston said.' Tears 'were streaming down his face . . . There were many occasions when he would silently and without any shame or embarrassment weep without speaking for many minutes.'[5]

Churchill did what he could for those who had suffered. After being approached in one town by the proprietor of a restaurant who'd lost his living, he instructed Sir Kingsley Wood, the Chancellor of the Exchequer, to arrange a scheme of compensation for shopkeepers, which eventually paid out through the War Damage Commission. Churchill happened to be at one of the commission's offices when a music teacher, whose piano had been destroyed, applied for temporary relief. 'As the official informed her that he was only able to give the maximum then allowed of £10, Winston interjected, "No, the maximum is no good in this case. Give her a piano now – before she has time to forget how to teach."'

Wherever in the country his visits took him, Churchill went to army camps and fighter stations – 'he had very deep feelings for service personnel', Walter was well aware.

In the early days with him, when he would be driving his dreaded Wolseley, he would often slow up suddenly when he spied a man wearing an ex-serviceman's badge who looked down and out. He would pull into the side of the road and give me a nod. I knew what it meant. Out I would jump and give the man he had spotted five shillings. Winston never carried any money in his pockets but would reimburse me later. Rarely did the recipients of this quite considerable sum in those days know where it had come from. For, as soon as I had passed over the half-crowns, Winston would be revving the engine to move off, and I would have to leap for the running board.

Walter relished the occasion on one of their wartime visits when

We were travelling in the car of the officer commanding that area [and] were halted at a roadblock by an army sergeant and troops with fixed bayonets. The car stopped and the officer jumped out and rebuked the sergeant at some length, accusing him of not recognising his flag. The sergeant, although very annoyed at this attack upon him, refused to allow him to pass until he had inspected everyone. After he was satisfied, he stood back to allow us to proceed. Winston's reaction was immediate. He jumped out and complimented the sergeant upon his strict adherence to his duty. As we drove away, I heard him say to the officer: 'Never rebuke a soldier for doing his duty.'

* * *

Churchill's work routine had been set in the 1920s and 1930s and didn't change in the Second World War: it simply intensified.

His day started with the newspapers in bed, followed by breakfast – 'a main meal to the Prime Minister . . . ham, bacon or beef (when meat was available), or cold chicken, mounds of toast with jam or jelly, and tea. He loved a good-sized sole, too.' And then, propped up on pillows wearing one of his vividly coloured quilted dressing gowns, 'two long pieces of foam rubber under his arms on a large bed-table, he would light the first cigar of the day and begin work'. Churchill didn't inhale, and his cigars often went out, and 'he would chew on [them] for an hour before realising [they] were dead. He smoked few, about eight a day, each one requiring relighting seven times on average.'

Having been through his official box, Churchill would begin dictating his dispatches and communiqués, his messages, criticisms, orders and demands, his secretaries typing furiously in relays on a silent machine at the end of his bed. If there were important visitors to be seen, he saw them, often continuing to dictate while they were there. Even as he directed a war, nothing was too small for his attention (as in a memo to the Ministry of Works to ensure a sufficiency of candles at the Annexe in case of a power failure). Around one o'clock he got up for his bath, sometimes continuing to dictate from it through the open door, then 'gargled, applied a nasal douche . . . shaved with an electric razor' and got dressed – Walter constantly surprised 'how a man of his bulk could do that so quickly'.

After lunch, Churchill repaired to his office until the late afternoon or early evening. Now he retired for an hour's siesta,

a daily rest period [that] was almost a ritual. He would leave his office, ask me to have him called, and then there was not another word from either of us. I would open his bedroom door, he would step inside and as he walked towards his bed he would remove his clothes, just dropping them on the floor. By the time he reached the head of the bed he would be completely undressed. He would put on his silk vest, make sure the pillow was his own [and] put the black satin band over his eyes . . . On many occasions before I had even picked up his clothes he was oblivious to the world.

He was up for a second bath and then dinner, with a bottle of champagne that he considered entirely medicinal.

And then his working day began again.

Churchill was a night person. It was at night, free of interruptions and clad in his air-force-blue woollen rompers, which he'd taken to wearing in Downing Street in case he needed to work in the cold air-raid shelter, that he framed and dictated his speeches and the long directives to the heads of government departments and the senior officers who were fighting the campaigns around the world – on becoming PM he'd indicated he'd only communicate all matters relating to national security in writing, to avoid misunderstandings.

The volume of communications that emanated from Churchill grew to such proportions that a third secretary was needed. Finding someone suitable wasn't easy: one of Churchill's foibles was a dislike of any new face in his inner circle. His unintentional glare and his growled 'Where's Mrs Hill? Or Miss Shearburn?' drove away several who came to fill the role (one found she had TB; another had a nervous breakdown) before someone who could take the heat arrived. Churchill's hours and his working methods – and his sudden mood changes, which, as May Shearburn put it, ranged 'from charming, amusing, light-hearted and talkative to moody, bad-tempered, irascible and silent' – took some getting used to. General Sir Hastings Ismay, head of the military wing of the War Cabinet Secretariat, once found Kathleen Hill in tears in the corridor and told Churchill off for bullying her. Instantly contrite, Churchill sent for her and asked her to take a letter: 'My dear Ambassador, I fully agree with you.' That was the extent of it – and he asked for it to be typed at once. When Mrs Hill returned, he looked at the letter and said, 'Beautifully typed' – and as she left the room in some puzzlement, Churchill turned a triumphant smile on Ismay.

Churchill's foibles, large and small, took getting used to as well; small: his loathing of paperclips (he put holes in his own papers with a punch he called his 'klop', securing them with green tags), which had to be removed from incoming mail before he saw them; large: his almost pathological aversion to whistling. Churchill hated noise – his bedroom window at Chartwell was puttied shut. But whistling, Walter wrote, 'seems to cut right through him, jarring him from head to foot. Within a few weeks of taking over as Prime Minister, he issued an order forbidding whistling in the corridors. On many occasions I have been given an order to dash out and warn an offender.

One day he was walking slightly ahead of me along King Charles Street, Westminster, on the way to Downing Street. Approaching him from the other direction was a boy of about thirteen years of age, hands in pockets, newspapers under his arms, whistling loudly and cheerfully. When the boy drew near, Winston hunched his shoulders, walked towards the boy and said in a stern voice: 'Stop that whistling.' The boy looked up at the Prime Minister with complete unconcern and answered: 'Why should I?' 'Because I don't like it and it's a horrible noise,' growled Winston. The boy moved onwards a few steps, then turned round and called out: 'Well, you can shut your ears, can't you?' With that he walked on. Winston was completely taken aback, and for a moment he looked furious. Then, as he crossed the road, he began to smile and quietly repeated to himself the words 'You can shut your ears, can't you?' and followed it up with a hearty chuckle.

Churchill's intolerance and his sense of humour were seldom far apart.

The pace Churchill set his staff was frantic: he drove them as he drove himself, expecting of them what he expected of himself. They gave it, but were often out on their feet. Mrs Hill went to bed in the afternoons with a hot-water bottle, but others who tried in some fashion to copy the Old Man's sleeping pattern couldn't keep to it. On his security rounds in the small hours, Walter from time to time silently entered the Cabinet Room at Number 10 or Churchill's study at the Annexe 'to find the Prime Minister and one of his secretaries on opposite sides of a table, both with weary eyes closed. More than once a secretary came to with a great shock at the next burst of dictation.'

May Shearburn told Walter how, in a less absorbed moment, Churchill once asked her if she was tired and when she stoutly denied it was informed, 'No, you wouldn't be – you are a soldier's daughter!' Another night, when Churchill was as worn out as she was, he looked at the clock to see that it was 1.30 a.m. Sighing, he said: 'It is early yet – we must press on.' He was surprised on the first Christmas Eve of the war when she thought she might have the next day off. 'I asked what time he would require me the following morning. "Eight o'clock, of course, as usual," he said. Perhaps some surprise showed in my face, for he then gave me a sharp glance and said: "Oh, did you want to go to church, Miss Shearburn?" "No," I told him, "I just wondered whether we should be keeping normal working hours on Christmas Day." In a kindly voice he said: "Oh, well, make it 8.30."'

Lord Halifax, who witnessed this exchange, was amused.

Coming back from Paris with Churchill during the period in which he was trying to keep the French fighting, he'd been told something very similar, as Walter overheard. Having just landed at Hendon aerodrome after two days virtually without rest, Halifax had been exhausted, and when Churchill suddenly announced 'We will have a Cabinet meeting at 10 p.m., [Halifax] was dismayed. "Surely not tonight, Winston," he protested. "We have had a long day; it will make such a late night." "All right," replied Winston. "We will make it 9.30 instead."'

Churchill was at least fifteen and as much as thirty years older than everyone other than Admiral Sir Dudley Pound, who was three years his junior, but he exhausted them all: his secretaries, his personal private secretaries, his ADC, Naval Commander Charles Thompson (who wasn't related to Walter), his other aides, the Chiefs of Staff (Pound regularly fell asleep at meetings). Once he had them all in the Annexe, any of them might be roused from their bed to help with some existing project or to formulate a new one. Such summonses included Frederick Lindemann,[6] who was Churchill's interpreter in all technical matters, and General Ismay, who later wrote: 'If he isn't fast asleep, he's a volcano.' Throughout the war, those close to Churchill existed on an average of five hours' sleep. Walter, up and about to see the Old Man to bed when eventually he went there, had even less.

*   *   *

Lloyd George was the first Prime Minister to have Chequers in Buckinghamshire as a country retreat after Lord Lee of Fareham gave it to the nation. As it happened, Walter had been there in 1921 during Lloyd George's house-warming. At the time Sinn Fein were threatening to burn the place down, and Walter thought they could have done if they'd tried – with its enormous wooded grounds and mile-long drive, Chequers was wide open.

'Had a terrorist gained access to the grounds, I would not have known: nor would it have been difficult for him to secrete himself in the thick bushes lining each pathway whilst I was continuing the circular patrol around the house – itself no mean distance.'

Going back in June 1941, when Churchill spent his first weekend there under infinitely more dangerous circumstances, Walter realised what a terrible security risk Chequers was: German bomber crews could easily take bearings on it from nearby reservoirs and other landmarks. 'The likelihood of killing Winston from the air was no greater than the likelihood of our killing Hitler in the same way, but invasion remained a possibility or the dropping of parachutists landing in large numbers – there were stories that the Germans would make an attempt to assassinate Churchill at Chequers.' The guard on the property consisted only of 'a small force of local policemen intended for little more than keeping intruders from the vicinity'.

Walter put his views to the Yard, who contacted the military authorities. Soon, 200 Guards were deployed,

ack-ack guns were posted in the neighbourhood; roof-spotters were placed on the leads of Chequers, and, just in case of the arrival of paratroops, Bren-gun carriers were stationed nearby. An air-raid shelter was also installed under the house itself . . . Winston was most interested in the construction of this, and together we inspected it when it was finished. To use the emergency exit meant crawling through a tunnel, and I wondered if, in the event of an air raid, he would enter the shelter. I am sure he had not the slightest intention of using it, although he wished the staff to do so.

There was a bombing scare one night when 'the sirens sounded and an enemy plane dropped flares and went back and forth – apparently over the building itself'. Walter informed Churchill, who told him to see that everyone went to the shelter. As for himself, Churchill said, '"Come and tell me when they drop the first bomb." None were dropped that night, but during the week that followed, when we were not in residence, bombs were dropped in the grounds, one within 200 yards, though this failed to explode.'

The guards on duty around the house were 'sharp', and Walter advised Churchill not to go outside at night, 'but he felt a certain frustration and protested that he really needed some exercise after long spells of dictation . . . I had to make arrangements for him to use one side door only. Every evening I was told the pass-word, which was rigorously enforced. He always made me go ahead. "I do not want to be shot," he would say. "What about me?" I would reply. "I do not want to be shot either." "Well," Winston said, "security officers have to take chances."'

Testing Chequers' security unannounced, a military security officer bluffed his way past the gate sentry; it was summer, the doors of the house were open and he walked in. 'Naturally this incident was viewed seriously, and the major did a service by drawing attention to the inadequate precautions,' Walter acknowledged. 'However, shortly afterwards another officer came to the gate. In view of the previous lapse, the guard was partic-ularly alert. The officer was stopped, interrogated and asked for various passes, which he produced. These seemed to be in order and indeed were quite correct, except for minor discrepancies which the guard could hardly be expected to detect. He got through and subsequently presented [another] adverse report.' Walter fumed, considering that the officer had abused his posi-tion and felt sorry for sentries everywhere who 'were often bullied when they asked for passes'. He hoped that the officer involved would try it again: 'It would have given me great pleasure to have put him under arrest for misrepresentation.'

After the incident, the gate guards were overseen by a few experienced men from the Met.

Almost every weekend when he was in England, Churchill went to Chequers (except, during the Blitz, when a full moon made the risk too great, in which case he went to Ditchley Park, home of his parliamentary friend Ronald Tree, close to Blenheim but two hours from London). These weekends, Walter commented, 'were as alike as two peas . . . really more like moving Number 10 Downing Street to the country'.

Leaving on a Friday afternoon was a performance. Churchill would give a time – 3.30, 5.30, 7.30 – prevaricating as to whether he'd have his sleep at Downing Street or not, then suddenly rush out, telling everyone else to hurry up. During the hours of indecision, three cars would be waiting at the garden gate. Invariably, Walter wrote, the party included 'Commander Thompson, one of the private personal secretaries, three secretaries, the valet, myself and another detective, two film operators and an electrical engineer [from the BBC – Churchill's addresses to the nation after the Sunday evening news almost always came from Chequers]'.

Churchill liked to travel fast, and the cars hustled through the outskirts of London, jumping traffic lights and taking traffic islands on the right. Sometimes he dictated to a secretary, trying to balance her shorthand pad on her knee; at other times he slept, his eyeshade as ever covering his eyes.

The arrival at Chequers 'was like a mini invasion'. There would also be several carloads of other people, who might include Cabinet Ministers or Chiefs of Staff, generals, politicians, civil servants and visitors from overseas. 'Most were, of course, connected with the war effort, [though] on rare occasions other guests were asked, including the famous pianist Moiseiwitsch and Sir Alexander Korda, the film producer.'

After his second bath of the day, Churchill dressed in his siren suit and went to dinner in it. 'He did not care what anyone else wore either, and his dinner table was almost always the ultimate in incongruity of apparel. After dinner he would retire for a moment, then come back dressed in one of his gorgeous dressing gowns for the film showing. I never saw an exception to this.' The weekend film was shown upstairs in the Great Parlour, with household staff and officers and men of the guard having a standing invitation. It was difficult to get new films, but Churchill, entirely uncritical, preferred old favourites like *The Great Dictator*, *Gone with the Wind*, Korda's *Lady Hamilton*; he also liked Laurel and Hardy. However many times he saw *Lady Hamilton*, he cheerfully cried. (Later in the war, when the Japanese were sweeping through Burma and had captured Mandalay, Churchill came in to see a film 'as the loudspeakers blared out the melody of "The Road to Mandalay". "It's a little late for that," he muttered grimly.')

Whatever the films, they 'seemed to relax his mind'. So, often, did playing bagatelle in the Great Hall, to which everyone adjourned when the show was over. Churchill only played, Walter noticed, 'when there was a problem on his mind . . . He played as if the game was of the utmost importance and made careful note of every score on a piece of paper.' Then, suddenly, the problem perhaps resolved, he'd launch himself among his guests. Soon, however, he'd announce: 'Come along, we must do some work now' – and no one he had business with during the weekend was likely to see their bed before three or four next morning.

Churchill worked in the Hawtrey Room (the Hawtreys owned

Chequers for 350 years) below the Great Parlour, and during the course of the war it was here that he crafted some of his memorable speeches, a few of which were also broadcast from here, as well as most of his nine o'clock addresses to the nation. One speech that May Shearburn typed at Chequers was Churchill's 'tomorrow the dawn will come' rallying call to the people of France (*'Français! Prenez garde, c'est moi, Churchill, qui vous parle'*) – a success when completed, an initial disaster when Churchill tried to translate it into French: his secretary spoke little French and Churchill's schoolboy grasp of the language, together with his speech impediment, made him incomprehensible to her.

All through the nights at Chequers, Walter, as ever, hovered, waiting to see the Old Man to bed. Sometimes, even when he'd finished work, he wouldn't go, returning to the Great Hall, a draughty place in the depths of winter when the fire had gone out, and put on records. His musical taste was simple: music hall (Harry Lauder's 'Keep Right on to the End of the Road', 'Poor Old Joe', 'Run, Rabbit, Run', 'Home, Sweet Home') and marching bands. 'There were times,' Walter wrote, 'when I approached the Great Hall to find [Winston] dressed in his blue siren suit or a vivid dressing gown – looking rather like a teddy bear – his hands thrust deep in his pockets and his head bent forward. He hummed the tune as he marked time, marched across the hall, did a smart about turn, marked time again and then repeated the manoeuvre. As the radiogram had an automatic record-changer, this march would often last a considerable time.' Churchill would be 'absolutely absorbed'.

Being at Chequers did Churchill good: 'he picked up: you could see it in his face.' In truth, he would have preferred to be at Chartwell. Before the Blitz and again after it, he was able to spend a few weekends there. But the big house was shuttered and empty, and he had to make do with the cottage that he'd helped to build. It was a squeeze: Walter and his colleague were put up in Westerham, about which he makes no comment, so presumably he considered the security adequate.[7]

Churchill went to his beloved home on other occasions, too, if only for an hour or two, when he was especially worried or tired. 'It soothed his soul,' Walter said simply.

*   *   *

'Hello, Thompson, got your gun?' Invariably that was how Churchill greeted his bodyguard: a private little joke between them from their time together in Cannes. They knew each other well, and Walter made himself indispensable; he carried a spare eyemask in case Churchill forgot his; a spare cigar case should Churchill's run out; he even carried Churchill's National Registration Card.

But they did fall out on occasions, mostly over Churchill's reckless flirting with danger but over other things, too. It irritated Walter that Churchill so often expected him to perform menial tasks. To some extent that went with the job, but while he was prepared to fetch and carry for the Old Man, he refused to do it when it interfered with his proper function. 'Once, when he asked me to pack up his papers as he was leaving his private train . . . I put my foot down. "I will do it with pleasure," I said, "but you must give me a chance to do my job. I cannot guard you if you rush off and leave me to clear up." Mr Churchill glared at me furiously and stalked out of the compartment. But he was waiting for me on the platform when I came out with the baggage.'

On a visit to Manchester, travelling overnight, Churchill not only didn't wait but left Walter in his sleeper to pack his clothes – his valet had joined up, and he hadn't yet got used to the new man and refused to take him out of London. Walter, fuming, laden 'with a number of official boxes . . . an exceptionally heavy large leather case containing his clothes, my revolver, his Colt, two respirators and a special official box' came after him, 'considerably hampered by all this paraphernalia', thinking enough was enough. The final straw came at the hotel, when Churchill told him to run his bath and Walter decided 'the matter must be cleared up for good'. What exactly he said to Churchill he didn't record, but he was 'agreeably surprised' by the response. 'You are quite right, Thompson. I had so much on my mind that I did not realise what the extra work meant to you. I will bring the valet in future.' But Churchill, being Churchill, added: 'Will you run me a bath now?' And Walter, being Walter, did.

The pair bickered constantly over Churchill's refusal to carry his respirator and steel helmet.

Needless to say, he always dumped them on to me. As I already had my own to carry, I was not too pleased about this, for they must have weighed at least twelve pounds together. In the end I got fed up and I said: 'I am sorry. I cannot carry these for you any more. You must carry them yourself.' He did not like this at all and started to object. I cut him short. 'You know hundreds of pictures of you are taken by the press every week. What do you think the public reaction is to you not carrying your gas mask and tin hat? You really ought to be setting a good example.' He still did not like it . . . [but] he carried them himself after that. Mind you, he still tried to leave them in the car when I was not watching.

Other incidents set them at loggerheads. After London had taken considerable bomb damage, Churchill issued an order that no newspaper photographs were to show public buildings, many of which the Germans claimed to have destroyed. When Walter instructed the photographers waiting at the garden gate of Number 10 to put down their cameras ('my reason being that the Treasury would have been pictured from their position'), Churchill countermanded him. Annoyed and feeling that Churchill had made him look foolish, Walter wanted to know why he'd gone against his own orders; he'd done the same thing when at the Admiralty but on that occasion Walter was acting on the instructions of the Yard, not the Prime Minister himself. '"They are all God's children," Winston replied. When he saw I was not mollified, he added: "They have to do something to get a little copy."' Walter understood the Old Man's impulsive kindness but not his inconsistency, and he didn't understand Churchill's attitude over an incident involving President Roosevelt's envoy and most trusted adviser, Harry Hopkins, who'd come to England for talks, although America still wasn't in the war.

Walter had left a colleague at Number 10 during a Cabinet meeting and gone to lunch. He'd emerged from a restaurant near Oxford Circus to see his police car, his colleague in it, going by at a great pace. Grabbing a taxi back at Downing Street, he established that the other officer, with the meeting still in progress, had slipped over to Scotland Yard to make an enquiry and when he'd returned Churchill was gone – to Hendon aerodrome with his ADC, Commander Thompson, to see Hopkins off. Walter had spotted his colleague in pursuit. Walter paced the pavement outside Number 10 until Churchill got back. 'I noticed that as soon as he saw me he turned to Commander Thompson and made some remark, at which they both laughed. As he left the car, he looked at me and said, "I dodged you that time, Thompson," and seemed quite pleased with himself.' What annoyed Walter was not so much that Churchill had again 'slipped the leash' but that he seemed to think it amusing that Walter was upset.

Usually, Churchill could win his guard over. Visiting towns, he occasionally put on his steel helmet, 'giving me a grin like a schoolboy doing as he was told'. Out and about the streets when the bombing was at its height – and Walter was yet again about 'to have my say' – Churchill, anticipating him, innocently remarked: 'You were going to say something, Thompson?' Once he told Walter impishly: 'I would not take you into danger except I know how much you like it.' Such moments, Walter admitted, 'completely disarmed me'. As did moments of unexpected humour. On a very cold night, Churchill, having watched the bombing for some time from the roof of the Annexe, sat down to smoke his cigar and, in answer as to his welfare, professed himself warm. 'A few minutes later a sentry who patrolled the roof came to him and said, "Excuse me, sir, but I wonder if you would mind standing up?" "What?" said the Old Man. "You are sitting on the chimney, sir. You are smoking them out below."'

Whatever his public confidence, in private, with the war going badly, the strain told on Churchill. Walter appreciated the pressures he was under and made allowances: the Old Man was 'always a temperamental man [who], once riled, goes off the deep end with a vengeance but immediately comes to earth and all is forgiven'. But there began to be appreciably less forgiveness in Churchill and,

because I was always on the spot, I was frequently the scapegoat for things that had nothing to do with me. One morning Winston asked me to give some instructions to have a matter attended to through the Office of Works that day. At three the following morning, as he left the underground room with the Chiefs of Staff, he turned on me in a fury, demanding to know why his orders had not been carried out. I was not aware of this, but having carried out his original instructions I felt I should answer back. This I did quite forcibly. What amazed me most was the fact that – unusually for him – he went for me in front of the Chiefs of Staff . . . Neither of us said good night when I saw him to bed.

The strain got to Walter, too. The Blitz had 'multiplied my hours of duty while reducing my periods of rest', and he reached the stage where he felt he couldn't cope. He asked the Yard to be temporarily relieved.

It was the second time that he went to the Yard about Churchill. The first followed the wounding of Sergeant Davies when he was at his wits' end as to how to keep Churchill out of trouble. The head of Special Branch told him 'it was not possible and "to do my best – no man could do more"'. This, however, was more serious. 'Nothing I seemed to do appeared correct in his eyes. I bored him. The necessity of my job bored him. My everlasting presence must have bored him to death. It even bored me. I asked if a temporary shift might be advised. At the time I felt thoroughly disheartened. I felt I was falling down. I even wished somebody would attack him so I could shoot the attacker.'

For the second time he was sent back and told to do his best – the Yard didn't want to be put in the position of telling the Prime Minister, in the middle of conducting a war, that his body-guard wanted to quit. Walter, a self-sufficient man not in the habit of unburdening himself, talked to General Ismay, who'd been present during the outburst that had made Walter go to the Yard. 'The general smiled somewhat ruefully and said: "I get it just the same, Thompson. You have broad shoulders – you can take it. If it gives him relief from his overtaxed mind, it is well worth it."'

CHAPTER 7

Winnie, Franklin and Joe

A few days' leave in the summer of 1941 did Walter a power of good. He came back at the beginning of August to learn that the Prime Minister was planning a secret journey. At first he wouldn't tell Walter where it was to, or why. When he did, he was 'rather like a schoolboy planning a day's outing ... We were going to meet President Roosevelt at sea.'

America hadn't wanted to get involved in the war – isolationist sentiment in the Senate was so strong that during the 1930s a series of neutrality acts were forced through. Franklin Roosevelt hadn't been able to support the Allies overtly, but in 1940 he was ostensibly concerned with the defence of the US: more warships being built, Atlantic patrols in US coastal waters and a shoot-on-sight policy against Axis submarines. In March 1941, however, using home security as his reason, he persuaded the Senate to supply Britain with credit to fight the war.[1]

Churchill had worked on Roosevelt from the moment he'd

become Prime Minister (his communiqués addressed 'From Former Naval Person to President Roosevelt'), and he was excited about the trip. It was less than two months since Germany had invaded Russia in breach of the 1939 non-aggression pact the countries had signed,[2] and now, he hoped, America would do more. The American President was 'very apprehensive about Winston crossing the Atlantic, but Winston said: "Damn the risk."' Waiting at Chequers before catching his special train to Scapa Flow, where he was to board the destroyer *Prince of Wales*, he was all of a fidget. 'What time were the cars ordered to be here? I am ready to go now' – a surprise, because he was invariably late for trains; as his wife said: 'Winston is a sporting man. He likes to give the train a chance.'

To spirit Churchill out of the country without word reaching enemy ears, photographs had been taken on the steps of Number 10 showing him buying a flag for a flag day that would take place a week later.

Churchill was in jovial mood on the way to Scotland.

After dinner he asked Lord Cherwell [Professor Lindemann] to work out how many pints of champagne he had drunk in twenty-four years at the rate of a pint a day. When given the answer, he wanted to know how many coaches, such as the one we were in, would be needed to carry that amount of champagne. When he was told that it would only take up part of the coach he said: 'I am very disappointed. I had hoped that it would have taken several coaches.' Sir John Dill, Chief of the Imperial General Staff, then asked Winston how many yards of cigar he had smoked, but Winston would not be drawn.

Since Germany had opened the second front, Churchill had been more his old self. Two days out, the *Prince of Wales* made a drastic alteration of course – two U-boats, one disguised as a ketch, had been sighted – but he was relaxed. He read *Hornblower*, bustled about talking to the crew ('who asked me for Winston's cigar butts or the bands from his cigars, which he was careful not to break'), played darts in the warrant officers' mess ('he was dissatisfied with the darts and went along himself to the Naafi and purchased a quantity of new ones, which he presented to the mess') and watched the nightly film in the wardroom ('he saw *Lady Hamilton* again'). As once more Churchill had left his valet behind, Walter was in constant demand, the signal booming over the Tannoy: 'Inspector Thompson aft to the Prime Minister's cabin.'

* * *

Placentia Bay, Newfoundland, into which they steamed, was an awe-inspiring sight of American naval might. Included in the party of eight that went aboard the USS *Augusta* to meet the President, the no-nonsense Walter was overwhelmed by the idea that 'he was not only seeing history but sharing the making of it'; he was no less overwhelmed by the Americans' display of ceremony (and their generosity, later, in sending over boatloads of individual boxes of fruit, cheese and cigarettes for every man on the British destroyer and the accompanying escorts). During the three days of the get-together, when Churchill and Roosevelt signed the Atlantic Charter of peace aims, a Sunday morning church service was held on the *Prince of Wales* for which Churchill chose well-known hymns and, Walter thought, the occasion 'could not have failed to make an impact upon the least religious man'. Roosevelt's bodyguard, Mike Reilly, wanted to introduce Walter to the President, but Churchill insisted on doing that himself. Roosevelt asked Walter if Churchill was 'troublesome' and Walter dutifully lied. As he said goodbye, the President implored Walter to keep Churchill safe. 'Take care of him. He is about the greatest man in the world. In fact he may very likely be the greatest. You have a terrible responsibility in safeguarding him. You have the responsibility of four or five million people, Thompson.' One wonders what exactly Roosevelt meant by 'four or five million'. What was possibly in his mind was that if Churchill died, and with him Britain's chances of halting Hitler, then the number of lives that might be lost globally could have been of that magnitude – a figure utterly unimaginable at that stage of the war.[3]

On one of his sudden whims, Churchill wanted to go ashore to climb a hill overlooking the harbour. Walter was 'astonished at the effort he put into it. He not only seemed full of energy, but he wisecracked all the time, keeping us all in fits of laughter.' A rainstorm soaked them to the skin, 'but it did not damp Winston's enthusiasm and afterwards . . . I could see some of the tension of the past two years had disappeared from his face'.

Churchill hadn't got all he'd hoped for at Placentia Bay, but he did have Roosevelt's assurance that America would protect all commercial shipping as far east as Iceland – to which the *Prince of Wales* now headed: after Germany's invasion of Scandinavia, Iceland had been occupied by the British as a base for North Atlantic operations and Churchill wanted to see the troops. Convoys on the way to England frequently used the route they followed, and news came over the Tannoy that a convoy was ahead of them. As they caught it up, it 'opened into two lines, allowing us to pass through the centre. There were over seventy ships, crammed with supplies and in some cases with aeroplanes on deck.' The destroyer passed through, then circled to pass through again before proceeding, 'Winston placing himself in such a position that all the men lining the decks could see him'. Churchill was 'stirred in his heart'; so was Walter.

The previous month, Roosevelt had sent a 'neutral' US force to Iceland. After the *Prince of Wales* docked there, Walter watched these troops as they marched but didn't think much of their 'Yankee slouch' compared with the British 'upright carriage'. He thought even less of being photographed with a gigantic bouquet of flowers that the Icelanders presented to Churchill and he was given to carry. The 'rather floral study' was pinned up in the *Prince of Wales*'s mess 'with appropriate remarks inscribed thereon'.

Placentia Bay hadn't brought America into the war, but four months later the Japanese attack on Pearl Harbor did.[4] Churchill heard the news on his small radio at Chequers. 'So we have won after all!' he wrote. 'Our history would not come to an end... I went to bed and slept the sleep of the saved and thankful.' And he headed back to see Roosevelt, worrying that the President might divert attention and resources from Europe to the Pacific. The British Empire across the Far East was collapsing before the onslaught unleashed by Pearl Harbor. An overall strategy was needed.

The voyage was made on the battleship *Duke of York*, which left the Clyde in a full gale, making headway at only twelve knots. They were so far behind the timetable that once they'd left the dangerous waters off the west coast of Ireland they dropped the protecting escorts 'and belted through the seas for two days'. U-boats constantly lurked off the Irish coast, in the main to pick off merchantmen. Had Ireland, which remained neutral during the war, not refused Churchill's repeated requests to use its west coast ports, British anti-submarine ships could have operated a further 180 miles out into the Atlantic.[5] Churchill was under constant public pressure to take the ports over. Walter asked him why he didn't and was told: 'That is the very thing we are fighting against. I will not do it!'

This time, Churchill had with him a large party, including the service chiefs, and 'meetings were held day after day. The Prime Minister had brought a mobile version of his War Room, complete with maps, charts and models; later he would set it up in the White House, and it would accompany him to all the major conferences of the war.' There were constant reports of U-boats in the area, and Churchill expressed the hope that they might be able to ram one.

Not the best of sailors, Churchill was seasick, his nerves jangled by the seamen's whistling as they swabbed the passageways; he sent his male secretary – he'd considered it inappropriate to bring a female aboard ship – to tell them to stop (the secretary, Patrick Kinna, hadn't the courage). He worked most of the day in bed, but he was up for meetings and to watch most of the films; several were Westerns and after one 'in which about twelve people were shot', he left saying: 'Now I think I will have a little peace and get back to the war.' As the battleship neared Chesapeake Bay, a number of American destroyers joined the *York* but couldn't keep pace. Walter later met a crewman from one of them who told him: 'I thought we were told to escort a battleship – not a goddamn greyhound.'

What is known as the Arcadia conference straddled Christmas, during which Churchill was given the grim news that Hong Kong had fallen. It was not unexpected: the colony was virtually on Japan's doorstep. Nonetheless, Churchill found it psychologically impossible to accept and, Walter saw, 'he reeled'. He was poorly and his doctor, Charles Wilson (later Lord Moran), had to attend to him. However he was feeling, when he addressed both Houses of the American Congress Churchill radiated optimism, and his sense of humour was unimpaired one evening

after a meeting in which the President had asked for certain details about North Africa and thought, wrongly, that

Winston was deliberately holding back on the subject. He was relaxing in his room at the White House after a bath, absolutely naked, thoroughly enjoying the warmth of the central heating, when the door was suddenly thrown open and the President propelled himself through the doorway in his wheelchair. 'You see, Mr President,' Winston said. 'I have nothing whatever to hide from you.'

Walter and his number two on the trip, Sergeant Charles Dudgeon, who received ties from Mr and Mrs Roosevelt as Christmas presents, witnessed the Secret Service destroy 'many parcels' of cigars sent as gifts to Churchill, 'in case they had been tampered with or had poison injected with a syringe'.[6] The Secret Service's method of guarding Roosevelt raised Walter's Cockney scorn: where Scotland Yard guarded Churchill with two men ('me in the front of the PM's car, my colleague in the one behind ... and we avoid as much as possible drawing attention to ourselves'), the President 'has a dozen men around him, and when his car stops they immediately surround it on all sides facing out ... telling everyone that the President is in the car. A bomb in the middle would finish them all.' Churchill's 'quizzical look plainly told me his opinion of the turnout'.[7] Walter was delighted when the Old Man came out of the Capitol and brushed the Secret Service agents away from him so that he could talk to the crowd.

On 28 December they left for Ottawa, where Churchill addressed the Canadian House of Commons, describing his last visit to France when the French generals were predicting that in three weeks England would have her neck wrung like a chicken. Peering over his reading glasses, Churchill added: 'Some neck! Some chicken!' – an impromptu that brought the house down. 'I was glad to have been present,' Walter entered in his notes.

Returning to Washington, Churchill saw in the New Year on the train by joining hands with his staff and the dining car attendants and singing 'Auld Lang Syne' 'in his hearty but not very tuneful voice'. But he was far from well and gratefully accepted a few days' rest on the coast of Florida. He swam off the beach without trunks ('If they are that much interested, it is their own fault what they see'); once a sand shark was close inshore and he went into the water on being told it was harmless, though he joked: 'I'd like to see his identity card, Thompson.' Refreshed after the break, he returned to Washington for five more days of conference, then went to Bermuda on the flying boat *Berwick*, the biggest aircraft in the world at the time, to rejoin the *York* for the homeward journey. The comfort of the *Berwick*, with its armchairs and sleeping berths, so pleased Churchill, who was anxious to get back home quickly because of the worsening situation in Malaya, that he asked if it could fly the 3,000 miles to England. Walter was in an acute state of anxiety, especially as the aircraft could take only ten passengers, meaning he was to be left behind to accommodate the service chiefs. He 'protested violently', pointing out that 'flying the Atlantic was still in its early stage', irrespective of the dangers of aerial attack, and it was 'a foolish thing to have all your eggs in one basket'. As ever, his protests were to no avail, and again Churchill hurt him by telling someone in his hearing: 'The Inspector is very sore because he is not coming with me.' Before making the trip, Churchill shook hands with those going by sea. 'When he came to me it was obvious from his expression that he wasn't quite happy about leaving me behind . . . the first time since August 1939.'[8]

The *York* didn't weigh anchor until news came through the following morning that the flying boat had arrived safely in Plymouth – but not, as Churchill told Walter later, without hazard. He'd awoken to find the *Berwick* in dense cloud and the pilot uncertain of his position. In fact, had the pilot held course for another five or six minutes they would have flown into the German anti-aircraft guns at Brest. Churchill was lucky twice over. British radar screens showed what was thought to be an enemy bomber, and fighters were scrambled to shoot the aircraft down. The cloud cover saved them from being found.

*   *   *

North Africa was the constant thorn in Churchill's paw, in large part due to the bitter split in French loyalties between the Vichy government and the Free French, who had General de Gaulle, in exile in London, at their head.

The attempt in September 1940 by a British and Free French force to take the French naval base at Dakar on the West African coast, as a prelude to getting the French colonies to rally to de Gaulle, was a disaster. The landing was repulsed with losses on both sides, and Churchill called off the operation after two days. A greater setback resulted from a decision Churchill made in early 1941 to withdraw experienced units from Libya (to shore up the situation in Greece) just as the Empire force of British, Australian, New Zealand, South African and Indian troops were poised to eject the Italians completely. In the confusion that Churchill's strategy created, Rommel and his Afrika Korps arrived unanticipated, broke out of the bottleneck in which the Italians were trapped – and the desert war swung back and forth for more than the next two years.

'The service chiefs, who had not approved of the switch of troops, openly criticised Winston's handling,' Walter wrote. 'Their views had the support of a few Members of Parliament, including Lloyd George, whose attack in the House received the sharp retort: "It was the sort of speech with which I imagine the illustrious and venerable Marshal Pétain might well have enlivened the closing days of Monsieur Reynaud's Cabinet."' Churchill got a resounding vote of 447–1.

When he'd returned to London from Placentia Bay, Churchill had been greeted by a reception committee of his entire Cabinet and a big crowd roaring their approval. Four months on he came back from the Arcadia conference, while the humiliation of the loss of Hong Kong was still uppermost in people's minds, to parliamentary criticism of his conduct of the war. The vote of confidence he demanded was 646–1 for him.

A Russian delegation headed by Stalin's Foreign Minister Molotov having been and gone in England and America in January 1942, Churchill was off to Washington again, laying plans for North Africa. Having found air travel infinitely preferable to sea, he wanted another flying boat and he got one, the *Bristol*. The *Berwick* had crossed the Atlantic in eighteen hours; the *Bristol* took twenty-seven before arriving at the Potomac River.

> My most vivid recollection of the long flight was of Winston lying on his bunk at the rear of the plane, dressed in the inevitable gaudy dressing gown and smoking a cigar. After some hours, Winston called me over to find out when we were due to eat. When I told him that owing to the change in time it would be several more hours, he exclaimed: 'My stomach is my clock. I want to eat when I am hungry – not by the clock.' . . . After that, meals were served about every four hours.

For the second time Churchill's leaving the country seemed to precipitate bad news. The 8th Army was in full retreat, the vital Libyan port of Tobruk had fallen in a single day – and ships carrying tanks to Libya on the tortuous three-month voyage round the Cape and through the Suez Canal had been sunk. But Roosevelt immediately diverted 300 Shermans (and 100 self-propelled guns) that were already en route to his own 1st Armored Division in the Middle East. So buoyed was Churchill by this gesture that he decided he wanted to tell the troops in North Africa himself. The Washington papers were full of stories that back in London MPs were calling for his head ('a real field day,' Walter recorded). The Prime Minister, however, returned in pugnacious mood to face down his critics – but not before a near encounter that happened as he left for England and of which he knew nothing at the time put his life in danger.

The Secret Service had wanted Churchill's flying boat *Bristol* to leave from the waterside Anacostia naval air base at Washington. The British Embassy, however, insisted that the departure should be from Colgate Creek at Baltimore's municipal airport, Harbor Field. What those on board the *Bristol* were unaware of as they lifted into the air was that on the pier, two FBI agents, one of them Roosevelt's bodyguard, Mike Reilly, had wrestled to the ground an airport worker armed with a gun who was overheard muttering to himself, 'I'm going to get that fucking Churchill. I'm going to kill him.' He was later judged insane (Churchill wrote about the incident in his history of the war, commenting that 'crackpates are a special danger to public men, as they don't worry about the "getaway"').

During the parliamentary debate about the PM's handling of the war, the matter of British tank production arose, including the new Churchill infantry tank[9] that had started coming off the assembly line the previous summer. 'The A22 tank was ordered off the drawing board and large numbers went into production quickly,' Churchill responded. 'As might be expected, it had many defects and teething troubles and when these became apparent it was appropriately rechristened the Churchill.' The

House, Walter was happy to report, 'was in the palm of his hand'. The motion of censure was defeated 475–27.

Later in the month Churchill and Molotov signed a treaty providing for full cooperation between Britain and Russia for twenty years. It was time to meet Joseph Stalin – and to give him the unpalatable news that the second front in Europe, which Roosevelt and Churchill had been promising, was on the back burner until North Africa was resolved.

*   *   *

Whatever his public resolve, whatever his indomitable belief in his destiny, Churchill was an emotional man who couldn't help taking every defeat and loss as personal blows. Normally his sheer spirit carried him forward. Sometimes his anger spilled over and those closest to him bore the brunt, as Walter well knew. But there were occasions when something happened that was too much for Churchill and he descended into deep depression. Such episodes didn't last, but while they did he lapsed into listlessness. As far as he was in any position to do so, Walter tried to keep people from him. There were nights when he sat by his bed.

Churchill was badly hit by a double disaster in May 1941: the loss of Crete to the first paratroop assault of the war (12,000 men were taken prisoner); and the sinking by the *Bismarck* of the battle cruiser *Hood*, the largest warship in the world in 1939, launched in 1920 when Churchill was Secretary for War. The *Hood* was blown to pieces when a shell struck the magazine; only 3 of a complement of over 1,400 survived. The sinking of the *Prince of Wales* – which had taken him to his Newfoundland meeting with Roosevelt – together with the *Repulse*, also hit Churchill hard. He'd sent them to Malayan waters without air cover because planes couldn't be spared; they fell prey to Japanese dive-bombers and torpedoes.

But the setback of the war that threw Churchill into black

despair was the capture of Singapore in February 1942, with the surrender of 130,000. Churchill had regarded the island, with its massive gun emplacements facing the sea, as impregnable. The Japanese, having swept through Malaya in two months, came 'through the kitchen door', as Walter put it, and took the 'Gibraltar of the Far East' in a week. The loss was ignominious: Churchill had expected every inch of ground to be defended and described the capitulation as the 'greatest disaster . . . in British history'. Walter recorded that 'for days he was miserable and despondent. When asked what had happened, he would shake his head dismally and say: "I really don't know."' He went to bed at Ditchley Park and asked Walter to stop all calls.

Thirty minutes later he sent for me – the telephone ringing had awakened him. Unfortunately, although the operator on the switchboard had stopped calls to him, a line from the secretaries' office had been left through to his room. It would have been some relief if this had been one of the occasions for an outburst of Churchillian invective [but] he was not angry – he was pathetic, and he said, in a miserable voice: 'Sleep for me is finished. I shall do some work.'

Next morning, Sunday, I took the newspapers to him. He was sitting up in bed eating his breakfast . . . I handed him the papers, but he just laid them down on the bed. Usually, at any time of the day or night, when newspapers arrived he would look at them at once. He spoke to me but his thoughts were obviously far away, and his face looked blank. I felt I must make some effort to try to get him out of his despondency. I suggested somewhat apprehensively: 'Don't you think, sir, that it would do you good if you took a trip next weekend to see some servicemen or establishments? It would do you good to get out into the open air.' He was looking at me with his head slightly on one side, but he did not answer. I tried again: 'You always sleep well after these trips. They seem to put new life into you. Why don't you make one, sir?' Still he stared into space. I was determined to rouse him. I felt that we knew one another well enough for me to try again – even if his wrath did descend upon me. 'Is it not a fact, sir, that these trips always do you good and make you sleep better?' Suddenly he looked straight at me and said: 'Yes, you are quite right.' 'Then why not take one next weekend, sir?' I said. 'I will,' he answered, and it seemed as though a great weight had been lifted from his mind, and he seemed to relax.

In August 1942 Churchill chose to kill two birds with one stone: he went to Egypt and then on to Moscow on the same trip. For it, Air Marshal Portal acquired an American Liberator – a huge B24 four-engined long-range bomber – from US Ferry Command, as well as a pilot and crew. That Churchill was to use an American plane 'caused a certain amount of heartburn with the RAF', Walter wrote, but added practically that a plane with American markings 'was able to fly over some countries where a British one would have been fired upon'.

The Liberator, named *Commando*, offered primitive accommodation, a far cry from the York transporter that Churchill would mostly use later in the war, which the RAF fitted out for him with a galley and his own private cabin. The Liberator

retained its service interior, but bucket seats were fixed over the side of the bomb bay for us . . . At times the plane was like an icebox and at others the heat was well nigh intolerable. The noise was intolerable. Sleeping was either in rigged canvas bunks or mattresses on the steel deck. An improvised table was made up of boxes and some of our baggage to have our meals ... My greatest surprise was that Winston put up with so much discomfort.

The route to Cairo involved a stop at Gibraltar, after which 'we were to go due south down the West African coast and then bear left. To Winston this was an utter waste of time. He decided we should go direct across French Morocco, although he knew only too well that British planes flying over that area had been shot down. To make matters worse, we were flying in broad daylight.' An escort of fighters, however, substantially reduced any risk.

In Cairo's oppressive heat, Churchill met the South African statesman Field Marshal Smuts, a man exactly his age and a firm friend, whose 'massive judgement' he sought about the way the desert war was being fought. He also built up his own picture of the military situation, inspected the Alamein Line, the last defensive position before the Nile, where the 8th Army had already engaged Rommel the previous month along their six-mile front – and assessed his senior officers. Then he ruthlessly sacked General Auchinleck as C-in-C Middle East, having come to the conclusion that 'the Auk' lacked aggression. He gave the job to Alexander and command of the 8th Army to Montgomery (his first choice, Gott, was killed when his plane was shot down two days after his appointment). Until now Montgomery had been in charge of the defence of the south-east of England. Churchill had met Montgomery during his tours of the region. He hadn't liked him – but he was impressed by his air of confidence.

It wasn't Moscow next stop: *Commando* took an overnight stop in Teheran, where Churchill slept at the British summer legation. Returning to the Liberator, he received a shock: two

Russian air-force officers were aboard for the ongoing flight that was

to fly, they said, by a route already laid down by them. Winston reacted to this by saying: 'I am sure my navigator knows the way.' He was put out at their presence and even more so when our pilot was instructed to climb high – the plane was not pressurised, and owing to Winston's health it was not advisable. An argument followed, at the end of which a more reasonable height was agreed.

Commando touched down in Moscow to be met by Stalin – replete in peasant smock and blue trousers tucked into long boots – Molotov and a galaxy of commissars and generals. Churchill inspected a guard of honour before the party were driven to a villa eight miles outside the city, followed by 'two black cars with ten security police'. The garden was surrounded by inner and outer walls, the ground between them stripped bare for surveillance; guards manned platforms around the perimeter.

Everyone, Walter wrote, 'felt very uneasy in this building' from which they weren't allowed to go unaccompanied. 'The guards were not supposed to be able to speak English, but I found they could. I suddenly realised that they were supposed to eaves-drop on every conversation the British party might have in the hope of picking up secret information that could be useful in the negotiations . . . I spoke to Winston about this in his bedroom. I warned him to speak with care. I told him: "It may well be that even this room has hidden microphones."' If it did, Walter added, it would be impossible to trace them all. '"In which case I will send them a message," Winston said. With that, he stamped his foot and said: "This is Winston Churchill speaking. If you have microphones in my room it is a waste of time: I do not talk in my sleep." Then he grinned at me and said: "I had better tell them again in the other room."'

Churchill the romantic was also a realist. When he'd been Secretary of State for War in 1919, he'd believed in Allied intervention in the Russian civil conflict and supplied the White Russians with arms, proclaiming that Bolshevism 'must be strangled in its cradle'. Now he had Stalin lined up beside him against Hitler. 'If Hitler invaded hell I would at least make a favourable reference to the devil,' he said.

His first face-to-face encounter with 'Uncle Joe', as he often called Stalin, in the company of Averell Harriman, Roosevelt's negotiator, was cordial enough, after Stalin calmed down about the postponement of the second front. The one following that, however, broke up almost before it began, with Stalin accusing Churchill of breaking his word and Churchill stalking out, 'banging down the corridors looking neither to right nor left. He struck a match on the Kremlin wall and, still walking, lit a cigar and puffed angrily. For the next two days we did nothing and Winston chafed at the delay [but] the Chiefs of Staff on each side were in conference.'

Throughout their stay, the party were plied with food and drink – 'the Russians were just as lavish with their hospitality as they were with their security guards' – and, at a time when food in Russia was scarce, large tracts of cropland being behind the German lines, they were uncomfortable about it, 'as well as having indigestion'. But the Kremlin banquet that Churchill and his colleagues were now invited to was staggering in its lavishness, and in the number of toasts made at it. During the four hours of the affair there were thirty or forty, with Walter toasted 'by the head of the security police as the Minister of Scotland'.

Stalin was in affable mood, chatting to Churchill through his interpreter, Pavlov. Churchill mentioned that he admired the goldfish in the garden fountain at the villa; 'Stalin offered them to him, either to take back to England or to have them cooked there.'

At the point where champagne, liqueurs and coffee were being served in the anteroom, Churchill was restive, passing a message to Stalin that he wanted to get down to business.

When the answer came back – 'You are here to enjoy yourselves. Mr Stalin is enjoying himself. He does not intend to have a meeting tonight' – Winston almost exploded. He made it clear that the plane would leave on Sunday morning, and if Stalin wanted to talk he knew where to find us. With that, he turned on his heel and walked out. The next day Mr Churchill was respectfully informed that Marshal Stalin was most anxious to have a private interview with the Prime Minister if he would be so kind as to come to the Kremlin at 6 p.m.

Walter was the only person with Churchill on this occasion. Churchill disappeared into Stalin's presence and Walter waited. After a while he was asked to leave and return to the villa. At first he assumed Churchill was leaving, but he didn't appear. Walter refused to go, considered bursting in on Stalin, thought better of it but didn't know what to do. He hung around the entrance, then 'walked up and down the road, my every move followed by the secret police, who could not or would not understand my questions'. Where was Churchill? Walter's imagination was working overtime before he saw a police officer he'd met when Molotov came to London. The man Walter knew spoke no English, but his companion did – and Walter found out that the Old Man was continuing his discussions with Stalin over dinner: the Russians simply thought Walter would want to go back to the villa for his own. As Walter wasn't having any of that, the pair invited him to eat with them.

At around two in the morning, one of Churchill's party, Sir Alexander Cadogan, came looking for the Prime Minister, and he and Walter waited together until Churchill emerged. Going back in the car, Cadogan asked how things had gone. 'Unless he is a bigger liar than I thought he was,' Winston replied, 'we have got somewhere.'

Even at this early hour the bread queues were forming in the streets, and Walter, 'the menu from the banquet still in my pocket', felt guilty. He felt worse four hours later seeing 'the same people standing, unserved, when we left for the airport'.

On the Teheran stopover Churchill decided on a quick visit to the young Shah and went to his summer palace at Shirnan for lunch. Persia (Iran) swarmed with German agents that British Field Security were still clearing out,[10] and he was given a military escort headed by two motorcyclists. At 8,000 feet, the climb and the heat brought the machines to a crawl, and Walter became angry because he thought the riders were deliberately going slowly. Only talking to them afterwards did he find out that the motorcycles, like all the vehicles the British had in Persia, were clapped-out 'recoveries' from the Western Desert.

Arriving in Cairo again, Churchill paid a second visit to Alamein. He slept in General Montgomery's caravan, dipped in the sea, wore a sombrero and carried an umbrella. He couldn't be kept from the forward positions and caused General Freyberg 'some anxiety'. Seeing 'sand spout up several times 200 yards away and being told that Jerry was sending a few shells over', he at once headed in that direction. Freyberg asked Walter how he could stop him. Walter advised him to tell Churchill 'it was his duty to see him safely away from the front', which Freyberg did. Churchill turned back. After going to see several regiments, he then went to the Sweet Water Canal, 'where many of our troops had been brought together for regrouping and training'. Here, he listened to their complaints and in no uncertain terms was told they 'felt they were being let down. Winston listened patiently – he had something up his sleeve.' Finally he revealed it: Roosevelt's Sherman tanks, which '"have passed safely into the Suez Canal and within days you will have them". Cheers resounded, and the large circle of men closed in on him. I had my work cut out to prevent his being knocked over by the troops, who all wanted to shake his hand and pat him on the back.'

Tanks were involved in another Churchill escapade, though Walter never transcribed the incident involving them into any manuscript and doesn't indicate on which of the many wartime visits to Cairo it took place. It involved the Abdin Palace – again – a morning when suddenly Churchill announced he was going there to see King Farouk and they went, alone other than for their driver. Outside the palace, Churchill asked Walter a question that he found strange: 'Have you got a white handkerchief and my Colt?' Disturbed about the revolver (Churchill hadn't asked for it since the flight to France in 1940), and then by being asked the time by his watch, Walter pressed Churchill about what he was up to. In answer, he was told: 'Thompson, I know exactly what I am doing. If I am not out in fifteen minutes, wave your handkerchief above your head' – and Churchill was through the door. For the umpteenth time in their relationship, Walter was on hot bricks as he waited in the courtyard.

Before the fifteen minutes were up, Churchill was back, 'a broad smile on his face. "There was a rumour that I might be assassinated in there," he said.' What was the handkerchief about,

Walter wanted to know. 'If you had waved the handkerchief, tanks would have rolled into the courtyard. They are all around us. That is what I was relying on.' Walter saw some of them as they drove away. He never did find out why Churchill had really gone to the Abdin Palace, unless it was for the pure pleasure of the danger.

Home again, Churchill involved himself in the planning of the invasion of North Africa from the west, having to accede to the Americans that Oran and Dakar were still so raw in many French memories that Operation Torch had to be seen to be led by America. Between 23 October and 4 November the third and most famous battle of El Alamein took place, opening with the greatest artillery barrage in military history. Rommel fled west. Two days later the Torch was lit, squeezing him between two armies. Tobruk was taken, and its church bell was heard on the radio; and in Britain Churchill ordered the church bells to be rung for the first time since summer 1940.

*   *   *

Roosevelt was keen that Stalin should attend the Casablanca conference that began in late January 1943, but he refused on the grounds that he was occupied with the battle for Stalingrad. So together the President and the Prime Minister decided their next priorities, including the invasion of Sicily (stepping stone to the Italian mainland), future operations in the Pacific and Burma, the ending of the U-boat menace once and for all[11] – and what to do about the French leadership.

Despite his strong dislike of the man, Churchill always favoured de Gaulle as the spearhead of French resistance. Roosevelt, however, had refused to let de Gaulle have anything to do with North Africa (and Walter could see why – 'austere, stubborn, always on his dignity: not the easiest of men to get on with'). Instead, the President had sanctioned Admiral Darlan as

C-in-C French forces in the theatre, as well as High Commissioner North Africa, leading de Gaulle in London to front a protest against a man he believed pro-Nazi – until his *volte-face* Darlan had been a member of the Vichy government. Darlan's appointment left the situation on the ground tense and confused (some French troops put up armed resistance to the Allies), and only his assassination on Christmas Eve 1942 stopped it from getting out of hand. But even then Roosevelt refused to consider de Gaulle, instead putting his faith in General Giraud, who'd recently escaped from German internment.

At Casablanca Churchill and Roosevelt sought a healing process.

'After a long day dealing with this matter, Winston went to his bedroom, and after saying good night to him I went to mine,' Walter wrote. 'After a while I heard him calling me. "I am sorry to keep you up so late, Thompson, but I must go over to see the President, for we have to marry these two bastards somehow"' – the two bastards in question being Giraud and de Gaulle. De Gaulle, Churchill added, was 'on his way to our villa – I was to patrol around the grounds to see that no one came near while they talked.

'I could catch snatches of their conversation because Winston always seemed to speak very loudly when talking in French. I was amused to listen to his pronunciation. He knew French grammar, but beyond that at times I failed entirely to understand what he said. From what I gathered, I was glad that it was General de Gaulle he was dealing with and not me.' At last, Churchill

came to the window and said that they were going over to see the President. I followed. Just as we reached a right turn of the road, Mr Murphy, one of the President's staff, with General Giraud, came face to face with us. When de Gaulle saw them, he hesitated and appeared to turn back. To my amusement, Winston put his hand into de Gaulle's back and said: 'Allez, allez.' The two Frenchmen then shook hands, but to me it seemed that de Gaulle's was a very half-hearted greeting.

In a break in the conference Churchill went to see the French battleship *Jean Bart*, which was being repaired in the harbour. He didn't go aboard, much to Walter's relief, 'for as we walked along the side of the ship the sailors on guard seemed to look at him sullenly. Perhaps they did not recognise the Old Man, but I and my colleague kept a wary eye out until we returned to our villa.'

The conference was demanding and Churchill was drained, but wanting a breath of fresh air he walked down to the sea, returning to the villa by a different route.

Nearing our compound, he saw [that] rolls of barbed wire were between the villa and us. I said: 'I'm afraid we shall have to go back the other way, sir.' This meant quite a trip around. 'No,' he said, 'we can climb over that,' and promptly proceeded to do so, forcing his way through first and me following through the gap he had made. Suddenly there was a shout of 'Halt!' – and we found ourselves looking down the barrels of Tommy guns held by the American sentries. An American officer came up and soundly reproved Winston, telling us that his men had orders to fire upon anyone attempting to pass through the wire. Winston stood with his head down whilst the officer was speaking, then thanked him and said: 'You are quite right. What I did was extremely foolish. I should have gone back.'

Churchill insisted on the officer accompanying him to Roosevelt, where he took the blame for what he'd done, his only defence being that he was very tired. 'The President listened and said: "Winston, you should be ashamed. My orders are to shoot anyone passing through the wire." They both smiled, but as we returned to our villa Winston was extremely subdued.' His mood soon changed. The 8th Army had captured Tripoli.

In high spirits at the end of the conference, Churchill persuaded Roosevelt to drive five hours to Marrakech to show him his holiday haunt of 1936, and stayed behind for an afternoon painting the Atlas Mountains, the only picture he is generally believed to have painted during the war.[12] He then saw Roosevelt off on his return flight to Washington (wearing his dressing gown and slippers to the airport), before taking off himself for a few days in Cairo. One morning he suddenly ordered a visit to GHQ Cairo – he'd noticed 'the number of army cars running around and waiting outside shops and hotels; during the lunch period it was a continual stream'. Churchill put a stop to that, then boarded his Liberator for Adana, near the Syrian border, where he met the Turks and tried to persuade them to abandon their neutrality. In a neutral country 'the service members of the party had to borrow civilian suits. There were some strange sights. General Sir Henry Maitland Wilson put his bulk into a suit belonging to Sir Miles Lampson, the British Ambassador, a much taller and slimmer man. The general had to use a considerable amount of extra turn-up in the trousers.' The meeting with Turkish President Inönü was in a railway siding in open country, Walter 'alarmed [because] the Germans were aware that it was to take place, though they did not know the location . . . Turkish troops were guarding the sidings, but my colleague and I sat all night inside the locked doors of Winston's coach, with our guns at the ready.'

From Turkey to Cyprus – another whim: Churchill's old

regiment, the 4th Hussars, were there – then back to Cairo and, reunited with *Commando* (temporarily left in Turkey when one of its wheels sank into the tarmac on the apron), onward on the 1,400-mile flight to Tripoli, 'passing along the line of advance from El Alamein and flying low . . . the massive arrays of wrecked tanks, mechanised vehicles, guns and aeroplanes spread along the desert'. The 8th Army was about to cross into Tunisia, soon to join hands with the Americans advancing from the west, and Churchill was so excited 'he almost embraced' the waiting Montgomery, in whose caravan he again spent the night. The next day he was driven into Tripoli. Little more than a week earlier, the city had been in enemy hands and Walter worried that the houses over-looking the route couldn't have been thoroughly searched and cleared. The 8th Army's ceremonial entry was extraordinary: 'Their vehicles looked as if they had just come out of barracks – shining like new. Their boots were polished, their trousers pressed, their equipment clean and their heads held high. "I really do not know where they got their polish," said General Montgomery. Winston chuckled as he answered: "Trust the British Tommy to find some when required."' He concluded his address by saying: 'After this war is over, it will be sufficient for you to say when you are asked "What did you do?" to reply "I marched with the 8th Army".' He was cheered to the echo. One soldier, a little bolder than the rest, called out: 'What about a cigar, sir?' Winston stopped and said: 'Why not?' and handed him his case. Churchill didn't forget the other two services: he visited RAF units, and the navy who were busy clearing Tripoli harbour.

Next, he flew to Algiers for a quick round of talks and a briefing with Eisenhower; toured the battlefield west from Tunis, which was littered with destroyed tanks and other vehicles, most of them German (Walter being struck by 'how peaceful it now was among the olive trees'); then, on the night of 5 February, he drove to Maison Blanche airport for the return to London. But one of *Commando*'s engines was playing up: a faulty magneto, the captain thought. The huge Liberator could have flown on three engines and, after several frustrating hours of nothing happening, Churchill was all for it. '"Do you think we should risk it?" he asked me,' Walter wrote. 'I am always cautious about these matters and said no.' Everyone disembarked (except Sir Charles Wilson, asleep and overlooked in the dark), to return the following day when the problem was rectified.

This small incident appeared to become significant three years later with the publication of Captain Harry Butcher's war diary, in which Eisenhower's naval aide claimed that Churchill had sent 'one of his detectives' to Maison Blanche to sabotage his own aircraft by removing a magneto wire, thereby deliberately preventing it from leaving – a story that quickly gained wide currency, although no one had a credible explanation as to why. Walter (in fact, the only detective with Churchill on this trip) appeared more baffled than angry, saying the 'extraordinary statement . . . is neither true nor does there seem any point to it. If Winston had not wished to return to London that day he would have said so. He would certainly not have allowed, let alone ordered, a detective with no specialised knowledge to interfere with any part of an aircraft.'

Yet Harold Thompson is adamant that his father told him he'd done what Butcher said. 'Dad talked about Churchill all the time, but never about things that Churchill wanted kept secret or things he thought other people shouldn't know. But he suddenly told me one day when we were working at the garage together [see Chapter 12, pages 251–2]. In fact, he didn't remove a magneto wire; he took the rotor from the distributor cap. I have no doubt that he did it. Dad knew his engines. It would have taken seconds. And nobody would have been any the wiser.'

But why? Churchill was anxious to get home; there was credible information that a prominent German agent was in Algiers with orders from Hitler to assassinate Churchill and Eisenhower was anxious for him to be gone – indeed Eisenhower was so worried he'd had his own B17 ostentatiously prepared for takeoff and had sent Captain Butcher to it with an armoured convoy, where he made a pretence of smuggling a party aboard before the plane flew. So why would Churchill have ordered Walter to disable the Liberator?

There is a possible explanation that now seems startling simple – that Churchill was in possession of an intercepted German radio signal that indicated an attempt was to be made to shoot the Liberator down.

If Churchill had such information – which would have come from Station X at Bletchley Park, where British cryptanalysts had broken the Enigma code[13] that the German believed impenetrable – then subterfuge was needed to disguise the real reason he didn't fly. That Station X was reading thousands of German high-level communications every day was the best-kept secret of the war. Churchill would have wanted the Germans' confidence in their ciphers to be maintained. And there was no better cover story than a mechanical breakdown of his aircraft.

Churchill certainly wouldn't have told Walter about Enigma – not even his private secretaries knew the details of his secret source of information, codenamed Ultra, which he received every morning, wherever he was. But Churchill wouldn't have had to: just telling Walter he wanted the Liberator grounded would have been sufficient to get his bodyguard to drive the twenty or thirty miles across the desert to Maison Blanche. Again, if this scenario is true, it explains why Walter felt it necessary to elaborate his narrative by writing that he advised Churchill not to risk taking off on three engines.

Churchill was dead tired, having travelled 10,000 miles in a month. Ten days later he had double pneumonia. So did Walter: 'We had probably picked up a germ in Tripoli.' Walter spent a few days in bed, Churchill a week, though he couldn't be prevented from working; he wasn't, however, well enough for nearly a month to go to Chequers. Walter came into his room when 'the nurse attending him was leaning over him with a glass of glucose and water, saying: "Come along now, drink this." After he had swallowed it, she said: "There: what did you think of that?" From the depths of the pillow came the deliberate reply: "Let it never be said that that was my favourite tipple."'

CHAPTER 8

Pain and Loss

On a Friday afternoon in early March 1943, Walter shot himself by accident – 'not driven to it by the responsibility of guarding the impossible Mr Churchill,' he wrote laconically.

When Churchill became First Sea Lord in September 1939, Walter moved into the flat over the Admiralty garage in Richmond Terrace Mews off Whitehall; when Churchill became Prime Minister in May the following year, Walter moved again, to the flat over the PM's garage in College Mews, a little further from Downing Street, behind Westminster Abbey.[1] He was here, having tea with friends, when the direct-line phone rang: the signal that Churchill was ready to go to Chequers. On duty, Walter carried his Webley in 'a patent chamois leather contraption of my own, on the inside and between the two buttons of the left breast of my jacket – I found it faster to draw and fire from this position than from a shoulder holster'; by long habit, when his jacket was off, he carried it thrust into his waistband.

Leaning over the back of a very wide settee, to replace the receiver, the automatic slipped down his trousers, hit the floor and discharged, 'firing a bullet through the calf of my left leg, [which] diverted into my right thigh and, as I was in a crouching position, went upwards into my pelvis, lodging against my hipbone. My right leg collapsed. I began to bleed severely . . . Scotland Yard had an ambulance for me in seven minutes.'

The news was quickly censored, but not before the *Evening Standard* carried an inaccurate version of it, saying that Walter had shot himself while cleaning the weapon; the traitor Lord Haw-Haw, who broadcast Nazi propaganda from Hamburg, had a wilder version: 'there had been a riot in London demanding that Winston stop the war and sue for peace, and in protecting him I had been shot.'[2]

Walter was operated on in St Thomas' Hospital. Churchill paid him a visit. 'Get well soon and come back to me,' he said. Walter's three sons, all serving in the air force, managed to get away to see him – Harvey had just returned to England on his first home posting in six years. Kate, who'd been evacuated to Rotherham in Yorkshire with her two daughters, Grace and Kathleen, didn't come, but Harold brought his son Peter, then ten, who remembers thinking 'it was a feather in my cap that my grandfather who guarded Churchill had been shot. I remember the wire cage thing over his leg – and finding him a bit frightening.' In his published account, Walter wrote that 'my recovering was quick', but it wasn't. He'd sustained a serious wound. 'The scar that was left on his leg was incredible,' Harold says. 'It was about an inch wide. There were nights when he couldn't sleep without a hot-water bottle and a rug or towel around it.' Walter's leg frequently felt cold for the rest of his life; he took to wearing combinations.

When he was on the mend, Walter was transferred to the

police convalescent home in Hove, on the Sussex coast. There, he received a telegram, redirected from College Mews: DEEPLY REGRET TO INFORM YOU THAT YOUR SON FT/LT F. D. J. THOMPSON DFC AND BAR 120392 MISSING FROM OPERATIONS ON NIGHT OF 11/12 MARCH 1943 STOP ANY FURTHER INFORMATION RECEIVED WILL BE COMMUNICATED TO YOU IMMEDIATELY STOP LETTER FROM COMMANDING OFFICER FOLLOWS. Churchill telegrammed: I AM MOST DEEPLY GRIEVED TO HEAR THAT YOUR GALLANT SON IS REPORTED MISSING AFTER HE GAINED A BAR TO HIS DFC STOP YOU HAVE MY PROFOUND SYMPATHY IN YOUR SORROW AND PRIDE.

For a short while there was hope. Three days later Air Chief Marshal Sir Arthur Harris, C-in-C Bomber Command, wrote trying to allay Walter's anxiety:

I personally feel confident in all the circumstances that he will turn up as a prisoner or that he may even be in the hands of friendly people in France. The services which he has rendered to his country are great indeed, & it is all the harder that he should be missing so near the end of his operational tour. Nevertheless, I am sure that you will be sustained not only by pride in his achievements but also in the knowledge that sooner or later we get news of the safety of at least 25% of those posted missing. Everything possible is being done to obtain news . . .

The letter ended: 'Keep a stiff upper lip.'

On 2 April Air Marshal Sir Charles Portal, Chief of the Air Staff, wrote to Walter c/o Downing Street. Fred's death had been confirmed through the International Red Cross.

Writing about his son's death might have been cathartic, but to Walter it was too painful. Nowhere, even in his notes, does he have anything to say about Fred's death: not a line about his feelings, what he said to Kate or anyone else, how the terrible news affected his recovery. Did he think of his own brother Fred, a year his senior, who'd died at ten and in whose memory he'd named his middle son? In the fragment of autobiography he completed he'd written that his brother's death, the fifth and last among his siblings, 'which reduced our family to three boys and three girls . . . was a bitter blow to my parents', but, looking for some solace, he'd added that had all eleven children lived 'it would have been next to impossible to have fed and clothed them all'. Perhaps that his son Fred had lost his life in the service of his country was some solace now. Harold doubts that his father cried. 'The only time I saw him cry was years later when he couldn't get a tyre off a car wheel – and those were tears of frustration. Churchill cried and tried to find out what had happened – Dad told me that. But Dad, I doubt it. After the war my mother went over to see the grave and met some of the French villagers who'd witnessed the plane come down – on the way back from Stuttgart, Fred's Stirling got hit right in the middle of the bomb bay and split in two. It crashed into what was a duck pond but became a lake, the impact blew such a great hole. The villagers tried to get the bodies out of the water, but the Germans stopped them. Eventually they did get them out and gave them a decent burial in the cemetery. I got in touch with the Royal Graves Commission and they had an inscription put on the tombstone. Mother went over on her own and then again with Grace and Kathleen. But not Dad. At the time he was knocked for six. But he dealt with Fred's death by not talking about it or letting things remind him.'

Fred was Walter's favourite son. Harold, as he admits, wasn't much good at school and Harvey 'was absolutely hopeless – when he left he took a job as an office boy just like me'. Walter didn't know what to do with either of them. Eventually he got Harold into a garage in a mews at the back of Selfridges as a trainee mechanic, and Harvey joined the RAF as a boy entrant to become an armourer. There was never any doubt about Fred, who, Harold says, 'was academically brilliant': he wanted to go into the police like Walter and in his late teens went away to police college. Later, he was attached to Paddington Green, Walter's old station, quickly following his father into Special Branch shortly before war broke out.

Early in 1941 Harold was on leave and went with Fred to see Walter at Downing Street. They were talking to him at the back gate when Churchill returned from the Annexe. He shook hands with them both, then, as Harold remembers, 'he looked at Fred, who was in plain clothes, harrumphed, and asked him why he wasn't in uniform. Dad told him: "He's in Special Branch with me." And that was it; we went our separate ways.'

Soon after, Fred quit the Yard and joined the RAF, the first Special Branch officer to leave his reserved occupation. Commissioned, he flew as a navigator with Bomber Command, transferring as a flight lieutenant to the elite Pathfinder Force[3] on its formation in August 1942. Why Fred did what he did, Harold doesn't know, other than 'he found it difficult, with two brothers already in the services'. No doubt he discussed his decision with his father, though there's nothing in Walter's published or unpublished writings about that either.

'What was hard to take about Fred's death was that he'd finished his stint – after forty-three missions, some of them on the worst raids to Turin crawling across the Alps, he was due to come off operational flying,' Harold relates. 'It was painful to think he'd only been married a few months as well. But what was hardest for Dad to take was that, in a way, he blamed Churchill for asking Fred why he wasn't in uniform.' Did Walter feel at some level that Churchill had indirectly accused Fred of cowardice? He'd had his own experience of such an accusation – during the First World War in Southampton, when the port was thronged with troop movements, his civilian suit had attracted attention and, as he wrote, 'on three separate occasions I was solemnly handed a little white feather. The third time this happened, the feather was thrust into the band of my hat, and I still squirm at the thought of the laughter that little symbol evoked when, unsuspectingly, I boarded a tramcar filled with blue-coated Tommies.'

Walter was out of the convalescent home by the end of April. Jeanette, Fred's French-born widow, had decided to join the WRNS and, having passed her medical, wanted to be posted to Felixstowe, where her father dealt with Wren training. Walter saw Francis Brown, one of Churchill's private secretaries, who on his behalf wrote to the Admiralty. And he sought a meeting with Churchill. He was angry that the newspaper version of his accident 'made it look as if I was incompetent. No man would clean a gun with a bullet in it, surely.' But he was worried that the report might have given Churchill a jaundiced view and that he wouldn't want him back. He asked Churchill bluntly: 'Have you still got confidence in me?' He was relieved at the reply: 'I have no doubts about you whatever, Thompson. You are a most careful person. Carry on as before.'

At the Yard, Walter ascertained that the catch on his .32 Webley was faulty. To his surprise, 'so were those on several of the same type in the armoury'. Not trusting the weapon (and having had 'my opposite numbers guarding President Roosevelt express disdain at the small-calibre pistol I carried'), he picked out a German Luger that had been among the many guns handed in to the Yard on the outbreak of war, obtaining special permission to use it.[4]

Two days before he was due to be signed off for work, the

Luger was in the holster of his jacket. Churchill was crossing the Atlantic for the fourth time.

*   *   *

Concerned about the Prime Minister's health after his recent bout of pneumonia, Lord Moran insisted he didn't fly. Instead, for the first time, Churchill went on a civilian ship – the *Queen Mary* – which sailed, comparatively empty (apart from 5,000 German prisoners), to the States to ferry back American troops. The security problem was greater than usual: the German legation in Dublin was known to have contact with merchant seamen coming into British ports. When the liner left the Clyde she was escorted by four cruisers and, from halfway across, by two American, one of them the *Augusta*. Walter's instructions from the Yard were that if the *Queen Mary* 'were damaged by U-boats, Churchill was to be the first into the lifeboats'. Walter had been warned that, 'remotely, there was the further possibility that he could be taken prisoner by a U-boat or in some other way'. From Churchill, Walter had it in no uncertain terms that that wouldn't be an issue. His Colt was loaded and 'I will use every bullet but the last. That is for myself. They shall never take me alive.' In the first year of his premiership, Churchill had made time during weekends at Chequers to go to a nearby shooting range; he hadn't had time since – but on the weekend before they left he'd had Walter set up targets in the grounds so they both could sharpen their marksmanship.

The twelve days of this, the third Washington conference, were acrimonious, with the large number of participants (125 on the British side, and there were representatives from India and the Far East) disagreeing about priorities; the Americans thought the assault on Northern Europe was the only thing worth talking about in Europe, and until then the Pacific and the assault on Japan were all that really mattered.

With Churchill surrounded by so many people, Walter saw less of him than was usually the case, and with American security men swarming everywhere he had little to do. While he kicked his heels, he wrote to Francis Brown, who'd confirmed to him that the Admiralty had fixed his daughter-in-law's posting to Felixstowe.

On 19 May Churchill addressed Congress for the second time. Then, thinking all wasn't lost on his plan to make a concerted push on Italy, he persuaded General Marshall, chairman of the American Joint Chiefs of Staff, to fly with him aboard a BOAC Clipper to Algiers (fly, whatever Moran counselled – that was the only option). There, Marshall became enthused by Eisenhower's support for Churchill, who had the satisfaction of seeing the French Committee of National Liberation set up – at long last the marriage of de Gaulle and Giraud ('I could not help noticing the very much greater cordiality that prevailed among the Frenchmen than previously,' Walter commented). Pleased with what he'd achieved in eight days, Churchill for the first time boarded the specially adapted York transport plane that the RAF had sent out to him and headed home – and into one of the oddest incidents of the war.

The day before his plane should have left Algiers, a commercial flight from Lisbon to London was shot down over the Bay of Biscay, fuelling the rumour that the Germans believed Churchill was on it – German agents at Lisbon mistaking Alfred Chenhalls, the business manager of the actor Leslie Howard, for Churchill and Howard for Walter.

In *The Hinge of Fate* Churchill wrote: 'The brutality of the Germans was only matched by the stupidity of their agents. It is difficult to understand how anyone in their senses could imagine that with all the resources of Great Britain at my disposal I should have booked a passage in a neutral plane from Lisbon and flown home in broad daylight. We, of course, made a wide loop out by night . . .' It was a painful shock to him that 'in the inscrutable workings of fate', Howard (who'd appeared in one of his favourite films, *Gone with the Wind*) had died, as had the twelve other passengers and four crew.[5]

The war moved on at an increasing pace. Mussolini was arrested, the command of Italian armed forces was handed over to King Victor Emmanuel and a national government was formed. As resistance in Italy crumbled, with implications especially for a strike upwards through the Balkans, Churchill quickly convened the first Quebec conference for August. In the meantime, Walter had been to Buckingham Palace to receive the British Empire Medal. 'I had met the King on many occasions and was well known to him. As he pinned the medal on my coat, he said: "You must have a difficult time guarding the Prime Minister."' Walter was more forthcoming than he'd been to Roosevelt. '"Yes, Your Majesty," I replied. "Unfortunately he will not do what he is told for his own safety." "That is just what I find," he replied.'

When the *Queen Mary* sailed for Halifax, Walter wasn't amused: '1943 is nothing but conferences,' he groaned.

With a few days to spare before proceedings got under way, Churchill took his daughter Mary, released from her anti-aircraft battery to act as one of his aides-de-camp on the trip, to see Niagara. The press asked Churchill if anything there had changed since his visit in 1932. Walter recorded his reply: 'Well, the principle remains the same: the water still keeps falling.' The Churchills stayed with the Roosevelts at their home at Hyde Park, New York. Walter 'hated Hyde Park. There was no peace there, security men all around in the grounds, at night a big searchlight overhead. The heat was oppressive and Winston couldn't sleep; one night he got me up to watch the dawn.' As at Chequers, Churchill told his bodyguard: 'You had better go ahead, Thompson. I don't want one of their bullets through my head.' Walter was still feeling the effects of Freddie's death – his nerves were on edge. 'I will take Chequers in the Blitz to a Roosevelt weekend with the children,' he wrote.

Again the Americans and the British were frequently at logger-heads – it didn't help that the British delegation was even more unwieldy, having risen to 200. Things became so heated that a break was taken in the middle of negotiations, and Churchill and Roosevelt went fishing twenty miles from Quebec. It did Churchill good, and Walter, too. The intensity of the way in which the Secret Service watched the President's every moment, three men with walkie-talkies in a boat cruising round and round him while he sat with his rod in the water, had Walter shaking his head; when humorously he tried to show he was on the job, the Old Man shooed him away for disturbing his fish. There was more fishing at Snow Lake when the conference ended. Walter caught a three-pound trout, the largest fish of the party, but 'put myself in the position of needing catching. With a Royal Marine I [went] out in a canoe. A hook caught in some weeds and we together leaned over one side to get it off. The result was as might be expected. We finished up in two feet of mud . . . Our plight caused a good deal of amusement and nobody was more gleeful than Winston, who called across: "What are you trying to do, Thompson, commit suicide?"'

The invasion of Italy began; Badoglio's government accepted surrender terms. Deeming Italy's decision to change sides as treachery, Hitler poured in troops, had Mussolini rescued by a glider team from his prison in the Apennines and set him up as head of an opposing puppet regime. And the groundwork was done for the first conference that would be attended by all three leaders, Roosevelt, Stalin and Churchill: Teheran. Before that, however, Churchill wanted a get-together with Roosevelt to thrash out purely British–American details of Operation Overlord, the planned cross-Channel invasion of France.

They sailed in November on the *Renown*, which had brought them back from the Quebec conference in August. The intention, as Walter recorded, was to sail to Gibraltar and then fly to Cairo, 'but the weather at Gibraltar was bad and so we steamed on to Malta'. They were sighted by a German reconnaissance plane and action stations were sounded, but the *Renown* entered Valletta Grand Harbour unmolested. In Malta

> there was a delay because the American Secret Servicemen who had been sent ahead to Teheran were not satisfied with the security arrangements there. Winston suggested that the conference could be held in Malta and in the meantime paid visits to see the damage done by German bombs – the Maltese were having to live under primitive and impoverished conditions, but that did not alter the warmth of the welcome when they heard that the British Prime Minister was with them.

In fact, unable to shake off a feverish cold, Churchill spent two days in bed (and asked the governor of the island, Lord Gort, 'to stop his cows from mooing').

The message came back from Stalin: Teheran or nothing. Teheran, then, it was going to be, 'so we pressed on to Egypt, where the military had taken over the Meta Hotel and a number of villas'. The entire conference area was stiff with barbed wire entanglements, troops, ack-ack guns and fighter aircraft.

Roosevelt had invited Chiang Kai-shek, the Chinese national general and president, to Cairo, and the President's preoccupation with him frustrated Churchill, who wanted to talk about Overlord. Churchill was also frustrated by Roosevelt's reluctance to work late and seemed to spend his time 'going continually from one villa to the other . . . he was unable to take his usual afternoon nap'.

On one of the five days that the Cairo conference lasted, Churchill gave Walter a letter to deliver to the Chinese leader, inviting him to dine with him and Roosevelt.

On my arrival at the villa I saw the First Secretary, who informed me that Chiang Kai-shek was with the President. I returned to our villa and explained to Winston why I was unable to bring him a reply. He was sitting in a chair looking at some papers, but when I gave him the news he jumped up and started to walk up and down the room. 'I should have been informed of this meeting so that I could have been present,' he said. 'He cannot do this to me – he cannot do this to me.' He seemed very distressed. The atmosphere cleared a little . . . but at times Winston appeared to be in deep thought.

Churchill did see Chiang Kai-shek, his wife and staff off at the airport on their 5,000-mile homeward journey; Roosevelt had wanted the Chinese leader to come to Teheran but Stalin excluded him on the grounds that Russia wasn't at war with Japan.

*   *   *

When they got to Teheran after a six-hour flight aboard the York, Walter quickly came to the same conclusion as the Americans about the security arrangements. It was chaos at Amirabad civilian airport. Crowds impeded Churchill's car. The military police Land Rover that travelled ahead of them, 'with the hood up, thus preventing them from seeing all around', went so fast that 'they were soon far ahead'. In the city itself, the Persian police and army, 'who were at every junction, came to attention and saluted as we passed. A lorry broke down in front of us. The crowds were so large they were all over the pavements and roadway, compelling us to practically stop . . . Many were so close they could have touched Winston.'

It was no surprise that Churchill was angry. Walter saw the Provost Marshal and told him in no uncertain terms that in future 'the military escort should keep close and the police on the roads should face the crowd, not the Prime Minister'. The Provost Marshal 'became indignant that I should interfere with military matters', and Walter thought it expedient to leave it for the moment. The following morning the Provost Marshal came to see him, eager to cooperate: up to sixty German paratroops had been dropped near Teheran. Rumours of assassination followed Churchill everywhere: the Middle East during the 1920s, America in the 1930s, France just before the outbreak of war, Cairo almost every time he went there during it, Casablanca. This time, however, the intelligence seemed solid – and Roosevelt and Stalin were also in potential danger.[6]

Mike Reilly, Roosevelt's personal guard, had already decided the mile-long route from the American Embassy to the British legation and the Soviet Embassy, which were quite close together, was a bad security risk – the curtains of dust raised on the bad roads made spotting a sniper almost impossible; and Roosevelt had accepted Stalin's offer to stay at the guesthouse inside the Russian Embassy compound. On Churchill's instructions, Walter went over the short distance between the Russian Embassy – where the conference was to be held – and the British legation. Another bad risk, he reported: 'The local inhabitants were being stirred up by German agents and were most threatening. But while they could be dispersed by British troops, they could reassemble at corners, where cars had to slow down.'

The result was that the road between the legation and the

Russian Embassy 'was closed at each end by the Persian army, who erected barricades and machine guns . . . and while the conference was in session I had searches made of premises overlooking the side of the legation'. Walter searched Churchill's room every night, and he or his colleague kept watch outside the door. Crowds continued to form at the heavily guarded gates; 'most of the time,' Walter wrote, 'I had my automatic in my hand inside my pocket, hoping that I should not be called upon to use it and thereby make a nice hole in my pocket.'

Teheran was a strain for Walter and he couldn't prevent showing it. On the first day of the conference, Churchill, in air marshal's uniform, appeared to get in the car but when a military policeman opened the rear door for him he refused to get in, saying 'it was Anthony's [Eden] turn to sit on the left'. When Walter intervened, Churchill then said he wanted to sit next to the driver – Walter's place. 'Please do as you are told, sir,' Walter snapped.

Superficially, the conference went well. The Russians were more affable than they'd been in Moscow, 'the Russian officers in full uniform on duty at the entrance to the Embassy giving the delegates as they arrived military salutes in the British style'. And a great deal of goodwill was created on the second day when Churchill presented the Stalingrad Sword to Stalin after a lunch given by the Shah of Persia, Walter carrying the case in which it had come from England and placing it on a table in the centre of the room. 'On one side stood twenty soldiers from the Buffs with rifles and bayonets fixed; on the other, twenty Russian privates with Tommy guns across their chests.' In a brief, moving speech, Churchill, wearing the uniform of an air commodore, read the inscription on the sword's blade: '"To the steel-hearted citizens of Stalingrad, a gift from King George VI in token of homage of the British peoples." The national anthems of the two countries were then played, and Winston handed the sword to Marshal Stalin, [who] smiled in pleasure, lifted it to his lips and in absolute silence kissed the scabbard.'

All, however, wasn't well at the conference. While Stalin agreed to join in the war against Japan once Germany was defeated, he called for Germany to be broken up, with Roosevelt supporting him against Churchill. Stalin also emphasised that the 50,000 officers and experts who formed the core of the German military machine should be summarily shot to prevent further aggression – a suggestion that made Churchill stand up and walk out. Both the other two leaders opposed Churchill's hopes for an operation in the eastern Mediterranean: Stalin, with his own plans in the Balkans, wanting the British and the Americans to limit their activities to the west; Roosevelt because he'd erroneously got hold of the idea that Churchill had intentions to expand British colonial rule. He also wanted to direct all his energies to the Allied invasion of France – the Russians had already pushed the Germans back almost to the borders of Romania and Poland, and he was anxious that they would be in Warsaw, Berlin and even on the Rhine before the Allies.

Usually, Churchill walked back from the Embassy to the legation. 'In such circumstances,' Walter wrote, 'he always spoke to me. But now he did not; he was noticeably tense.' There was more than future strategy to Churchill's sombre mood, as Walter found out by asking around: 'Roosevelt, being resident at the Soviet Embassy, was in constant contact alone with Stalin . . . Roosevelt [also] appeared to be avoiding any meeting with Winston. When Winston invited the President to lunch with him, he declined this invitation on the grounds that the Russians might feel that he and Winston were privately making their own arrangements' – a brazen excuse, Walter thought, all things considered.

The rebuff upset Churchill greatly – until now he and Roosevelt had had an 'easy intimacy', although that had been less evident at the Cairo conference. What hurt Churchill more, however, was that the President constantly tried to win the Russian leader's regard at his expense. 'Winston loved humour and could give out much of it himself, but at a conference of such magnitude . . . humour and jokes directed at him caused him to feel very distressed.' Angrily, Walter added:

I am sure from what I saw that the President felt that his personality was strong enough to overcome any doubts in Stalin's mind. His view of Stalin was emphasised on the occasion he remarked to Mr Bullitt, the American Ambassador in Moscow: 'Stalin doesn't want anything but security for his country, and I think that if I give him everything I possibly can and ask for nothing in return, noblesse oblige, he won't try to annex anything and will work for a world of democracy and peace.' What a tragedy!

What Walter took away from the presentation of the Stalingrad Sword was less a sense of occasion but 'the look of intense admiration from the President as he looked up into Stalin's face'.

Throughout the conference Churchill was hampered by a throat infection he'd had in Malta and at times was unable to speak; Moran was in constant attendance. Those around him saw a worrying deterioration; Churchill was known for his astonishing memory, especially of military detail, but was showing moments of forgetfulness. He rallied, however, for his sixty-ninth birthday, and he insisted on hosting a dinner party, telling Averell Harriman: 'I have one or two claims to precedence. To begin with, I come first, both in seniority and alphabetically. In the second place, I represent the longest-established of the three governments. And in the third place, tomorrow happens to be my birthday.' There were cocktails, served in an anteroom, for the thirty-four guests. When Stalin arrived with his security officers, Churchill escorted him in, at which one of the security men 'entered the dining room, walked round the tables looking at the place cards and, having reached the seat allocated to Stalin, put his hands on the chair, stepped back two paces and stood to attention'. That, Walter decided, 'could not be permitted'. He attempted to persuade the man to leave. When he wouldn't, Walter propelled him out, not just into the hall but down the staircase and into the front entrance, 'where I indicated he should remain'. Feeling there might be repercussions, he told Churchill what he'd done. 'He smiled and said: "Thompson, strength is the only thing the Russians understand. They will drive you to the limit, but when you stand your ground more often than not they will relent."'

Toasts were drunk throughout the dinner in the Russian fashion, 'the proposer leaving his seat, touching glasses with the person whose health he proposed, and then returning to his place'. Stalin, more jovial than any of the British had ever seen him, toasted everyone, including Churchill's butler, Sawyer (twice), who was rushing about trying to keep the glasses charged. Walter recorded the toasts in some detail, the Big Three's to one another all proclaiming friendship. In view of the manner in which Roosevelt had treated the Old Man during the conference, one wonders what Walter thought, or what he thought of the words 'with great affection' on the card Roosevelt included with Churchill's birthday gift of a blue and white porcelain bowl. As it was, he kept his thoughts to himself. But he did enjoy the moment that occurred when Stalin was proposing one of his many toasts, 'with Pavlov, his diminutive interpreter, standing by his side. The frequent movements around the table had ruffled up the carpet, and, as Pavlov began to translate, a waiter carrying a magnificent ice-pudding tripped over it, flinging the whole thing over him. Drenched in pudding from the crown of his head, the little man solemnly finished before he allowed the waiter to mop him down.'

Walter probably enjoyed Churchill's remark hours later even more. As he went to bed, he said: 'That waiter was a bad shot, Thompson.'

The departure from Teheran was better organised than the arrival. As a diversionary tactic, military policemen in civilian clothes were driven to the airport, where, trying to look as much like VIPs as possible, they boarded a plane, which promptly took off (landing again on an unused strip on the opposite edge of the city). The British and Americans would have liked to know when Stalin intended to leave to coordinate movements, but the Russians refused to divulge the information. Roosevelt left from the old military airport he'd come in to near the American Embassy; Churchill left from Amirabad, five miles out in the opposite direction, the entire route lined with some 800 British troops with tanks and gun carriages, trucks blocking every inter-section and marksmen on the roofs of strategic buildings.

His exit was slightly undignified, but Walter had decided it was expedient. 'Having been very concerned at the lack of secu-rity on our arrival, I was determined to take a definite line of my own. We left the legation in a beaten-up army truck with a number of battered trunks covered with dust on the top, Winston lying down on the back seat. Nobody paid the slightest attention to us.' Churchill grumbled but complied. He lit a cigar as he got in. Walter took it from him.

Roosevelt broke his return trip to Cairo for more talks with Churchill and, without Stalin as an audience, was amenable.

Churchill felt their discussions were fruitful (which another attempt he made to bring Turkey into the war wasn't). On the day before Roosevelt left, he took him to the pyramids – a trip that Walter had first made with Churchill over twenty years before. It was at this location that the President revealed whom he'd chosen to spearhead Overlord. Churchill had originally envisaged a British commander but at Quebec had changed his mind, appreciating that as America would represent the overwhelming majority of the invasion force, an American should be supreme commander. He'd assumed it would be General Marshall. In fact, it was Eisenhower. Walter found it interesting that the pyramids were 'a place where part of the history of the Second World War was decided'.

CHAPTER 9

Death's Door, D-Day
and Doodlebugs

But Churchill wasn't well: he was listless and complaining of pains in his back. General Smuts saw him and was shocked by the way he looked. 'He really fussed over Winston,' Walter saw, not for the first time aware of the 'genuine affection' between the two men. The unflagging round of the wartime conferences, the huge distances involved, the stress and the intense nature of the negotiations had already cost Admiral Pound his life: he'd suffered a stroke at Quebec four months earlier and died soon after the *Renown*'s homecoming. Here in Cairo, General Ismay had collapsed with exhaustion on touchdown and was immediately sent back to England. Yet Churchill was intent on pressing on: a quick trip to North Africa to see Eisenhower, Alexander and Montgomery, and then the battle front in Italy.

Flying on 11 December, the York hit a problem as it

approached Tunis: the main airfield at El Aouina was closed down and they were diverted to a small, deserted landing strip some miles away. For nearly an hour Churchill sat on a packing case while the radio operator tried to find out what was wrong. The answer was a cruel irony: El Aouina was closed down for the arrival of the York.

Another takeoff, another landing. Walter told Lord Moran 'that I thought [Winston] was ill. "I think he is only tired," he answered. "But I will watch him."' That wasn't good enough for Walter. 'Well, sir, I have been with him many years and I believe he is ill,' he persisted, without getting anywhere.

The party drove to Eisenhower's villa (popularly called the White House) on the shore of the bay at Carthage, and Churchill went straight to bed. He slept fitfully; within hours his temperature was 102 degrees. Moran diagnosed pneumonia again. 'I was asked to take a turn in the night watching over him,' Walter wrote. 'I suggested that I should stay up for the whole night, as I was used to doing so in my job and Winston would not be disturbed seeing me around. Before I went on duty at 11 p.m. Lord Moran told me to listen to the tempo of [his] breathing, and if there was any sudden alteration I was to call him immediately.'

Walter sat outside the double doors of Churchill's bedroom, through which he could distinctly hear his 'fast, stertorous breathing'. At about 2 a.m. the sound ceased. 'Sick in my stomach', Walter crept into the room. 'All was silent. I reached the bedside. Still silence . . . I don't remember in the whole of my life such a feeling of shock and fear.'

In his published account, Walter continued: 'I leaned over the bed and brought my head down almost to Winston's pillow. He was breathing quietly and steadily. With a feeling of terrific relief – though it was some hours before I recovered from the first shock – I went to report to Lord Moran. He came to the bedside, listened and said: "He is breathing better now. You were quite right to call me."'

Yet a draft of the moment carries the implication that something else might have happened: the sentence 'I don't remember in the whole of my life such a feeling of shock and fear' is immediately followed by 'I went to report to Lord Moran' – from which Philip Nugus, the executive producer of the television series[1] that parallels this biography, speculates that when Walter heard Churchill's breathing stop, he acted to ensure that Churchill didn't die. 'If the draft is what Walter meant, there's no doubt in my mind that he resuscitated Churchill by giving him mouth-to-mouth or heart massage,' he says. 'He may not have thought Churchill was clinically dead. But here was a man who knew first aid, who knew that in such cases there are minutes in which it's possible to bring someone back. He wasn't going to let the boss die. I am absolutely sold. I'm equally convinced that if he did resuscitate Churchill he never told him. It was such an intimate thing to do – it crossed a barrier.'

The less controversial explanation of the addition, of course, is that Walter realised he hadn't said what he'd intended to say and therefore fleshed out the paragraph to make the matter clear. No one will ever know. Harold Thompson emphasises that his father never told him he acted in such dramatic fashion to save Churchill's life. There again, a comment Walter scribbled after Moran's own account was published following Churchill's death in 1965 perhaps lends Nugus support: 'In describing the incident . . . Lord Moran says that I informed him that Winston wanted him. That is incorrect . . . The shock and fear I had experienced at not hearing his breathing caused me to go to Lord Moran.'

Whatever happened that night, Walter resumed his vigil outside Churchill's door.

A little while later I heard Winston moving about in the bedroom. I went in and found him groping around the dressing table. He looked at me with heavy eyes and asked for his sleeping tablets. I knew that they had been removed and played for time, pretending to look for them. 'Can't you find them, Thompson?' he said. 'No, sir,' I answered. 'Shall I call your valet?' I knew he would not permit the valet to be disturbed. 'No, it doesn't matter,' he said, and climbed back into bed. I went over to see that he was comfortable. He lay back on the pillow and said dreamily: 'Thompson, I am tired out in body, soul and spirit.' 'No, not in spirit, sir,' I answered. 'You are just very tired after a strenuous time. Now that the conferences are ended, I hope that you will be able to get a little rest.'

He lay back for a few minutes with his eyes closed. Then he looked at me and repeated: 'Yes, I am worn out. But,' with returning animation, 'all is planned and ready.' Suddenly he sat straight up in bed and flung out his arms, crying: 'In what better place could I die than here – in the ruins of Carthage?' 'Don't say that, sir,' I pleaded, as he sank back into the pillows. 'The world needs you.' He sighed and dropped off to sleep as suddenly and peacefully as a child.

Moran, as he later wrote, expected Churchill to die over the weekend: his pulse was 130 and irregular, and he was in no shape to fight off infection. And the pain along his collarbone, Moran suspected, indicated that he'd suffered a small heart attack – as he had in Washington on Boxing Day 1941. He hadn't told Churchill then (he'd told the Prime Minister he'd had a 'heart disturbance' and his circulation was sluggish) and he didn't tell him now. In the meantime he sent signals to Algiers and Cairo seeking specialist medical help. Brigadier Evan Bedford, a heart specialist with Middle East Forces, arrived (with a portable X-ray machine), as well as other army doctors and two nursing sisters. Moran's diagnosis was confirmed.

'Gloom settled on the villa,' Walter recorded. Clementine flew in from London. Churchill hovered between life and death and Walter quietly seethed about Moran, who'd been the Old Man's personal physician since 1940.

What puzzled me is that Lord Moran, knowing that we should be absent from England for some weeks at the conferences, had apparently not made any provision for the treatment of chest troubles, to which he knew Winston to be prone. At Carthage, where we were in rather an isolated spot, he complained that there was no chemist. No doubt a number of drugs, including antibiotics, were necessary, but I should have thought he would have carried some with him. I have wondered what Winston would have said to me at Carthage, or in any other place, if someone had pointed a gun at him, and I had said: 'Sorry, sir, I cannot do anything. I have left my gun in London. Perhaps I had better send for the military to come and guard you in the meantime.'

Nowhere in his writing does Walter devote more than a few lines to anyone other than Churchill. But there are pages in his unpublished notes about Moran, whose book, detailing Churchill's many illnesses, he considered a breach of confidentiality:

A privileged position such as that held by Lord Moran must of necessity give the occupant access to much which . . . is not intended for publication. Its disclosure – even after a lapse of time – can be disturbing and even harmful to individuals . . .[2]

He mentioned more than once that [in Teheran] he saw Winston with his head in his hands and that he was a spent force. I saw Winston right through the conference and I realised the difficulties, which he was doing his best to overcome against strong opposition. Of course he was tired – his average allowance of sleep was about four hours a night and an hour during the daytime. At the same time he had on his shoulders not only the weight of the war but his political work as Prime Minister. Not many men would have stood up to the colossal amount of work which Winston got through.

Sarcastically Walter wondered whether 'some of the time [Moran] devoted to compiling his diary might not profitably have been given to his patient'. Elsewhere Walter wrote: 'Since reading his book I have wondered how Lord Moran would have stood up to the work which Winston covered during these years. By comparison, the duties of the former constituted more of a kind of holiday around the world.'

All his life Churchill was prone to illness: he'd had pneumonia twice before he was twelve; he'd suffered acute appendicitis in the 1920s, and, in the 1930s, while visiting German battlefield sites for background to his *Marlborough*, ended up in a Salzburg sanatorium with paratyphoid fever; constantly he had head colds, dyspepsia and skin conditions. But he also had the constitution of a horse and it came to his rescue now. To everyone's amazement, he turned the corner. Within days he was being the difficult patient he always was, rejecting the healthy diet of Eisenhower's personal army dietician and demanding good English food (the cook was dispatched from the *Renown* at Gibraltar).

And, of course, sitting up in bed working, laying plans for Anzio (agreed in Teheran) to attempt to break the deadlock in Italy – where Field Marshal Kesselring's fifteen divisions were dug in south of Rome, the Allies' advance stalled against the German line that pivoted on the Benedictine monastery of Monte Cassino.

Every day Walter and Cyril Davies patrolled around the villa. The first day he was up, Churchill told Walter: 'I saw you and your colleague carrying on just the same while I was ill. It was pleasing to see you pass and re-pass the window.' It pleased Walter that the Old Man had noticed: 'These little mentions have great meaning.'

Two days after Christmas, having accepted from Moran that he wasn't strong enough for an English winter, Churchill boarded the York for Marrakech, which he loved so dearly, to continue his convalescence. 'Strict limits,' Walter wrote,

> had been laid on altitude [because of the strain on Churchill's heart], and an RAF doctor flew with us with oxygen apparatus. We flew at about 7,000 feet and were making a detour to avoid the Atlas Mountains. Winston, however, said he had no intention of nosing along narrow passes below the peaks and demanded we go the direct route over them. Those in attendance on him were against the idea, but he had his own way. So we climbed carefully to over 10,000 feet.
>
> At each stage Winston asked the doctors to check his pulse, and on being told that it was all right he roared with gusto: 'Of course I am all right! I don't need to be told this! I'm announcing it!'

Weak as he was, for a brief spell he persuaded the pilot to let him take over the controls and Walter felt distinctly nervous;

Churchill's flying, he thought, was out of the same drawer as his driving, and he 'gave me and others in the aircraft anxious moments. Once he veered to the right, causing the escorting fighters to take avoiding action. He then decided to climb, and after a while said, "Now we'll do a gentle dive," and the plane dived at such a speed that I thought we were going out of control.'[3] Churchill was pleased with himself, but 'he was very tired when we landed and went straight to bed. For the next few days he took things easily, sitting out in the sunshine among the orange and lemon trees, but carrying on his work as usual.'

There was a high tower in the villa grounds, and one evening just before sunset Churchill called Walter into his room and said: 'I want to go to the top.' 'I protested: "But you cannot climb all those stairs." "I know," he said. "You are going to carry me up and down." He was no lightweight but Sergeant Davies and I carried him up in an improvised chair with poles across the bottom which allowed us to hold them at each end. It was certainly heavy going . . .' Churchill's intention was to paint the sunset and Walter erected his easel. But 'he was still unable to do all that he thought he ought to be able to . . . He sat there looking out over the blue mountains for some time and then said: "Take me down, Thompson."'

There was no lack of visitors: Beaverbrook from England, the big British and American generals in Tunisia, others including Harold Macmillan (resident Minister at North African Allied Headquarters) and Duff Cooper (the British representative of the French Committee of National Liberation). De Gaulle came to lunch, bristling from more imagined rebuffs – Churchill had ignored the French governor-general of Tunisia when he was in Carthage and was ignoring the governor-general of Morocco; Churchill was treating North Africa as if it belonged to him – but the Prime Minister stayed cheerful and persuasive. After lunch he 'took [de Gaulle] by the arm and led him down to the swimming pool. Here they remained for a long time in deep conversation. They appeared to be on excellent terms.' Indeed they were. The discussions had gone off so well that de Gaulle had invited Churchill to take the salute with him the next morning at a parade of the French garrison.

Walter had some misgivings: although the Germans had been led to believe he was in Aswan in Egypt, Churchill had been advised not to show himself in public. As if there was any chance of that when his mind was made up, Walter thought. The Old Man 'was much moved by the tremendous welcome he received from the garrison. The cries of "Vive Churchill!" rivalled the cries of "Vive de Gaulle!"' The reception Churchill received at a small African village on market day was no less enthusiastic, even though the natives had no idea who he was. 'He was wearing his sombrero and, as he moved towards them, gave the V sign . . . Some returned [this] and looked for approval of their cleverness from their friends . . . The native telegraph then came into operation. Everywhere we went thereafter Winston was saluted as we went along.'

As he got better, Churchill 'wanted to get out, and then we would be off for daily picnics in the mountains and foothills'. One excursion took them to Demnat, eighty miles to the east of Marrakech, where the party spread out their picnic on a small plateau near a bridge spanning a little gorge, at the bottom of which was a pool from a rushing mountain stream. Churchill decided he was going to climb down. 'Lord Moran objected, but Winston said he felt strong enough. Carefully he made his way along the narrow pathway cut out of the cliff. And when he reached the bed of the gorge he climbed across the rocks to where the water cascaded out of the cliff side.'

On the way back up, Walter went first 'with Winston holding

on to me, but we made heavy going of it'. Churchill tried to gain breathing space by holding 'a one-sided conversation with a goat' before admitting it was too much for him. Lady Diana Cooper, Duff's wife, hurried down the cliff with a large tablecloth and the suggestion that it could be used as a kind of sling. With Walter on one end and Cyril Davies on the other, 'we had him to the top in no time – much to the amusement of the guests above'.

On 14 January 1944 Churchill was in the air again – but only as far as Gibraltar, where the battleship *King George V* waited to take him home. The York was at Gib, too, and, impatient to get back, Churchill enquired whether the weather forecast favoured flying. Moran was anxious: the weather was fine. Fortunately it closed in, and in the end Churchill went by sea. When they'd been on the *Prince of Wales* two years earlier, Walter had 'tried to assist him up and down the ladders [and] he was most indignant . . . "Do you think I have never climbed a ladder before?"' Then Churchill had had repercussions, 'for his legs and knees ached to such an extent that he had to have massage from a member of the medical staff on board'. Aboard the *King George V* Churchill simply wasn't able for the ladders. But he made 'his usual visits of "inspection" to various decks, [and] it was a funny sight to watch a husky Royal Marine sergeant, with his shoulder at Winston's rear, heave him up the narrow gangways. Winston was aware of the chuckles – and a grin would appear on his face.'

Churchill's special train was waiting at Plymouth to take him to London. Ninety minutes after arriving at Paddington he was in the Commons for Question Time. He'd been away two months.

*　　*　　*

By rights he should have slowed down, but he didn't: he ran at full throttle, engrossed in Overlord and other plans, and dashing around the country. 'The time was ripening and Winston was here, there and everywhere watching preparations for the invasion,' Walter, striding out at his side, wrote. 'He visited docks, aerodromes, training grounds and stores. Everywhere he took every opportunity of talking to those who were to participate.' At the end of March he spent two days with American forces – their first sight of him – in Oxfordshire, Wiltshire and Hampshire, where in Winchester he 'saw a large force of US paratroops on parade, examined their equipment and watched a mass drop of several hundred men'. He also handled a bazooka and a US carbine and took on Generals Eisenhower and Bradley at target shooting.

Walter fetched his younger daughter Kathleen, now eighteen, from the evacuated Bank of England near Winchester to see the Old Man. Even when she was in Rotherham, Kathleen had tried to get to London twice a year to visit her father. Once she'd arrived to find Walter already gone with Churchill to Chequers. 'When Winston learned of my plight, he got one of his secretaries to drive me there and I was invited to stay the night. The following morning I was shown into his bedroom and he shook my hand.' On another visit she'd stayed in Downing Street and on another at the Annexe. In Winchester, in the middle of being involved in the most colossal operation in the history of warfare, Churchill made time for her and asked her how she was. 'His kindness is an everlasting memory,' she says.

The last day of March found Churchill touring British units in Yorkshire, where he 'was deeply impressed by the speed and agility with which the huge men of the Guards Armoured Brigade jumped in and out of their tanks'.

Churchill was 'constantly in and out of SHAEF[4] on the outskirts of London'. Walter was as impressed as Churchill by the telephone links to Washington and Moscow and even more by the secret radio wavelengths that 'enabled the planners to contact military chiefs in various parts of Europe and even bombers in flight'. Through April Churchill was deep in discussions with the Prime Ministers of the Commonwealth who came to London: Mackenzie King of Canada, Curtin of Australia, Fraser of New Zealand, Huggins of Southern Rhodesia and Smuts, his old South African friend. Smuts, Huggins and Mackenzie King accompanied him around the towns on the south-east coast and 'at Denze Marsh we were shown the terrible devastation which flame-throwers can cause'.

The following week Churchill was in Portsmouth, out in a motor torpedo boat looking at the floating piers and the hundreds of massive concrete caissons and other parts of the Mulberry artificial harbours that were to be towed to the Normandy beaches and which now were being massed in the Solent.[5] Where, Walter wondered, 'were the Luftwaffe? Surely German intelligence must have known that we were getting ready? The ships and various parts of landing stages well offshore were an absolutely sitting target.' In fact, German air reconnaissance was so successfully nullified by the RAF that Field Marshal Rundstedt, in command of Army Group West in France, remained in total ignorance.

Near Southampton, in a vast camp of Allied troops, Churchill stopped his car when he saw men parading for a meal.

'I want to see this,' he said, and got out. He went across to the cooks who were serving and said to the men: 'Show me what you have got. Do you get enough?' 'Yes, sir,' they answered. He still was not satisfied and found his way to the mess tent. He thrust in and said in a loud voice: 'Do you men get enough to eat?' His entry was so surprising that for a moment there was silence. He repeated: 'Do you get enough?

Now is the time to say. I want to know.' There was a shout of: 'Yes, sir – quite enough.' He continued his enquiries with the cooking staff. He wanted to see exactly what was being served before he expressed himself satisfied.

Walter expressed himself satisfied, too: 'This was the right kind of inspection, for nobody knew that the Prime Minister was coming. It was so unlike some visits by VIPs, when everything is "laid on" only to revert to normal once the inspection is over.'

A week before the intended invasion date of 5 June, the whole south coast of England was sealed and all troops confined to camp. Two million men, 10,000 trucks, 3,000 heavy guns and 1,500 tanks moved towards the invasion ports. On 3 June Churchill's train pulled into a siding at Droxford in Hampshire, close to Eisenhower's HQ, and he was out and off, 'keyed up for the invasion', descending on ports and beaches to watch equipment being loaded into the landing craft.

The Old Man was in his element. He moved among the vehicles talking to everybody. The troops laughed at his sallies and some of them were not slow in answering him back. The whole atmosphere was one of expectation and tense nervous excitement.

The next day he stood watching the troops embarking at Southampton. Many of them touched his coat as they passed and called for a speech. He did not want to speak, he was too full of emotion, so he called out: 'Good luck, boys.' A soldier called out: 'Have you got your ticket, sir?' 'What ticket?' asked Winston. 'One like this, sir,' said the soldier, holding up a piece of paper. 'It entitles me to a free trip to France.'

'I wish I had. If only I were a few years younger, nothing would have kept me away.' The tears came to his eyes...

Disappointed that he hadn't seen as many men as he'd planned, Churchill went by boat down Southampton Water to view the gathering armada.

Have you got your ticket, sir? Walter could almost hear the Old Man thinking. 'Twenty to twenty-five – those are the years!' he'd once said. Well, he was way beyond them in chronological terms, but not in spirit. Walter wasn't surprised when Churchill suddenly announced that he was going with the invasion force and began to make arrangements for his accommodation on HMS *Belfast*. But when the Prime Minister went to inform Eisenhower, he got a blunt no. Churchill argued that the Supreme Commander had no jurisdiction over who made up a British ship's complement. That was true, Eisenhower said, but, as Walter recorded: 'The general then pointed out quite forcibly that if Winston went over, it would add to his personal burden.' There the matter simmered until the next day. When he was making his final visit to Hampshire, Churchill received a letter from the King: if the Prime Minister insisted on sailing, then he himself, as the head of the three fighting services, was also obliged to go. 'That,' Walter added with deliberate understatement, 'altered the position entirely.'

Churchill gave in, but he was bitterly disappointed. So, two days later, was de Gaulle, for whom Churchill had sent his own plane to Algiers. Having been kept out of the picture until now for security reasons, he arrived with his feathers ruffled and he became bad tempered when Eisenhower gave his demand to be with the invasion force the same short shrift he'd given Churchill's.

The weather worsened. Gales whipped the Channel. The men in the battened-down ships endured seasickness in cramped conditions. At 4 a.m., D-Day was postponed for at least twenty-four hours and Churchill decided to return to London, inviting de Gaulle 'to return with us and have dinner on the train. But he refused . . . seriously displeased'. Added Walter, poker-faced: 'The train journey would have been both quicker and more comfortable.'

Millions knew that Operation Overlord was launched on 5 June many hours before the BBC announced it: through the night they'd been kept awake by the roar of more than 10,000 planes taking off from the airfields, carrying with them the three British and American airborne divisions or the 6,000 tons of bombs that were to blast the German coastal defences between Cherbourg and Le Havre.

Exactly a week later, Churchill was on French soil, four years to the day after his last abortive meeting with the French government. Rome was already liberated, the first European capital to be so. 'The Germans' determination to stop the advance in Italy occupied considerable resources and men and played into the Allied hands on D-Day,' Walter mused.

With Smuts and Field Marshal Sir Alan Brooke, Chief of the Imperial General Staff, Churchill sailed in the destroyer *Kelvin*, transferring to an amphibious landing craft to come inshore, resplendent in Trinity House uniform. Walter was in for an immediate blow: he was separated from his charge. In a war zone all decisions were in the hands of the military authorities, and as a civilian Walter was ordered to remain on the beach. Disconsolate as Montgomery whisked Churchill away to the château at Creully five miles away, where he'd set up his tactical headquarters, Walter wandered about.

It was a strange feeling to be the solitary civilian among so many troops. Some press correspondents I knew came to my rescue . . . I walked with them some distance along the beachhead and saw a hastily dug grave, at the head of which stood a rifle surmounted by a steel helmet. A wooden cross had been placed there with the words: 'Here lies a Canadian soldier.' After walking for a few miles, we sat on a raised part of the beach and ate some sandwiches, but it was a shock to notice that I was sitting near a rack of German hand grenades. I did not touch them, but a soldier seeing me glancing at them called out: 'Don't touch them or anything. You see – most of them are booby traps.' He also told me to keep to the trodden parts of the sand or the roads.

Getting the message that he would catch up with Churchill at Courselles, Walter walked on, arriving 'at a small village where wounded Allied and German soldiers were being embarked on small landing craft. A continual stream of all kinds of vehicles brought the wounded men, and, as one boatload embarked, another came into position for loading.'

All the time, no doubt, he worried whether the Old Man's recklessness was leading him into trouble. Of course it was. Having been to look at the British Mulberry at Arromanches and the terminal point for Pluto (PipeLine Under The Ocean – more accurately under the Channel) that was to deliver fuel to the Allies, he climbed to the exposed platform of a lighthouse (his knees, presumably, holding out). Everyone with him was as alarmed as Walter would have been – a direct hit would have brought the lighthouse down.[6]

Seven hours after landing, Churchill arrived at Courselles in a Jeep, just as 'three German fighter-bombers dashed over the coast, dropped some bombs very wide of the ships and streaked for home. One, however, fell victim to our Spitfires and came to earth blazing from end to end.'

192

Once the party had re-embarked, the *Kelvin* cruised along the coast about six miles out

until we lay off the *Monitor Roberts*, watching her bombard the German artillery defences. An order rang out and we fired several salvoes into the German positions. No reply came, and at last we turned for Portsmouth. As we were walking from the ship to the train, General Smuts said to Winston: 'I think the captain of the ship was rather cross with you for ordering him to fire on the German batteries.' 'Why?' asked Winston. 'Because the destroyer was well within the range of the German guns and they might have fired on us.' 'That's what I did it for,' Winston said. 'I wanted them to fire!'

Shortly after our return, questions were asked in the House of Commons concerning the risks the Prime Minister ran and were told that no one could stop him going on journeys which he thought necessary.

Churchill always told Walter that he took no unnecessary risks; as Walter knew all too well, Churchill's idea of 'unnecessary' was flexible.

Within hours of *Kelvin*'s docking, the first flying bombs struck London.

*   *   *

At the beginning of 1944, Hitler had retaliated to the Allied air offensive on Germany by returning to night-bombing the capital. The 'Little Blitz' had lasted until April. Churchill was advised to move out during it and, predictably, refused, showing his old interest in proceedings from the Annexe roof.

On 13 June came something worse: the first V-1 flying bombs, soon christened doodlebugs. In one of the first raids, the Guards'

Chapel on Birdcage Walk was struck on a Sunday morning (Mrs Churchill actually saw it happen), killing 119 of the congregation, including many people Churchill knew. When he and Walter returned from SHAEF headquarters that evening, 'we visited the scene and saw the grim work of rescue still in progress'. On the last day of the month the Churchills visited the ack-ack gun sites that had been trying to deal with the onslaught, at one of them – a plotting battery – with their daughter Mary. The barrage balloons were up again, and the heavy guns were moved from London along the coast from Dover to Beachy Head, 'the system of defence . . . to fire at the bombs on the south coast and to let the RAF chase those which got through the gun belt'.

It was impossible for people to show the resigned indifference that they had during the Blitz; what they dreaded was the noise of a doodlebug's motor cutting out, which indicated it might be coming their way. In the first five weeks, 3,000 of these missiles came over, and for Walter 'this form of attack brought with it, for me, a deal of worry'. It was the same old story: Churchill wanted to go for his daily walks in St James's Park – or head for the roof, 'anxious to see one for himself'.

On one occasion in the park, with 'the angry buzz of a flying bomb receding towards the East End of London' and Churchill 'walking jauntily' ahead of him, 'unconcerned for his own safety, hands in pockets and hatless', Walter snapped.

I was virtually at the end of my tether with the Old Man. I would dearly have loved just to walk away and leave him . . . Before receding eastwards the flying bomb had buzzed over Westminster. At any second its engine could have stopped and the machine plunged earthwards to explode . . . Previously I had pleaded and cajoled . . . Now I shouted at him: 'For God's sake, sir, if you don't care about yourself, at least have a thought for me.' . . . He was about to make one of the angry retorts with which I had become so familiar over the years. Then he nodded slowly. 'Very well, Thompson. We will go in,' he said.

But he still wanted to see a doodlebug. 'He told me: "Thompson, I'm going to be notified as soon as the next is heading for London. I want to see it, and you must take me up."' As before,

we had to pass through a number of rooms to the top floor, and all these rooms had to be opened by keys. Sentries had to be given a password by me, even when the Prime Minister was there.

In the interests of safety, I was naturally most anxious that Winston should *not* get up on the roof when there were flying bombs about. Sure enough, when [he] was notified that the next one was heading for London, he demanded that I take him upstairs at once. He missed seeing it. Came another, and he missed that. A third was notified as approaching, but he didn't see that either. It wasn't that the bombs had not reached London; they had already exploded. The reason he missed them was because I was deliberately making sure he missed them.

After the third time he was angry. 'Thompson,' he growled, 'what is happening? Why are we not getting to the roof in time to see these bombs?' I said nothing. He went on: 'Thompson, you are not fooling me. I know what you are doing. On all previous occasions when you have brought me up here I have passed through to the roof without difficulty. You have always known the various keys to open the doors. Now you are fumbling with your keys . . . [and] you are operating the lift so that the doors will not open because they are not level with the floor. You are delaying my arrival on the roof with deliberate intent. You do not want me up there.'

I confessed this was true. 'I know that if one exploded near you it would kill you. I must try to prevent that.' Churchill considered that, then said quietly: 'All right, we will not come up again.' He kept his word.

There was worse than the V-1s to come – the V-2 liquid-fuel rockets that arrived at a height of fifty miles and were capable of supersonic speed.[7]

The first arrived on the evening of 8 September – 'the kind of evening when a blue sky, a warm sun and a still calm give a deceptive feeling of peace,' Walter wrote. The 'colossal explosion in Chiswick . . . left a far deeper crater than a flying bomb and the explosion was heard throughout a radius of several miles. A complete security blackout was clamped down. The official cause was given as a burst gas main. This was the start of a series of burst gas mains . . .'

There was no defence against the rockets: the explosion on impact heard before the sound of the engine was the first indication that one had arrived; fortunately many suffered mechanical failure, and many that did strike did their damage deep under ground, such was the force with which they struck. But until the launch sites were destroyed, four to six came over daily and, Walter noted, 'for the first time under bombing, there were signs of shaken morale . . . wartime strain on the nerves was beginning to have an effect'.

*   *   *

Towards the end of July, Churchill was back in Normandy, landing on the Cherbourg peninsula to meet up with Montgomery once more. He watched American activity at Utah beach, went to see how things were progressing at the British Mulberry at Arromanches (in an amphibious craft that made him sick), visited British army units and field hospitals and went on a hedge-hopping tour of several RAF camps in a captured Fiesler Storch, with Walter earthbound. A fortnight later he set off for Cherbourg again, but halfway across the Channel the weather closed in and the pilot said he'd be unable to land. Churchill wanted to go on and agreed to turn back only when told that a Dakota ahead of them had just crashed on the airstrip, with everyone killed. But, Walter wrote, 'Winston was furious. He jumped out of the plane and turned to one of his staff. "My blood is up," he said. "I will fly tonight. Get on to the Air Ministry and find out the weather forecast. I mean to go." He got to Montgomery's headquarters early the next day.'

Three days later he was in Italy, at Posillipo on the Bay of Naples, where his first visitor was Marshal Tito ('Winston took a very special interest in this conference, for his son, Randolph, was operating with the partisans in Yugoslavia'). It must have amused Walter no end that Tito's heavily armed guards so heartily availed themselves of the hospitality that they fell asleep in the basement and their man left without them.

Churchill had missed D-Day, but he 'was on the spot for the next excitement: "D-Day" on the French Riviera.' He was aboard the *Kimberley* but, unknown to him, under instructions from Admiral Cunningham (who'd replaced Pound as First Sea Lord) the destroyer stayed six miles out to ensure his safety. Churchill watched the bombardment from sea and air and the dropping of 14,000 parachutists, but he wasn't close enough to the action for his liking. Finally, bored, he went to his bunk to read a novel, writing in the flyleaf: 'This is a lot more exciting than the invasion of southern France.'

A swift visit to the Monte Cassino front – Rome for discussions with Italian Ministers (and an audience with the Pope) – London for the opening of Parliament, 'and we were on the move again', on the *Queen Mary* once more, for the second conference in Quebec. Stalin's refusal to attend next involved Churchill and his Foreign Minister Eden in an additional journey – 'they had to act as intermediaries between the President and Stalin. Almost as soon as we arrived back in England we were airborne again en route for Moscow.'

In Quebec, the main decision had been for the British to send a fleet to the Pacific; in Moscow, Churchill was anxious to get clear-cut answers on what territories the Russians intended to keep under their control. He was especially concerned, after the German massacre in Warsaw – which happened while the Russian army, just across the Vistula, stood by and did nothing – to try to settle the Polish Question. As ever, Stalin was evasive. But the general atmosphere 'was in marked contrast to that of August 1942. The Russians seemed far friendlier. Cordiality was everywhere.' Walter hoped 'for a long period of Anglo-American-Soviet cooperation in the post-war years'.

At a performance of the Bolshoi Ballet, 'the whole audience rose and gave Winston a remarkable ovation. Winston insisted on Stalin going forward with him . . .' At a lunch at which Stalin 'gave a toast to the future collaboration of the United Nations', Churchill in reply 'lauded the Red Army, and in his generous praise of them declared: "I have always believed and I still believe that it is the Red Army that has torn the guts out of the filthy Nazis." I was told that this last phrase presented the interpreters with something of a problem. Ultimately, however, I believe that the translation, if a little crude, left nothing to be desired.'

On 19 October Stalin came to the airport to bid Churchill's York farewell.

Paris was liberated. The three major powers gave formal recognition to de Gaulle's provisional French government. And on de Gaulle's invitation, Churchill went to the city for Armistice Day, this time in a Dakota (escorted by Spitfires) rather than the heavy York, accompanied by his wife and Mary.

There was no doubt in Walter's mind that Paris posed something of a security risk – no one had any idea how many Germans might still be hiding in the city – but like everyone else he was swept up in the occasion. Just before the eleventh hour of the eleventh day,

the Prime Minister, in RAF uniform, accompanied by General de Gaulle, left the Quai d'Orsay in an open car. I stood on the running board. Flags of the Allies were fluttering from most of the buildings. Windows were jammed. The crowd went almost hysterical with delight.

On the stroke of eleven, a single gun was fired for silence . . . There was not a murmur. Another gun announced the end of the two minutes [and] Winston and de Gaulle, each carrying a huge wreath, walked side by side to the Tomb of the Unknown Soldier, [after which they] and Mr Eden walked abreast – refusing the cars that had brought them – from the Arc de Triomphe down the Champs-Elysées through crowds that the French police had the utmost difficulty in controlling.

It took the military parade nearly an hour and a half to pass the saluting base.

Churchill wasn't done with this visit to France. The next day he went by de Gaulle's train and then car to visit the French troops who were about to launch a major attack on the mountainous Vosges frontier but was turned back by heavy snow. Instead, he reviewed a march past of other French troops at Valdahon as freezing darkness fell. By the end of the day, Churchill had been in the open for ten hours, in melting snow and a biting wind. Walter worried about him: for all his energy, the Old Man had been intermittently unwell since Carthage. In Quebec, to which Moran took not just a brigadier who'd been part of the medical team in Carthage but also a nursing sister, Churchill had felt wretched; and on his return a bout of fever had confined him to bed for a week (the King had come to his bedside in the Annexe to sign Montgomery's promotion to Field Marshal). In Moscow a recurrence of fever at one stage had forced him to bed yet again.

Whatever his concerns for Churchill's health, Walter suddenly had to worry about his own.

CHAPTER 10

Things Catch
Up with Walter

He was nearly fifty-five: a decade too old to be a personal protection officer in peacetime, never mind war. In five years he'd travelled 200,000 miles, mostly in aeroplanes big and small and in destroyers, and almost every other kind of transportation, often in great comfort and in extremes of heat and cold. In five years he'd never had enough sleep, on hand for every hour of Churchill's manic eighteen- or twenty-hour day, never going to bed before Churchill and sometimes being summoned after they both had. A once excellent sportsman, he was out of condition and he smoked too much. And for five years he'd lived constantly on his nerves.

In truth, the burden of guarding Churchill and the unflagging pace of his duties were beginning to be too much for him; he was worn down by his fragmented life, the moments of high tension interspersed with the long stretches of doing nothing, there at many of the most important meetings of the war – yet 'a spare part', as his son Harold describes it. Above all, a single thought never left his mind. Roosevelt had told him Churchill was possibly the greatest man in the world and not to let anything happen to him; Smuts had similarly charged him, saying the Old Man was 'one of the greatest men who have ever lived'. Walter accepted the responsibility but 'was always horrified about one prospect: that, as the man in charge of his safety, if anything ever happened to Winston I would be the most unpopular man in Britain'. The repercussions haunted him: 'Loss of job, face, pension and every other right to hold up my head in Britain for the rest of my days.' Walter never equated his task with Churchill's remark about de Gaulle that 'The heaviest cross I've ever had to bear was the Cross of Lorraine' – but it was a cross he finally would have liked to lay down.

There were other factors that contributed to Walter's finding himself back in the police convalescent home in Hove. Fred's death was still raw in his memory (the very place he was in an unwelcome reminder). In the coldest winter for fifty years, his leg hurt badly. And he'd become jumpy about the doodlebugs, to the extent that he couldn't sleep at all. It was hard at a distance to tell the difference between an incoming V-1, a car or a motorbike, and he loathed the drone and the cutting out of the motor, as many others did, too – so many Londoners had left the capital that it seemed quite empty.

But he was still there. So was Churchill. The V-1s and the V-2s posed a threat that he could do little about. And they posed that threat not only to the Old Man but also to May Shearburn, who, having left Churchill's employment, found herself removed from the safety of the Annexe.[1] It mattered to Walter because he and May were lovers.

* * *

Walter's marriage had been one of contentment in the early years when his life was more orderly as an on-the-beat copper and then as a general Special Branch man; he was especially content during the First World War in Southampton.

Coming back to London in 1920, the family was broken up for a time, while he and Kate looked for somewhere to live – Harold, then five, and Fred, three, went to Rotherham on the train in the care of the guard to stay with Uncle Bill. 'I don't know if he was a relative or a family friend, but we called him Uncle Bill,' Harold says. 'He was the trainer of either Rotherham United or Rotherham Town, as they were at the time, and then he went to Sheffield Wednesday – as kids, we always had football gear!' The family were reunited – in a flat in Norwood – but, with Walter's duties with Churchill taking him away so often, they moved again, this time to Westcliff-on-Sea, where his parents and one of his sisters lived. He was happy living here, too, playing football in a local side with his younger brother Ernie, who later emigrated to Australia.

To some extent life was more settled when Walter bought a house in Venner Road, near Sydenham railway station, in 1924 (Churchill having become Chancellor and moving into 11 Downing Street) and brought his parents back to live with them (his mother, who'd run a sweet kiosk in Westcliff, as she had in south London, died the following year). Kate taught the children to cook, the three boys included. They had sing-alongs around the piano (Kate at the keyboard, later Harold on the violin) in which Walter joined. They attended dos at the CID social club, which Walter organised, having had to give up the secretaryship of the Yard athletics club. When he did have time off, he was content to dig his garden or tinker with his motorbike. He was at home as often as the demands Churchill made on him allowed – 'but he was never there for any length of time,' Harold remembers. He knew when Walter came home because he slept in his mother's bed and in the morning would find he'd been moved back to his own. Walter's job became less onerous after 1929 when Churchill lost office, and during those two years the family were very close, in Harold's memory, at least as close as most families are.

As a father, Walter was firm but, Harold thinks, fair. He certainly wasn't like his own father James. 'I well remember the occasion when my eldest brother [James, like their father], who had joined the Scots Guards, was home on leave,' Walter wrote in his fragment of autobiography. 'At lunchtime, something annoyed him and he turned round and swore at my youngest sister. My father, who was cutting the joint, put down his knife and fork, turned to my brother, saying, "When you hear such words from me you can use them . . ." With that he knocked my brother down and then went on with what he was doing.' 'Dad believed in discipline but he wasn't harsh,' Harold elaborates. 'A clip around the ear for putting dents in his cricket bat or a cricket ball through the kitchen window is the most I remember. Mind, you knew about it if he just grabbed you by the skull with one of those massive hands.' In Walter's house, however, everyone did as they were told. No one was allowed to miss a main meal, which was always eaten together; no one stayed out later at night than the hour he set. Just as his parents had made him attend the local Wesleyan chapel, so he made his children; like him, his sons joined the Boys' Brigade. Kathleen Bucknall, the baby of the family and eleven years younger than Harold, sees her father's rule somewhat differently from her brother: 'He was a good dad, but he was very strict with the others, too strict, I think. He was certainly softer with me.'

A clue to Walter's feeling about his family can perhaps be read into an observation he made about the Cabinet Minister Jimmy Thomas, whom he guarded after the first time he left Churchill. 'One thing I do admire about him,' he wrote, 'is that he is a happy family man. Nothing pleases him better than to have his children and grandchildren around him. Christmas is *the* time of the year for him, and he revels in struggling round crowded shops buying huge quantities of presents.' In the early years of his marriage, Walter felt like that. Sometimes he took the family down to Brighton, where Kate's wealthy relatives owned at least one pub and were also fishmongers and, remembers Harold, 'we got refreshments in the bar and fish to bring home. That was a family outing, it really was.'

For several years Walter rented a hut on the beach at Rushington near Littlehampton where they all played cricket and football and he taught the children to swim 'and tried with Mother, though I don't think he succeeded,' according to Harold. Later he rented a patch of shingle at Littlestone near New Romney in Kent where not just his family but members of his extended family, Harold's wife Winnie and her younger brother and sister, pitched tents during the summer. 'Holidays, Christmas – wherever Dad was, the family congregated,' Harold says. 'At Westcliff, one of his sister Emily's boys, Bernard Dow, even ran a furniture repair business from a shed at the bottom of our garden.'

When Harold married at eighteen, Winnie was added to the Venner Road household, and soon their son Peter – by which time Walter had bought another house not far away in Charlecote Grove. The family were there only about eighteen months before it was sold and they moved back to Venner Road, which in the meantime Walter rented out. Money appears to have been the reason. 'We weren't financially embarrassed, but it was a struggle at the time,' says Harold, who at fourteen and a half left school to lend a hand with the family finances. 'Mother was very ill for a long, long time after Kathleen's birth, and she had to have home help. Dad asked me to help out, and that's when I took up this job as an office boy. I didn't earn very much money but it helped, and I think I did a paper round to help out a bit more.'

'It was a heck of a lot of people in one house to look after,' says Peter Thompson, a retired lecturer in computing, now seventy-one and living in Croydon. 'Granddad Thompson liked people being around him, though I don't think he appreciated what hard work it all was. He came and went and wasn't there for long stretches. Old Granddad Thompson was a bit senile, which didn't help. These were the days before washing machines. Nan Thompson was a saint.'

Whatever Walter's heartfelt feelings about family, the lengthening periods he spent away from home gradually put more and more strain on his marriage. In 1929 he wrote in his notes that his marriage was in trouble: 'My long hours had created a rift that would never heal.' It appears he tried to heal it: until he returned to Churchill's side in 1931 to accompany him on his American lecture tour, what anecdotal evidence there is suggests that he and Kate at least rubbed along; but shortly after his return from America he was writing 'my marriage is in tatters'.

His eye began to rove. One day Harold was driving to his brother-in-law's when he saw his father's car parked outside a house that meant nothing to him. 'I didn't know why he was there, whether he was supposed to be working or what. I did wonder if he might be in trouble. I knocked the door and Dad answered, and there was a woman I didn't know standing behind him. "I'm coming home in a minute," he said, and he came home and told Mother he was seeing someone else. I can't to this day tell you who she was.'

The marriage, Harold remembers, 'broke up very slowly. Dad began to gradually withdraw. There were no bad feelings, just a feeling of separation between the two; you couldn't say there was a root cause. Mother had a pretty tough job with five children, but her life was her children – just as Churchill was Dad's.' Kathleen doesn't see it like that. 'Dad's leaving was a time of great sadness and difficulty. My mother was terribly unhappy for a long time. During the war I used to go back from Winchester to Rotherham to be with her when I could. In fact, I was there when the telegram came about Fred. I remember her saying, "Why did it have to be Fred?" Of all the family, Fred was the one who looked after her; he was her big friend, and mine. He was the one who stood up to Dad; he would have had a lot to say about his leaving Mother.' On one thing Kathleen agrees adamantly with her brother: 'It was Dad's devotion to Churchill that destroyed the marriage.'

*   *   *

May Shearburn, daughter of a Royal Engineer major stationed in Alderney when she was born, wasn't looking for romance when she went to work for Churchill in April 1939. She'd been engaged at twenty, but her fiancé had died of tuberculosis. She was now thirty-two and very independently minded.

Walter, it seems, was smitten from the beginning. On his first night patrolling Chartwell as Churchill's private bodyguard, he came in from the grounds at 2.30 in the morning, just as she was finishing transcribing some of Churchill's dictation, to ask her if she'd like a cup of tea. She made him laugh by telling him that when Churchill had interviewed her and asked if she minded working late she'd replied that she'd once been secretary to the manager of a theatre and was used to finishing at 11.30 p.m. Now, she said, she realised why Churchill 'had smiled so wryly'.

The development of May's relationship with Walter, whom she called Tommy (which introduces some confusion into the narrative), is contained in a detailed account of her service with Churchill that she compiled in 1943. The very nature of their jobs meant they were constantly in each other's company and she

found myself, at first almost unconsciously, relying more and more on the unobtrusive help which Tommy gave me. In the long years he had spent with Mr Churchill he had come to know him so well that he could give me invaluable advice in most circumstances . . . When we were going on longer journeys it was Tommy who saw to it that help was available when I needed it, particularly when it meant carrying a good deal of the office with me – not to mention an office typewriter in its special box.

In London, 'when the boss was safe in his Admiralty office or, after he became Prime Minister, in the Cabinet Room or the Annexe, Tommy still had to be in arm's reach, and as he had no place of his own to wait, other than the corridor, it was natural for him to sit in my office. He would often have to sit there for hours, and soon we got into the habit of going to lunch together.' May knew he was married, but 'there was never any suggestion from him that our relationship was other than that of two people thrown together by our work, being friendly to one another'.

Their friendship deepened.

More and more, Tommy and I went about together whenever we could snatch a few hours off at the same time. We often went to an inn, the Grafton, near Leicester Square, where the sherry was marvellous and, for a time, steaks were still on the menu. There was another restaurant near Victoria Station and a nearby cinema that we sometimes visited. We went to one or two shows: *Black Velvet* with Vic Oliver, then married to Churchill's daughter Sarah, as the star, and the Noël Coward play, *Blithe Spirit*. When Winston gave me a grudging two hours off on Christmas Day 1939, I took Tommy across to Notting Hill for a Christmas dinner cooked by my mother. A few days later, given two days off for working through

THINGS CATCH UP WITH WALTER

Christmas, I went to Weston-super-Mare, the Somerset resort where my sister Kit then lived. Tommy drove me there . . . and there was a mad chase back through fog, eating ham sandwiches hurriedly prepared by Kit, after a telegram told Tommy that Churchill was leaving on a journey at midnight.

In the winter of 1940, 'on a cold Saturday afternoon, I found myself enthusiastically shivering in the stands at a soccer match – the first I had ever attended in my life – cheering for Tommy's favourite team, Tottenham Hotspur. Afterwards, in a little café near the stadium, we hungrily enjoyed sausages and mashed potato, or "bangers and mash" as the football fans said.'

Exactly what Walter was thinking or hoping during these months he didn't commit to paper – his feelings, as always, remained private. The furthest he went in print was to add to the story of Admiral Pound spelling *Scharnhorst* and *Gneisenau* for May on the train: 'I was always unusually interested in [Churchill's] encounters with Miss Shearburn, for I had the greatest admiration for all her qualities.'

Right from the moment she refused to give him Churchill's revolver, he admired her feistiness yet found it endearing that she was frightened by bats and moths – 'the big furry kind,' she wrote,

which he was willing to deal with when they invaded my quarters; and this sent him up in my estimation as few other things could have. I never had to seek his help to cope with bats – though there was an occasion at Chartwell, during that first summer, when I would have given much to have been able to call on him. I was taking dictation in Mr Churchill's study, which had all the windows flung open to the hot night and all the lights blazing. A bat flew in [and] I found it well-nigh impossible to concentrate on shorthand with this evil monster encircling the room. Even Mr Churchill's concentration was not impervious to my inattention. 'What *is* the matter?' he asked irritably, and he demanded an explanation. He got one – but it obviously astonished him. 'I will protect you!' he said – which might have been comforting but for the fact that he promptly forgot the existence of anything but work, and I was left to suffer agonies until I could escape to the office.

A number of May's encounters with the Old Man, which Walter either witnessed or which she related to him, ended up in his books (though she usually appeared only as 'the secretary').

What kind of determined person May was is evidenced in her own account. There was, for example, the story of Churchill's fortnightly article for the *Daily Telegraph* just before the war, which was published simultaneously in Paris.

They were seldom dictated until the last minute – partly for reasons of topicality – which meant a race against time to get them typed and dispatched to London. As they frequently had to be put on a passenger train for London, with the necessary arrangements being made for them to be met and collected, it also meant that the typescript for Paris could not get there in time by mail. The solution was simple, I was told . . . The newspaper office in Paris could be reached by telephone, and the article could be dictated over the line. I felt, not unreasonably, that the simplicity of the arrangement was somewhat overrated when it meant dictating about 2,000 words over what might be a very bad line to a secretary at the other end whose English left much to be desired.

When the Churchills moved into the Admiralty at the beginning of the war, there was the question of what May and Kathleen Hill were supposed to do about eating and sleeping:

From the point of view of meals there seemed to be little difficulty, as there were ample canteen facilities at the Admiralty throughout the twenty-four hours of the day. We would, of course, have the additional expense of paying for our own food, but that was one of the hazards of war! Sleeping accommodation, however, was another matter. Even had we been successful in finding rooms within reasonable distance of the Admiralty, it would have meant a pretty early start for Mrs Hill to be there on duty by 8 a.m. each morning. In my case it would have been even more difficult – and I did not relish the thought of making my way back to digs any time between 2 and 4 a.m. – particularly if, as we anticipated, heavy air raids were to become a regular thing.

However, I looked around Admiralty House pretty thoroughly when we first moved in there . . . The floors below the [Churchills'] flat as far down as the ground-floor level were occupied by offices and the public rooms. But having made friends with some members of the Office of Works, the government department responsible for accommodation, I learned that it would be possible, if I could obtain the necessary permission for the work, to turn two rooms in the extensive basement that were in variable states of disrepair into bedrooms.

May got the permission, and she rounded up 'furniture of a sort'. At first she and Mrs Hill 'had unwelcome company in the form of swarms of mice. But once the four-legged inmates had been dispatched (by courtesy of the same Office of Works), we were reasonably comfortable – and, more important, within reach of the office and work.'

May's first wartime trip to France 'made history in a way – women never went to sea in warships' – but she did, with Churchill aboard the destroyer *Codrington*. The party stayed in Paris overnight, then went to Arras, leaving a disappointed May behind to await their return. Shortly, however, she got a call from Walter saying Churchill wanted her. 'I realised, of course, that I couldn't just go and buy a railway ticket to Arras,' May wrote,

so I approached the naval attaché who would be the natural one to help me as I was working for the First Sea Lord. He met my request with a flat refusal. It was out of the question, he said; it just couldn't be done. No one, particularly a civilian and a woman at that, could roam around the countryside at will. From his point of view he was, no doubt, right [but] I didn't intend to accept his refusal lying down. He said he would contact the military attaché and see what could be done. Very shortly I went to see the military attaché and once more went through the now-familiar routine of his explaining that I was asking the impossible, and my insisting that when Mr Churchill wanted something done – *nothing* was impossible. Finally he procured a safe conduct for me and I was on my way. Tommy met me at Arras station and took me to the military HQ where Mr Churchill was staying. Without further ado I found myself in the familiar routine of dictation from the First Lord. No comments were ever made, nor questions asked as to how I managed to get there – Mr Churchill, as was his wont, simply took it for granted that he had given an order and it had been obeyed.

Normally, documents that Churchill worked on went with an official messenger in an official box, but Churchill sent May back to Paris with the box. Arrived at the hotel, she rang the naval attaché's office to arrange for its collection – 'only to find that he had gone home for the night and it would have to remain in my charge until the following morning. Its official value had been made quite clear to me by Mr Churchill, and I spent a rather disturbed night – having locked the box in the wardrobe in my room and put the key under my pillow.'

There was another occasion when May was entrusted with an official box on one of the visits Churchill paid to Scapa Flow.

At the last minute he found that he still had some unfinished work [and] told me that I would have to travel part of the way with him, leaving the train at Carlisle and returning to London with the box. He said that a sleeping compartment on the return journey would be arranged for me – as much, I gathered, for the protection of the official papers as for my comfort! – and he stressed the importance of the safe arrival of the papers, asking me what I would do if, during the train journey, I were to be attacked and the safety of the box threatened. I replied that I would scream at the top of my voice, thereby attracting all the attention I could to my plight, and at the same time kick my assailant's shins with all my strength. This seemed rather to amuse him, and he commented: 'I believe you would – and I believe it would work!'

Perhaps above all the stories about May and the Old Man that Walter cherished was the one about whistling. One quiet, sunny Sunday morning May was doing the early-morning duty when the silence was pierced by the sound of someone whistling, and

Churchill, 'peering at me over the top of his reading glasses, said sternly: "Open the window and tell him to stop that noise." I went to the window and saw an inoffensive civilian crossing Horse Guards Parade – and whistling. "Go on," urged Mr Churchill. "Call out to him to stop." We were on the top floor of the building and I doubted if my plea would reach the culprit. In any case I felt it was going a bit too far: the man was on a public highway.' So she refused. And Churchill accepted it.

It was on the *Codrington* that May (who admitted that she was aware of 'tiny pointers for the future') suddenly realised the depth of Walter's feeling for her. In the American edition of his book, he wrote:

I was, of course, no end pleased to find her aboard, and thereafter not at all surprised at the stir she caused. It's a wonder we made land. Miss Shearburn, it being known instantly somehow that she was 'Miss', was escorted to one place after another, from bridge to gun turrets to the torpedo room to the wardroom and back. Her name had been included in the list of the party to the destroyer, and one of the officers recognised the name and greeted Miss Shearburn with the news that he was a friend of her brother, a naval commander. She was not only given every possible attention; she was given more than she needed . . . She loved it, too.

The bantering tone appears removed from the truth. 'On the bridge,' May's version reads,

I was intrigued by the ASDIC equipment – the device for sending out sound waves [that] could indicate the presence of enemy submarines. I asked how it worked then – remembering the wartime need for secrecy – added hastily, 'That is, if it's all right to tell me, of course.' The officers laughed. 'Surely,' one said, 'we are allowed to tell the First Lord's secretary anything she wishes to know.' Tommy, who was naturally there to guard the boss, was a little chilly to me for much of this trip. At one point in the tour the officers invited me into the wardroom. We were all drinking and talking happily when I caught sight of Tommy standing in the doorway. He wore a black expression. Ah! I thought.

He had a black expression shortly afterwards on a visit to Scapa Flow where May wasn't allowed beyond Thurso, the furthest point on the Scottish mainland, where the navy threw a dance for her. She was 'flattered and amused' and 'in that perverse way' she 'enjoyed it even more when a glance from Tommy showed me that *he* was not too pleased by the attention I was getting . . . We had never spoken of romance but, as in the wardroom of the *Codrington*, I thought, Ah!'

*   *   *

If Churchill or anyone else were unaware of the closeness of Walter's and May's relationship, the story of the official box that went astray was revealing.

In the version that Walter published, he described it as 'an incident that . . . brought down upon my head the just wrath of Mr Churchill'. May's version is more forthright and certainly doesn't see Churchill's wrath as just.

We had been down to the country home of the Digbys – the parents of Randolph's first wife – for the weekend. On our return, due to our late arrival for the train, there had been a certain amount of confusion over the official boxes. A

Treasury messenger was travelling with us and it was his job to see that the boxes were put on the train. However, when the train started, Tommy found that one was missing. He came into my compartment to ask if I had it with me; when I said I hadn't, he pulled the communication cord, the train stopped and the guard arranged for us to wait at the next station and have the box sent on.

Mr Churchill, of course, instantly demanded to be told why the train had stopped and took Tommy to task over it. This happened very frequently: when things went wrong, the Old Man was apt to blame him, when the matter was no concern of his whatever. I gathered from Tommy that the Old Man suggested that part of the blame must lie with me, but Tommy stoutly denied this. A few minutes later Mr Churchill sent for me, and I immediately apologised 'for overlooking the box'. We were both spoken to very severely [but] he appeared to be slightly pacified by the fact that we both accepted responsibility.

Walter's version added: 'I am not sure that he did not guess the reason why we were trying to lift the blame from each other's shoulders.' May's isn't equivocal: 'For a long time Churchill had shot me disapproving looks when he saw Tommy and me together.' Really, Walter knew that the Old Man knew: in numerous places his anecdotes end with the words 'Winston misses nothing' – though he did miss the little exchange of glances between the couple on the occasion when a nearby bomb put out the Annexe lights and Churchill came up to ground level to see the extent of the damage. May followed behind General Ismay and Walter, but Churchill sent her back down with the words, 'Go back to your rabbit warren!' . . . and May, smiling to herself,

Man of the people: during the Blitz Churchill visited the bomb-damaged towns, encouraging, uplifting and helping where he could, with Walter either in a car with him, or close behind

Boss and bodyguard in Canada, 1942.

Left: strolling together in Halifax. Below: After a visit to a training airfield in Ottawa, Walter lights the Old Man's cigar

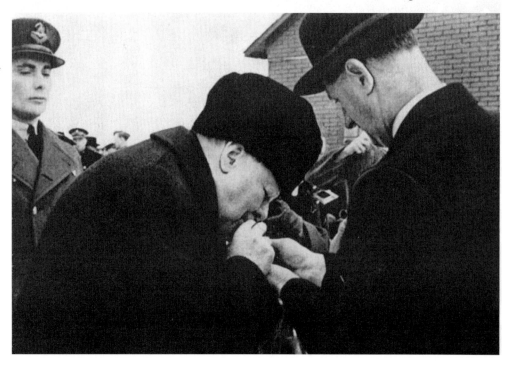

Churchill leaves Downing Street during the war

An open car on VE Day for Churchill and
Walter. But when Churchill went out a second
time and tried to walk, his bodyguard feared for
his life in the crush of the crowd

Walter's family in the 1920s. From left to right: Kate, Harold, Kathleen (seated), Grace, Harvey, Walter and Freddie (cross-legged)

Walter's three sons: Harold, Freddie and Harvey

One of the first Pathfinders, Freddie (second left) and the rest of the crew died when their Stirling was shot down over France

A member of the French Resistance stands in front of the wreckage

The graves of Freddie and his fellow crew – a place that Walter could never make himself visit

Marjorie Wigley was part of Walter's tangled love life and they might have married if he hadn't gone back to Churchill in 1939. Her leave pass in 1945, after she'd married someone else, was for a meeting with Walter that was almost certainly their last

Walter didn't need the 'tremendous arm power' he'd used cutting the lawn at Chartwell – when he moved to Hill Head in Hampshire he bought a sit-on mower to cut his own

Walter and May, who exchanged photos expressing their love in 1939,
became a double act in the 1950s, lecturing about Churchill

'Dad would have taken a bullet for Churchill – it's as simple as that'

went. Walter's pet name for her was Bunny, because of the way she wrinkled her nose.

When the relationship developed into an affair and how long it continued before Kathleen Hill, Churchill's senior secretary, went to Clementine about it one can only guess. What followed, however, was that Clementine went to her husband and demanded Walter's dismissal. Churchill refused to agree to this – and it was May who had to go and did, in the summer of 1942.

Clementine (Clemmie to all the staff as well as her husband) was annoyed that May had paid the price for Walter's infidelity. She liked May, who at Chartwell and then the Admiralty helped with her correspondence, before she got a full-time secretary of her own. When May's bedroom at Number 10 was destroyed in the blast from the bomb that hit the Treasury, she gave her 'a beautiful black suede handbag containing a cheque and a note saying that it was to help replace some of the things I had lost'. Again, when May contracted measles, Clementine 'made a number of phone calls to try to get me into a nursing home, alas without success as none of them was prepared to take infectious cases. She finally got me a private room in the Fulham Fever Hospital and, when the ambulance came to Number 10 to collect me, she gave me a large pot plant to take with me.'

Walter was a different matter. Clementine didn't like him or, at the very least, his constant presence. He'd lived at Sussex Square in the Sinn Fein days, and at Chartwell, and here, twenty years on, he was in the Annexe too (admittedly with many other people), outside the door of whatever room her husband was in. At both Sussex Square and Chartwell, Walter wrote in his unpublished material: 'I was a perpetual annoyance to her.'

Sometimes she refused to feed him. 'One day, Winston returned home [to Sussex Square] for lunch just before 2 p.m., thirty minutes late, and the staff, with whom I had my meals, had already finished theirs. Owing to Winston's lateness, there was quite a rush on to attend to him so that he could return to his office. I went along to the cook for my meal, as I usually did, to be told that Mrs Churchill had made no provision for me and there were to be no meals for me in future.' This, Walter wrote, 'did not bother me in the slightest', and, having arranged for a uniformed officer to watch while he was out, he 'went up the basement steps and to a local café'. On his return,

Gertrude, one of the parlourmaids, told me to go to the dining room, as Winston wanted me. 'Where have you been, Thompson?' he asked. 'As you were late home for lunch and all the staff were so busy attending to your meal, I thought it would help if I went outside for mine,' I said. He looked straight at me, knowing full well that I was not speaking the truth. He turned to his wife. 'You are sure, Clemmie, that the sergeant's meals were arranged for?' She looked straight at me as she replied, 'Of course, Winston, they have always been there for him.' I could not let her down, so I apologised, but her look told me quite enough, for she had deliberately stopped the meals, as she so often did in later years.

At Chartwell, Clementine even ordered Walter out of the house. 'I was informed by her secretary that I was no longer to be accommodated and that I must make arrangements to go to the village. Moreover, that I should use my allowance for my accommodation. Of course, I had to notify Mr Churchill that I should have to be away from Chartwell, not only at night but to go to the village for my meals. This he refused to accept, so I was on his orders reinstated . . .' Cryptically Walter added: 'The atmosphere was not to my liking.'

From Clementine's point of view, it's fair to assume, Walter was almost an eavesdropper on her personal life. He was there during her domestic arguments: in the early days about the state of Churchill's clothes; about the trees she had cut down at Chartwell (which 'gave her considerable satisfaction' but caused Winston 'displeasure and hurt'); about the time she took over getting dressed (once, according to a tale Walter told Harold but didn't commit to paper, her response to Churchill's question about how long she was going to be was, '"When I am ready I will come down", and with that she stripped off, had another bath, changed all her clothes and kept him waiting quite a long time'); about her personal extravagance.

On that last topic Walter wrote:

One weekend we were to travel to Chartwell. Winston was at the wheel of his two-seater open car and I was in the dickie seat, when his wife appeared dressed in a most gorgeous black dress decorated with gold thread. Winston voiced his delight. 'Clemmie,' he said, 'you look beautiful. What a lovely dress.' 'I am so pleased you like it, darling,' she replied, as she took her seat beside him. It was not until we were out in the country that the dress was again mentioned. Winston gazed sideways and quietly said: 'And what did it cost?' She replied: 'I dare not tell you.' 'I thought not,' he said. 'I am sure it was very expensive.' 'I will tell you later, Winston,' she replied. 'But there is no harm in knowing now, in view of the fact you have bought it.' The car almost came to a standstill when she said: 'Two hundred guineas.' 'I suppose,' he said, 'you have not paid for it yet?' 'Let us talk about it later,' she replied. Dead silence followed and not another word was said . . . the weekend was far from a happy one.

Another dress that Clementine bought put Walter in the middle of an argument. She had returned from a visit to France, having bought the dress but she hadn't paid Customs duty on it and Churchill, furious, at once wrote out a cheque and 'to my embarrassment . . . spoke strongly to us both' – although Walter's part had merely been to go to Victoria Station to pick up the luggage.

The antipathy that existed between wife and bodyguard continued in the war. On one occasion during Churchill's visit to bombed cities when Clementine went with him, Walter walked in on her when she was in the bath. This certainly didn't endear him to her. He was aware of her hostility even in little things, right to the end of the war – like the disagreement he had with her over whether a large cake sent to Churchill as a Christmas gift should be destroyed or not. Walter thought it should ('I could not take any chances') but compromised and, in time-honoured fashion, 'had enquiries made of the senders of the cake by the police in the town from where the cake came . . . Apparently two elderly spinsters had saved part of their rations during 1944 and had handed them to a local baker who had made the cake . . . When I told Mrs Churchill that it was all right, she replied: "I told you it would be so."'

It seems that Clementine was in some sense jealous of her husband's bodyguard. Other than in the Chartwell years, and especially during the war when she saw her husband very seldom, Walter was always with him. Walter understood how she felt and, seeing 'how much happier [Winston] seemed when she was at his side', he kept his own counsel. He chose to offer no word of criticism about Clemmie – though he added with a trace of satisfaction: 'Actually, during the war years I spent more time with him than any other human.'

The five days that Walter spent with Churchill after May's

dismissal weren't the most pleasant they had together. 'Winston was very upset about the business . . . and he refused to speak to me,' Walter mourned. Churchill was still maintaining a stony silence when they went to Chartwell on a rare wartime visit and Walter decided to confront him. 'I told him I thought it was about time he stopped being peeved with me over his secretary. "She was the best secretary I ever had," he said, frowned, grunted and walked on. But he started speaking to me again after that.'

Walter wasn't able to bring himself to write that May had been dismissed, never mind why; his preferred version was that the pressure of work 'left her close to a breakdown'. 'It was too much for anyone and she had to resign, deciding to take a quieter job at the BBC.'[2]

*　　*　　*

Walter's personal life was more complicated than May could have known at the beginning: he was still seeing a woman named Marjorie Wigley – his partner in the grocery enterprise. For nearly three years until Churchill recalled him, they lived together in Oakfield Road at the bottom of Anerley Road, where the bigger of the shops was located. 'Whether my mother was an equal partner, I don't know,' says Hilary Greenstreet, who breeds sheep and runs holiday lets at her farmhouse in Bude on the Devon–Cornish border. 'But she did put money into the business. And she had experience of dealing with customers, which Wally, as she called him, didn't – she'd been a housekeeper at Haddon Hall in Derbyshire and then worked as a manageress in a big hotel chain.

'Apparently they fell out a lot – a lot of tiffs caused by working together. But their relationship was extremely deep, I know, because, quite frankly, my mother never stopped talking about him.'

A postcard that Walter sent to Marjorie from the Ritz in Paris on 15 November 1939, three months after meeting May, indicates a bond between them: 'Have arrived quite safe and staying at the place shown in the picture. Expect to return Sunday evening. Love, Wally.' A letter dated 27 December 1941 that he wrote from the White House in Washington is banal in content, but strongly suggested they were still involved:

Dear Marjorie,

I have just heard that a mail is going out today and we can send a letter, unfortunately they did not tell me until late so that my note will have to be short.

We shall be over this side until at least the end of next week, you can write to me for they will send your letter on. Very hectic this business over here, little time to spare, and all on the alert wondering what might happen also surrounded by 'G' men – nearly drives you silly.

How did you get on at the garage? Sure you must have been fed up to the eyebrows; I have been here but hope to get back soon. All work and no play makes me feel I want a break badly.

Now my dear you must excuse me, you know we cannot write much.

All my love dearest.

Ever yours,

Wally

Whether or when May found out about Marjorie is swallowed up in the past. But as Walter's feelings for May deepened, his relationship with Marjorie ended. He had sold the lease on the smaller shop on his recall to duty, but she tried to keep the bigger one going. However, as the men who worked there went into the services, she gave up the struggle, at some point getting Walter's agreement to get rid of it. Soon afterwards she went into the WRAF, becoming a sergeant at a balloon barrage unit in Farnborough in Hampshire.

In their many conversations together while May was still Churchill's secretary,

> bit by bit Tommy poured out his troubles to me . . . One day, in some emotion, he showed me a letter he had received from his younger daughter. It was a sad little note which told of the other girls at school who had daddies who came home on leave. The unspoken message was that she didn't have a daddy. The letter drew me up with a jerk. Though we had never spoken of marriage, I realised that we had dropped into a way of thinking vaguely that we might have a future together. But I told Tommy that he ought to try to patch up his marriage, and he agreed.

In October or November 1942 Kathleen, Grace and their mother came down from Rotherham and for nearly two months lived in the mews flat. Kathleen, who'd been down in September to be bridesmaid at Fred's wedding, wasn't told why they'd come, but she realised a reconciliation might be in the offing. The Bank of England had left a small office open when it had evacuated to Winchester and she applied for, and began, a traineeship; Grace, a hairdresser, found a job, and Kate became a temporary alteration hand in Selfridges clothing department. 'My father didn't sleep at the flat or eat with us – I think he and Mother met a few times for tea,' Kathleen says. 'One day my mother said, "This isn't working", and we went back to Rotherham, basically to pack up – the bank knew there were family problems and gave me leave.'

In early 1943 Kate answered a newspaper advert for a live-in nanny to the family of an RAF flight lieutenant stationed near Andover in Hampshire. She and her daughters moved there, Grace soon being drafted into war work at a local factory making trailers for transporting aircraft parts; Kathleen rejoined the bank at its temporary home outside Winchester. Kate was to stay in Andover until Harvey, her youngest son, returned from serving in Rhodesia in 1946, when she went to live with him and his wife Helen at various RAF stations in the UK; other than when Harvey did a tour of duty in Cyprus,[3] she was to continue living with them for most of the rest of her life. She was needed: the couple eventually had twelve children. 'Helen relied on Mother,' says Kathleen. 'As the daughter of the governor of the Seychelles she'd been used to servants – she wasn't at her best domestically.' Harvey had become a Catholic to marry, and Kate converted to Catholicism. 'I think she was looking for some comfort in life,' Kathleen adds.

Walter never formally proposed to May, who'd been at pains to establish with Kate that 'there was nothing left of their marriage long before I arrived in Tommy's life'. One thing that held him back, she wrote, 'was the feeling that he would never survive the war because of Churchill's habit of continually walking into danger'. It was a fate to which, until he became serious about May, he had perhaps resigned himself. 'Every time he went abroad with Churchill, Dad would ring me up and say, "You know where my will is",' Harold says. During 1944 Walter increasingly worried that this indeed was what was in store – another pressure that undoubtedly contributed to his collapse. And he very much didn't want it to be the case. Lying in the police convalescence home, he was conscious of the fact that the war would soon end. He wanted to be there when it did.

CHAPTER 11

Parting of the Ways

'Having a strong constitution, I quickly regained my health and in a matter of weeks I was back with Winston,' Walter wrote ebulliently. He hated to admit either the seriousness of what had happened to him or that he was ever absent from Churchill's side, and this time it had been for five weeks; in fact, he didn't admit his breakdown in anything that was published.

Since October 1944 there had been escalating trouble in Greece, where, in a vacuum created by the German retreat, ELAS communist troops had tried to overthrow the government. In the April of the previous year, five warships of the Greek navy mutinied in Alexandria in support of the communist EAM Party, as had the First Greek Brigade outside Cairo. Churchill hadn't hesitated to deal decisively with these outbreaks, which were quickly quelled, and he didn't hesitate now, ordering British troops in Greece to meet force with force. In the meantime he suggested to the King of Greece, exiled in London, that as an interim measure a regency should be set up. The King was obstinate. As fighting continued in Athens and the possibility that the country would fall into communist hands was very real, Churchill decided that only one course was open to him – to go there and sort it out for himself.

The decision, made suddenly on Christmas Eve, spoiled Christmas 1944 for all those who went with him; at least when they took off from Northolt on Christmas Day it was in a new plane, a Douglas Skymaster (later famous as the commercial DC4), lent by the Americans, which was luxuriously fitted out and could make the trip in one hop.

The situation was highly dangerous; Churchill was persuaded to stay aboard the cruiser *Ajax*, anchored in Athens harbour, and travel by armoured car. Throughout his visit gunfire crackled over the city – on the night the Skymaster landed, its undercarriage was riddled with bullet-holes. At the British Embassy, where bullets frequently thudded into the walls and windows, the staff slept in the corridors for safety and lived off army compo rations. On the first morning Churchill was there, the Ambassador, who'd continued working in his office with his desk moved into an angle of the room, walked in to find him sitting reading his dispatches in full view of a rebel machine-gun post. Once, as Churchill emerged from the Embassy to enter his vehicle, a volley of rifle fire killed or wounded several people in the street and he was showered with plaster from the Embassy wall.

All parties in the conflict were brought together in the Greek Foreign Office where, Walter noted, 'Winston told the Greeks frankly that the British government was tired of nonsense'. It was, he added, 'a strange scene. The only light in the large room was supplied by hurricane lamps. There was no heat. All the delegates sat huddled in their overcoats.'

To Walter's irritation, Churchill had been heavily criticised in the press at home for involving the British army in a fight with what many saw as anti-Nazi freedom fighters (and in America for imperialist ambitions) and had faced a vote of censure in the House. The climate was somewhat changed when he returned – and the truce he'd won had within a week led to the ending of the civil war. The *Manchester Guardian* praised his swift intervention as 'one of those flashes of courage and imagination which will always cause his countrymen to forgive his occasional errors of judgement'. Not everyone agreed. Wrote Walter: 'The opponents of Winston's handling of the Greek situation were far from satisfied, although the vote had gone against them, and, following more adverse criticisms in the press, another vote of censure was put in the House early in the New Year.' He added with evident satisfaction: 'This again was defeated, by 340 to 7.'

After what Walter referred to as 'the Greek interlude' – and another flying visit to Eisenhower as the Germans were driven back towards their own border – came the most important conference of the war at Yalta, which, he pointed out, 'Marshal Stalin . . . always referred to as the Crimea conference'. Again, Stalin wasn't prepared to travel outside his domain.

Churchill's Skymaster arrived via Malta at Saki airfield across the mountains from Yalta on 3 February 1945,

then started off on a journey of over a hundred miles along incredibly bad roads. Along the whole route were Russian troops, mostly women, who saluted as each car passed. At road junctions, sentries, again chiefly women, controlled the traffic. They were exceedingly smart at this work. They worked with a red flag in the right hand and a yellow one in the left. After signalling drivers to proceed, the red flag was passed to the left hand and a salute given in one movement.

Yalta turned out to be a dismal place, the harbour waters jagged with sunken ships and many of the buildings of the old resort wrecked by the Germans, though not the Lividia Palace, where the conference was held. All three powers fielded the usual big teams; the British sent the liner *Franconia* to Sevastopol to provide extra accommodation as well as a communications centre.

Even before the Big Three got there for this, their second meeting, Stalin had made clear his intention about Poland – the country over which Britain had gone to war with Hitler. Ignoring the Polish government-in-exile in London, he declared his puppet Lubin Committee as the country's provisional administration. Churchill pressed for free elections in Poland and the other countries that Stalin had overrun (hoping that the Allied armies might be able to push far enough east at least to prevent Soviet occupation of Czechoslovakia and Yugoslavia). Stalin made promises he had no intention of keeping. Roosevelt, aged and ill, was more interested in getting Stalin into the war with Japan and gaining his support for the setting up of a United Nations.

Churchill was marginalised: the war belonged to Russia and America now. Walter wrote angrily about 'the absolute submission of Roosevelt to Stalin. Again, here, the President had absolute faith in Stalin and Russia.' Charitably he added that 'it should be borne in mind that all those present realised that the President was a very sick man and resistance to Stalin seemed to be beyond his capabilities'. He might have added that all those present realised that the Prime Minister, for all his resolution, was less able than once he'd been to counter Stalin's wiles. Churchill knew, and didn't forgive himself. Weeks later, in London, Walter would make 'one of my usual visits to him, following the morning secretary leaving his room', and find him very depressed, 'his thoughts far away . . . "Why, Thompson, did they allow the President, almost dying on his feet, to be at Yalta?" It was depressing to see him as tears rolled down his cheeks. I did not know what to say to him. He continued: "All Europe will eventually suffer from the decisions made at Yalta." Again I could not answer him . . . not feeling able to talk on matters beyond my knowledge.'

Instead of flying home at the end of the week-long Yalta conference, 'to Winston's astonishment' Roosevelt went to the Middle East for discussions with various rulers; Stalin took his train back to Moscow to plan the final assault on Berlin; and Churchill

made another spectacular visit to Athens . . . The scene that met Winston's eye when he appeared with Archbishop Damaskinos [the man Churchill chose as regent] on a balcony overlooking the Unknown Warrior's Tomb was of a seething mass of people, cheering, clapping and delirious with delight. The audience was almost certainly the largest he ever addressed. [They] listened intently whilst [he] spoke, cheering him to the echo when he said: 'Speaking as an Englishman, I am proud of the part that the British army has played in protecting this eternal and immortal city from violence and anarchy. Let right prevail; let party hatred die; let there be unity; let there be resolute companionship; Greece for ever; Greece for all!' The whole occasion was a better answer to Mr Bevan [the Labour politician regarded as Churchill's 'one-man Opposition'] and the other malcontents than all the debating points it was possible to make in the House of Commons.

That night Churchill slept on the Skymaster before it took off for Egypt. At Aboukir he went on board the cruiser *Aurora*, where he intended to stay the night. But Roosevelt arrived unexpectedly on the *Quincy* from Ismailia and, having lunched with him, Churchill flew to Cairo for talks with

the Emperor of Ethiopia [Haile Selassie], now happily restored to his throne, the portly and unpopular King Farouk [of Egypt], the King of Saudi Arabia, and the Syrian President . . . King Ibn Saud al Faisal [of Saudi Arabia] stayed in a hotel in the desert on the shores of Lake Karoon as the guest of the British government. The European food was not to his liking. A room in the hotel was cleared. Members of his own staff roasted whole sheep for his table.

The day that Winston went to lunch with the King was one of the most picturesque that I can remember. The King was protected by his official bodyguards with their polished sabres and daggers. Their robes were most colourful. In his party were princes, sheiks, his official food-taster, his astrologer, his fortune-teller and the royal purse bearer. Presents were exchanged. Winston received a jewelled sword and dagger, the hilt of which contained a magnificent diamond, and a set of ceremonial Arab robes in a beautiful hide case. The King was given boxes of exquisite perfumes of very rare varieties.

The result of the conferences at Cairo was that the countries there represented declared war on Germany, as did Turkey. Better late than never, perhaps!

The war hurried on and Walter with it: 'The troops under Field Marshal Montgomery had by this time commenced clearing the enemy from the northern tip of the west bank of the Rhine.

The Prime Minister resolved to visit these troops and place his feet on conquered German soil . . . [He] visited Julich and its defences, near Aachen, in the Siegfried Line. He chalked on a huge shell the words "Hitler personally" and then fired it himself from a 2,400-millimetre gun across the Rhine.' Shortly afterwards, when British and Canadian troops were about to cross the river, Churchill was back, intent on making the crossing himself. Eisenhower had no intention of letting him do any such thing, but when he left Churchill at Buderich the Prime Minister suggested to Montgomery 'there would be no harm in paying a brief visit to the other side, as I think it was his due', wrote Walter. The war front had swept far ahead, and Walter wasn't worried. Churchill went over in a landing craft and did see a shell explode, but there wasn't much else to see and he soon came back, disappointed. The schoolboy in him wasn't satisfied and later in the day he crossed again (in a Jeep, over a just-completed pontoon bridge), making the return in an amphibious craft.

It was Churchill's last visit to a battle front, no doubt much to Walter's relief, though he makes no comment; nor does he have anything to say about the end of the German rocket attack on England – the last V-2 struck Orpington on the day after they got back from the Rhine. Walter's writing during 1944 had been vague as to places and times as, clearly, he headed towards his breakdown; now it was short on detail, events mostly dismissed in a sentence or two. He was, clearly, impatient: he wanted the war to be done.

But how Roosevelt's death touched Churchill, and touched Walter. He wrote: 'I had only left the Prime Minister in the early hours of the morning when he was going to bed, but on reaching my room his bell rang. I went at once to his bedroom, and as I opened the door he was walking across the room away from me, saying, "Terrible, terrible." When he turned towards me I saw

231

there were tears running down his cheeks. "Have you heard the awful news, Thompson?" he asked. "No, sir," I replied.' Churchill told him, praising 'what [Roosevelt] had meant to this country and the world', their differences in Teheran and Yalta forgotten. As Churchill himself was to write in his history of the war, the last time he'd seen Roosevelt he'd 'had a slender contact with life', and his death couldn't really have been a surprise; yet Churchill was inconsolable. 'He continued walking backwards and forwards, frequently repeating the help which he had given to us, and said: "I have lost a great friend. Now we have to start all over again." That night will remain for ever with me, Winston's grief such that I remained in the room with him for some time until he felt he could obtain some sleep.' The next day Churchill drew Walter aside to say solemnly: 'Moreover, it is Friday the thirteenth.'

Few tears were shed over the deaths of two other men that April.

Winston had just arrived at Chequers for the weekend, and as he entered the Great Hall he was informed of Mussolini's death. He was elated and with much emphasis he said: 'Ah, the bloody beast is dead.' Three days later he received the news of Hitler's death, but on this occasion he went to a window and looked out, remaining there for some time without any remark . . . In view of some doubt existing in people's minds as to whether or not Hitler was dead, I asked him if he thought Hitler had committed suicide. Quietly he replied: 'That is the way I should have expected him to have died. That is what I should have done under the same circumstances.'

At 7 p.m. the following evening, 1 May, the BBC interrupted programmes to report the surrender of the Germans in Italy. Another news flash at 10.30 p.m.: Berlin had fallen. On 7 May the Germans surrendered unconditionally, and the country waited to hear that the war was officially over. Churchill hoped to broadcast on the 6 p.m. news but, although 'he spent a great deal of time on the long-distance telephone' to the new American President, Harry Truman, he had to wait until the next day so that America and Russia could make simultaneous announcements. But 'crowds were assembling throughout central London waiting for the news. As the day wore on, they became increasingly impatient and Winston decided to indulge their legitimate curiosity without anticipating the end of the war. An announcement was released that the following day was to be Victory in Europe Day. That told everybody what they wanted to know.'

For days Churchill had been showing his age and spoke to Walter 'about going over to France for a rest'. Ascending stairs, 'he would put his arm through mine [and] the way he leaned on me made he realise how worn out he was'. But in typical Churchill fashion he was galvanised when, at 3 p.m. British Double Summer Time on 8 May, he spoke from the same room at Number 10 from which Chamberlain had made his fateful declaration of war:

Yesterday morning at 2.41 a.m., at General Eisenhower's headquarters, the representative of the German High Command . . . signed an act of unconditional surrender of all German land, sea and air forces in Europe to the Allied Expeditionary Force. Hostilities will end officially at one minute after midnight . . . but in the interests of saving lives, the cease-fire began yesterday to be sounded all along the front. The German war is therefore at an end . . . We may allow ourselves a brief period of rejoicing, but let us not forget for a moment the toils and efforts that lie ahead. Japan, with all her treachery and greed, remains unsubdued . . . Advance Britannia! Long live the cause of freedom! God save the King!

The years dropped from Churchill on VE Day (and Walter rediscovered his interest in description). As Churchill had insisted on an open car to go from Downing Street to the Commons, to make a statement, Walter, knowing the unintended dangers presented by a dense crowd, had arranged for 'sufficient police officers in the car to cover him from all sides'. He wrote: 'What a struggle there was; we did not need to have any engine power – our car was almost carried along as the people went mad with delight. Laughter and cheering were mingled with tears of happiness and relief . . . As a matter of fact, my colleagues and I even forgot for a moment and cheered with the rest . . .'

When Churchill left the House to attend an audience with the King at Buckingham Palace, he asked Walter for a cigar: Walter reached for the case of spares he always carried

because his was so often empty. It wasn't there. In the excitement of the day I had forgotten. Churchill was unperturbed but insisted on stopping at the Annexe to get one, remarking: 'I must put one on for them. They expect it.' Ever the showman, he lit it in front of the crowd. Later in the day, from the Ministry of Health balcony, he beat time as the crowd sang 'Land of Hope and Glory' and was greeted by roars of laughter when he spoke and had just said 'The lights went out' – and the floodlights which were on him from the opposite side of the road went dim . . . a quite accidental theatrical effect. He could not understand what had happened and looked to me for an explanation, but realised the aptness of his remark and chuckled.

In 1939, when the crews of the *Ajax* and *Exeter* were fêted at the Guildhall after driving the pocket battleship *Graf Spee* into Montevideo harbour – where she was scuttled by her captain – Walter thought he was 'never more needed to save Winston from his friends'. Then, 'every sailor wanted to shake his hand or pat him on the back and I saw him flinch . . . These boys put real beef into their "pats". I literally covered Winston's back with my body.' The day after VE Day, when Churchill was surrounded not by hundreds of sailors but by tens of thousands of well-wishers, he was to find out he was even more needed.

The afternoon, when Churchill drove in the open car through the West End to the American and Soviet Embassies and paid a visit to the French Ambassador, was carefully managed – Churchill was surrounded by mounted police. But in the evening he impulsively decided to go out again, and Walter, having sent the open car away, had the Old Man's saloon waiting, with the police car standing by.

'He looked down his nose at the saloon and said: "Where is that open car?"' Walter wrote.

> When I told him it was not available, he said: 'I will walk, then.' 'Impossible, sir,' I objected. 'The crowd is too dense.' He took no notice. On reaching Whitehall he realised I was right and that he could not get through, so he announced: 'I shall walk between the two cars.' But the crowd at once closed in. I begged him to wait for the mounted police, but he refused. He was in danger of being trampled on. Suddenly he climbed on the back bumper in front of him and I assisted him up.

Then after a while he climbed along the car roof on all fours until he could sit in the front with his legs dangling over the windscreen . . . the crowd cheered their heads off.

The situation mightn't have been so jolly. 'Dad told me he was really frightened for Churchill's life,' Harold says. 'He thought he'd be crushed against the cars or be knocked under them. Even when Churchill was up out of the way, people were still climbing on the running boards trying to reach him. Dad had to get quite physical; he was striking out in all directions. He was mortified that he actually broke one woman's arm.'

*   *   *

For most of the population, VE Day was the end of it: only those with loved ones fighting in the Far East were concerned about the campaign against the Japanese. People began to pick up the pieces of their lives as they continued to contend with shortages and rationing – and concentrated on the first general election for ten years.

Churchill had wanted to hold the coalition together until victory was won outright. 'This, too, was the considered view of many of the more responsible members of the Labour Party,' Walter wrote, 'but the extremists on the left were making it quite plain that they intended to try to force the issue at the first possible moment . . . To me it seemed a thousand pities that a man of Winston's age, who had given nearly six years to planning day after day, night after night, the defeat of the enemy, should be mercilessly thrown into the party arena . . .'

The coalition was dissolved, a Conservative caretaker administration was put in place and campaigning headed towards polling day on 5 July, with the results to be declared three weeks later, allowing time for the service vote to come back from overseas.

And after twenty-four on-and-off years, the Walter–Winnie

partnership was over. At the beginning of June Walter suddenly told the Old Man that he'd been examined by the chief police surgeon, who'd told him: 'You aren't getting any younger, Thompson . . . I want you away in the next few days.' What Churchill's reaction was Walter doesn't record – he was writing very little again. He wrote nothing about being on the election trail that took Churchill around the country in his special train, but he must have been there at least at the beginning, although clearing up his affairs with the Yard would have taken him away from time to time. Detective Inspector Lumsden Hughes, who'd stood in for Walter during his convalescence, was appointed to accompany Churchill to Potsdam, near Berlin, where the final major conference of the war was scheduled for July – which Churchill would start as Prime Minister and which Attlee would finish as Prime Minister, after the election turned Churchill out of office in mid-summit, the most extraordinary loss of power in modern politics.

Walter's last job was to brief the Marine guards who were to accompany the British delegation to Potsdam. Nineteen-year-old Neville Bullock was one of those who volunteered for the assignment. 'There were thirty or forty of us, and we went up to London from Plymouth and stayed at the Union Jack Club,' he says.

Before we went to Germany the job was to guard a garage at the back of Sloane Square that was full of the documents for the conference – cases and cases of them. I called Inspector Thompson sir. I was in awe of an inspector from Scotland Yard. I came from a police family: my dad was a policeman and my aunt was the first policewoman in Leeds; and I became a policeman after the war. He [Walter] taught us about 'safe distance' – how you were to be close to whoever you were guarding but not so close as to invade personal space. I don't think I ever saw him smile, but he was very professional.[1]

In April, when the coalition first showed signs of breaking up and 'a political battle was in the offing', Churchill had gone to Chartwell. The grounds were tangled and overgrown, but as he and Walter walked around 'for a few hours he relaxed and was happy . . .' Before leaving for London, 'he went into the house to change his shoes. He gazed out of the windows, then with a smile he said: "Well, Thompson, if they throw me out in three months' time, I shall come down here and be as happy as a sandboy . . . and he said he would like to build some cottages on his land for ex-servicemen to live in.' Churchill didn't, of course, expect to be thrown out, and, he told Walter, 'he wanted to put things right that happened at Yalta'. But he was mistaking the enthusiasm with which he was greeted everywhere as a vote of confidence for the future. In fact, he was misreading the mood of the electorate, who turned away from his emphasis on the world picture; people wanted a government that concentrated on putting the country back together, and for it to be a better place. And he was to find that the service vote would go strongly against him: men overseas blamed him for their not yet being released, and many feared that when they did get home there would be the level of unemployment that followed the First World War.

And Churchill might have remembered that he'd written in *My Early Life*: 'Those who can win a war well can rarely make a good peace, and those who could make a good peace would never have won a war.' On a sunny spring day at Chartwell, what would happen at the polls had yet to unfold, but perhaps Walter had some foreboding, for 'the thought flashed through

my mind: I wonder how long you would be happy with no political work to do?'

On the morning of 30 June Walter told the Old Man that the
Yard had confirmed that

I was leaving him for good that night. He appeared hurt as
he looked at me, but did not speak to me then – neither did
he do so during the day. Officially I was relieved of my duty
at 6 p.m., but I waited until 11.50 p.m. before he sent for me
– actually I was finished with him and with Scotland Yard at
midnight.

As I entered his room he was sitting in a low armchair with
his head bowed. He did not look up, but stretched out a hand
towards me and clutched my fingers . . . [and] still clutching
my fingers, but without raising his head, he began to go over
the years we had spent together.

They shared a great deal that was personal, and even intimate.
Walter had lived in Churchill's home almost as a member of the
family. On occasions he'd run Churchill's baths, picked up his
clothes, sat beside him when he couldn't sleep, carried him when
he was ill, applied a heat lamp to his back and shoulders after
he'd been knocked down in New York – he'd even given him
his medicine, 'which otherwise, Mrs Churchill impressed upon
me, he would certainly forget to take if left to himself'. Once,
when the Old Man was travelling with Sir James Craig, the
governor-general of Northern Ireland, along a leafy Belfast road,
Walter ordered the driver to stop, produced a medicine bottle
and measured a dose into a glass. Craig told him: 'I knew Scotland
Yard men are versatile. But I've never before heard of one engaged
as a nursemaid.'

There was unquestionably a friendship between the pair: never on an equal footing, of course, but a friendship nevertheless. Churchill had around him statesmen and strategists, politicians and diplomats, thinkers, entrepreneurs and many others to satisfy his omnivorous needs and interests and with whom he could cross intellectual swords. But Walter met a different need: he was someone with whom Churchill could simply let go, someone who on occasions was a sounding board to what ordinary people were thinking, a kind of backstop – and, of course, a man whose presence made Churchill feel safe, who could be relied on utterly to do his job with subservience to no one: anticipate problems and eliminate them, and, when an unanticipated problem occurred, deal with it.

Churchill simply liked having Walter around and thought so much of him that he wouldn't tolerate him being slighted. Throughout the 1920s, when he went often to the theatre (and Walter accompanied him in his capacity as bodyguard), Churchill would have him sit with him if a seat was available. One night 'the manager came forward in the foyer with effusive greeting and began to lead Winston into the auditorium', Walter recorded in his notes. 'As he did so, the manager turned his head and murmured: "We have no room for you." Winston stopped in his tracks, turned to me and said: "What was that, Thompson? Did I hear aright? No room for you?" "That is right, sir." Winston handed his ticket to the manager. "If there is no room for Thompson, there is no room for me," he said. And we went straight back home to Sussex Square.'

On another occasion Churchill was the guest of Lord Curzon ('a great statesman and a greater snob . . . the one public man in my life whom I can honestly say I strongly disliked') and the housekeeper arranged for Walter to stay in a cottage on the estate.

On the morning after our arrival, Lord Curzon caught sight of me and asked who I was. When told, he fumed: 'I'll have no detective on my premises.' So I had to go to Basingstoke for a bed. We left on the Monday to go to Blenheim Palace . . . The route lay across country and Curzon came to the car, which I was driving, and began giving me instruction about the route . . . I answered by saying, on the first occasion, 'Yes, my lord,' and afterwards, 'Yes, sir.' 'Do you know,' he demanded, 'to whom you are speaking?' 'Yes, sir,' I replied. 'Then address me correctly,' he said. As it happened, the way I addressed his lordship was absolutely correct, as laid down by the best authorities in these important matters. I told his lordship so, forcibly. I enjoyed doing so, but the most heart-warming moment of the whole unpleasant incident came just before we left when Winston turned to Curzon and said: 'Thompson was perfectly correct in his manner of addressing you.' He got straight into the car and we drove away, leaving a very angry aristocrat behind us.

What incidents Churchill chose to remember as he said goodbye to his bodyguard, Walter doesn't say. But when he came to speak of the death of his mother, before which Walter had offered to give blood that might save her, and 'tears rolled down his cheeks', Walter 'felt considerably embarrassed and wanted to get away, especially as his head had remained bowed. After another pause, he said: "Goodbye, Thompson, you can come and see me any time, anywhere."'

In this oddly emotionally charged scene, Walter, 'puzzled that not once had he looked into my face', went to the door, calling back: 'Goodbye.' Suddenly Churchill looked up, his head and a finger raised in a gesture Walter knew well: '"When you came to me in August 1939," he said, "I told you I had something to do. Subsequently I said that I had a mission to perform. Now, Thompson, before you go . . . that mission has been accomplished." No words of mine could express adequately my pride at having worked at his side, and there was a huge lump in my throat as we parted.'

Churchill had given Walter a substantial cheque, not just in gratitude for his years of service but as a wedding present. Four months earlier, on 15 February, he and May Shearburn had married, 'when it was clear that the Allies would win,' she wrote in her wartime account, continuing: 'Without telling anybody, we slipped quietly into the registry office at Caxton Hall, a short walk away from the Prime Minister's home. I gave my address as 10 Downing Street, but the newspapers never noticed. Perhaps all the good reporters were away at the war. Tommy only told Winston when he was leaving his service.' May did, in fact, tell one person, her younger sister Stella (always called Kit), who'd evacuated to Australia with her four-year-old daughter Jan. 'My mother got a letter in the January saying the date was fixed and would we be back,' Jan remembers. 'We didn't have a hope in hell of making it. The earliest boat we could get was April, and we weren't home until the end of May. I was heartbroken. As a not quite ten-year-old I wanted to be a bridesmaid.'

It was a time of Thompson weddings. In December 1944 Walter had given away his elder daughter Grace when she'd married in Andover. A few days after VE Day he'd given away Kathleen, who'd been to see him exactly two years earlier 'to get his permission to marry, as I was under twenty-one. It was the first time my father had met Eddie, who was in the Fleet Air Arm. When Mr Churchill heard of our intentions he arranged for us to be taken by car to Waterloo to go back to

Winchester, and he promised that my father would be at the wedding. I found out later that the car was the same one used for the VE Day celebrations – and after those it was covered in dents!'

There is a coda to Walter's own marriage.

Among his papers is a day pass for WRAF Sergeant Tradewell, stationed at Farnborough, to visit Inspector Thompson at 10 Downing Street, valid from 0700 to 23.59 on 30 January 1945. Marjorie Wigley had married Percy Tradewell, a widower with three daughters, who was home on leave from Ceylon (Sri Lanka), where he was harbour master in Colombo, on 12 September 1944, in Dore parish church, Sheffield. Did Walter want to tell Marjorie that he was marrying May? It seems more than likely; this, too, then, was a final goodbye.

One other letter exists from Walter to Marjorie, which was written on 26 March 1945 from Downing Street, and the tone, while affectionate, shows how the relationship had changed:

Dear Marjorie,

Thanks for your letter, please do not think I expected you to pay Payne's bill, I sent it to you because I could not understand the furniture being allowed to go without payment. It is a most unusual procedure. If you will return it to me I will forward the cash to them in a few weeks time.

Am so sorry all your nice clothes are spoilt, that is the worst part of clothes remaining in the store. Yes, I managed to get the cycle but it was all a rush. I saw Payne for a minute, had to go over during my lunch hour. I shall need new inner tubes. We are right on the top line now, there are 3 of us guarding the boss, owing to some threats following the hanging of Hulton.

Let me know when you are coming down this way.

Hope you have some luck for yourself. I thought it was another gentleman you had to write to at the Colonial Office where Stanley is the present head there. Let me know what they say.

   Must now close,
   Fond love
   Wally

CHAPTER 12

Brought to Book

As the chief police surgeon said, Walter wasn't getting any younger. But he'd recovered from his collapse and one would have expected him to remain at Churchill's side until Japan's surrender two months later and the job was properly done, or at least until Churchill's unexpected electoral defeat. In fact, Walter chose not to record the real reason for his sudden decision to go: Downing Street and Scotland Yard were trying to prevent publication of a book he'd written about his war years' experiences.

When exactly Walter told Churchill he'd written the book, and exactly what passed between them, isn't clear. But the subject first surfaced in an eight-word memo that Churchill sent to one of his private secretaries, J. M. Martin, on 20 May, in which irritation or even anger is evident: *Pray vet the alleged book by Inspector Thompson.* Five days later Martin returned the memo, penning on the bottom: *I have asked Inspector Thompson to show me the book when he gets the typescript back from Scotland Yard.*

At the Yard, Sir Philip Game had told Walter that he had no objection to publication if Number 10 was satisfied. But Number 10, in the person of Martin, was not. He wrote to the Commissioner, Sir Harold Scott, on 7 June, telling him that *the book contains much which it would be quite improper for anyone who has worked here as a member of the Prime Minister's staff to publish, certainly for many years to come. To save you reading the whole book, I attach a copy of Chapter 7 (entitled 'The Private Life of a Prime Minister') and various extracts containing passages the propriety of publishing which is questionable from various points of view.* Downing Street, he went on to explain, had objected to the Air Ministry the previous January about the proposed publication of a book by a pilot who'd frequently flown Churchill, adding: *I should have thought that there would be strong objection to the publication of such a book on the part of the Police authorities, since, if permission is given to Inspector Thompson, it will be difficult to withhold it from many others at Scotland Yard, for whose 'inside' narratives of cases they have investigated publishers would no doubt offer large sums. Before I submit the matter to the Prime Minister I should be glad to have your views.*

The next day Scott returned the manuscript, with a letter saying that he entirely agreed with Martin's view *that publication of this sort of Reminiscence, so soon after the event, is undesirable and that a self-denying ordinance, similar to that laid down* [by the Air Ministry] *for Transport Command, should apply to police officers who are in close contact with the Prime Minister or other members of Government.* Later the same day Scott sent across a second letter, indicating that Walter had handed him a note, addressed to Churchill, seeking leave to resign – as a reservist still in service he couldn't simply go. Scott was, he said, 'disposed to accept' the resignation but warned that then *we should have no* power *to censor his book.*

At this stage Walter evidently thought that by removing himself from the Yard's jurisdiction he'd be free to publish or, at least, would only have the Old Man to persuade; at this juncture he was probably optimistic. In the foreword to Walter's first book, Churchill had written: 'Inspector Thompson was my faithful vigilant guardian for many years, and I think he is quite justified in putting down his impressions and recollections of our travels in different countries.' That, surely, was all that he'd done this time. He was soon disappointed that Churchill didn't take that view. Exactly what Churchill said to him neither committed to paper, but on 18 June Churchill sent a note to the Commissioner saying that *Inspector Thompson has placed himself entirely in my hands in the matter, and has assured me that he will not publish the book if this is not in accordance with my wishes. Permission should not be given for publication at the present time. The passage of years may however reduce objections to disclosures of this character . . .*

Scott, in the meantime, had been busy. He'd consulted the Yard's solicitor and the Home Office legal adviser, and on 15 June he'd written to Martin explaining that, while paragraph 6 (a) of the Discipline Code as Breach of Confidence that applied to Walter in service could no longer be applied once he resigned, Section 15 of the Police Pensions Act might be: *Under this Section a pension may be forfeited by the Police Authority (i.e., the Home Secretary) if the pensioner publishes in a manner which the Police Authority considers to be improper any information obtained in the course of employment in the Police . . . Probably the Inspector would accept our advice in the matter but it is satisfactory to know we have a weapon at hand if needed.*

One wonders if the book came up during the farewell

conversation between Churchill and his about-to-be-ex-body-guard on the night of 30 June. Perhaps neither thought it an appropriate topic on the occasion.

Sometime before the war, as an investment, Walter had bought a tiny bungalow, Southways, a quarter of a mile from the sea at Greatstone near New Romney on the Kent coast, where the little light passenger railway runs to Dymchurch and the power station at Dungeness. It was to here he'd moved and it was here he listened when the election results were declared on 26 July. The Old Man's astonishing loss of office disgusted him ('One of the saddest days of my life,' he noted) – but at the same time it gave him hope of getting his book into print. Perhaps he was too eager; perhaps he should have considered that the Old Man was not only exhausted but was likely to still be depressed after what had happened to him. But Walter didn't; only a week later he wrote:

I am being asked repeatedly by the Kemsley Press whether I am now in a position to give them permission to publish the serial of my book. As you will remember, I have a contract with them for the serial rights for Great Britain only. Jarrolds, who are publishing the volume, are also anxious to know when they will be at liberty to do so.

I would be most grateful if you could let me know as soon as possible whether you are now agreeable to my publishing. If you are, would you consider giving me a foreword so that the book may go forward.

Walter concluded by hoping that Churchill was 'now able to get a well-earned rest after your strenuous efforts during the war', and added his wife's sincere good wishes to his own.

He heard nothing. On 22 August he wrote to Mrs Hill and a flurry of correspondence with her ensued. What was now clear came as a shock: whereas Walter believed his agreement with Churchill was not to seek to publish while Churchill was PM, Churchill believed the agreement was 'not for some considerable time' – as indeed he'd intimated to the Commissioner on 18 June – irrespective of whether or not he was in office.

A despairing letter to Churchill on 27 August seeking an interview at Chartwell went unanswered. However much Churchill felt he owed Walter (and when he'd written to the Commissioner on 18 June he'd taken 'This opportunity to place on record my sense of personal indebtedness to Inspector Thompson for his long and faithful service'), he was still feeling shattered and he was unwell, suffering chronic digestive problems that were diagnosed as diverticulitis. The letter he dictated to Kathleen Hill, which went out over her signature on 3 September, was curt, ending: *If however you persist against his wishes, and contrary to your definite promise, it will be necessary to submit the material to the Chief Commissioner of Police at Scotland Yard, and any words attributed by you to Mr Churchill on any occasion would have to be deleted.*

Churchill, meanwhile, had contacted the Yard, which brought pressure to bear; on 13 September the Deputy Assistant Commissioner saw Walter to point out in words of one syllable that his pension would be forfeit if he stepped out of line. He was evidently in a state of hurt and bewilderment when later that same day he wrote to Churchill:

It is apparent from your letter of the 3rd inst. that I have unwittingly caused you annoyance. I sincerely regret this and would respectfully point out that but for the publishers pressing me for publication I, personally, would not have approached you, at any rate for some time.

I would like again to assure you that I have never had the slightest intention of publishing either in book form or article any matter relating to you without your permission. I am indeed sorry that you should have thought I would break my promise to you.

I trust that you will accept this explanation and apology and that the misunderstanding which has arisen will not in any way deter you from considering my material when you think the time right and proper.

In 1945 Walter's pension was £353.12s. per annum: rather better than in 1936 but no fortune. He had to find work to supplement it, and he wasn't proud. For a while he was involved in pest control in some way, then he collected rents for New Romney Council,[1] for which he was soon elected a councillor.

In September 1941 the king had appointed Churchill as Lord Warden of the Cinque Ports,[2] *The Times* reporting that 'It is understood that Mr Churchill will not be installed or take up residence until after the war'. On 14 August 1946 the investiture took place at Dover, which held so many poignant wartime memories for Churchill and Walter who, 'living within a few miles, wished to be present'. He was still intermittently keeping notes and wrote:

It was a great occasion, but I was not fortunate enough to obtain a ticket to attend the actual ceremony. However, after the luncheon I made my way to the entrance of the hall, where Winston caught sight of me. He turned to his wife and said: 'Look, Clemmie, who is here!' With that he came forward and with obvious delight laid his hand on my arm and asked: 'Why were you not at the luncheon and the other ceremonies,

Thompson?' I replied that the answer was quite simple. I had not got a ticket. He reproved me with a smile and said that I was not to make such an excuse again. If he was coming to my district and I wanted to see him, he would make sure that I obtained tickets if a letter was sent to him.

Walter's pleasure in re-establishing contact with the Old Man is evident. But this time he didn't rush his fences about his book – he realised that he'd damaged their relationship, however unwittingly. He waited nearly two more years before contacting Churchill at the end of May 1948 to see if he'd now agree to publication. On 1 June Churchill's letter to Sir Harold Scott showed that on a personal level at least his attitude had become sympathetic: *I do not see much harm in the material myself, but of course there is the question of anyone in his position writing at all. However, three years are passed . . . I propose to say in reply that the responsibility in this matter is not with me but with [you] . . .* Not surprisingly, Scott chose not to disagree with Churchill about the harmlessness of the material but, leaving aside 'the bad taste of such disclosures', he intended to tell Walter, should he communicate with him, that he maintained his position. In fact, Walter waited four months before he sought Scott's reconsideration. He can't have been surprised at the reply.

At about this time he contacted Harold, then working for a motor company in Barnet, to tell him there was a garage for sale at nearby Littlestone. 'If you're interested,' he said, 'we could look at the cost and see if it's a possibility.' Harold says: 'Greatstone and Littlestone were all one, really – Dad's end was mostly holiday homes, Littlestone was more residential. So we had a look and bought it. He helped me financially – he was always there for me throughout my life. I think he always felt guilty about asking me to leave school before I should have done when the family finances were tight.' The garage, White Lodge, was a good business, repairing vehicles and farm machinery (Harold and his second wife Jean ran a taxi service on the side too), 'and Dad came and worked on the pumps and did the accounts and the stock and one thing and another'. Walter now also got involved in the local football club. 'Here we go again,' Harold thought. He adds: 'It didn't matter what the weather – hail, rain or snow – he'd be out on that field on match day, walking round and round, assessing every player's performance for the next committee meeting.' Two other retired policemen in the area also took an interest in the club, and when the three were together 'they complained about being taxed on their pensions when they'd already paid tax on their original earnings'.

Walter was back in regular touch with Churchill (Harold remembers correspondence[3] and thinks his father went to Chartwell from time to time). In any event Churchill felt warmly enough disposed that when Walter and Harold were proposed for membership of the New Romney Lodge on 18 November 1948, he seconded them.[4]

Walter's finances were evidently on a sounder footing by 1950, when he had a bigger bungalow, Cornerways, built on the piece of land adjoining Southways that he'd purchased at the same time. When he and May moved in, May's younger sister Kit, whose marriage had broken up in the war, and her daughter Jan came to live next door. At some point Walter's luck on the book looked up as well: he struck up an acquaintance with the publisher Christopher Johnson, a regular customer at the garage. What transpired one can only speculate, but Walter obviously told Johnson about the manuscript and the problems he'd run into with it, and Johnson, knowing that Jarrolds had long since pulled out of the contract, spotted a publishing opportunity for his own imprint. Soon Walter was back at his manuscript, which had been typed on various machines over a number of years – Harold had typed up some of it from his father's 'big broad handwriting' when he'd been on leave from the RAF. 'It was a labour of love to Dad,' he says.

The original typescript was long, much of it simply a report of the progress of the war culled from newspapers and, while Jarrolds had been prepared to publish it as it was, Walter now realised, with Johnson's advice, that he needed to cut it and sharpen the focus on his involvement with Churchill. Jan, in and out of Cornerways when home from boarding school, remembers that Walter (Tommy, of course, to her) 'used to sit in his armchair dictating to May sitting at the table typing, both smoking furiously. She would then correct what she'd typed and sort out the grammar where it needed to be sorted. She knew him so well that where she altered anything she usually knew how he would say something. If he didn't like something, he'd say so, and she'd do it again. They were very intense. If I came in, then I'd get a dirty look from him and be quickly dispatched.'

Like Walter, May had fallen foul of Churchill's aversion for ordinary cigarettes when she'd first gone to work for him. 'Soon after my arrival [at Chartwell] I was warned about this idiosyncrasy,' she'd written,

but nobody told me how keen was his sense of smell. One evening that summer I was working alone in the office, smoking a cigarette as I typed. Suddenly the door opened, and Mr Churchill walked in. It was highly unusual for him to visit the office, and I started with guilt. I slipped my cigarette in an ashtray and made sure the typewriter was between it and my visitor. He wrinkled his nose. 'What,' he demanded, 'is that horrible smell?'

Opposite the open window there was a large stretch of sloping woodland, and it so happened that foresters were burning down the gorse that evening. I pointed to the rising smoke, intimating that this might be giving offence to his nostrils . . . He said nothing, but I could see from his face that he was far from convinced. No doubt he realised that in the office I was on my own ground. On the other hand, he secretly admired quick-wittedness in others, as long as they did not lie to him, and I had not lied.

There was no Churchill to reprove the couple at Greatstone, and they smoked so much 'You couldn't see for the fug,' says Jan. 'Years later, I inherited some of their paintings and got them restored, they were so dreadfully nicotined. One frame looked like gold but was ordinary wood underneath.'

The first intimation that Walter had finally decided to go ahead with publication ('I took a chance,' he admitted in his notes) came to the Yard's attention in February 1951 when the editor of the *Empire News* wrote informing them that his newspaper was negotiating for the serialisation rights and asking if they'd check the material from a police point of view. The Yard bristled. The *Empire News* refused to be warned off, and on 6 March Scott wrote to Churchill, again raising the ultimate weapon of the Police Pensions Act. Three days later Churchill, who'd had another stroke in August 1949 and yet another in February the following year, responded in a tone that seemed tired and, in his unwillingness to consider taking action, hinted at the affection that at bottom he held Walter in: *I should be very sorry if he lost his pension. It is good of you to write to me about this, and I hope it will come to nothing.*

The *Empire News* duly heralded its exclusive and ran it for an extraordinary eleven weeks. In October Johnson brought out *I Was Churchill's Shadow* – retitled from Walter's original *I Guarded Winston*. The book carried a dedication 'To My Dear Son Fred', with part of a poem written by May:

> Your Spirit lives in every plane that flies;
> And when the daylight fades, and courage dies,
> We will remember that you faced the night
> And through the darkness found a brighter light.

'May wrote a lot of poetry, but only for herself,' says Jan. 'Tommy thought the poem was beautiful. He wasn't a man who showed much emotion, but using the stanza, which in a way brought May and Fred and Churchill together, meant a lot to him.'

There was no Churchillian foreword as there'd been for Walter's first book, *Guard from the Yard*, but Walter sent him a copy to Chartwell, inscribed: 'To Winston, with best wishes, Tommy' – in private, Churchill had often addressed Walter as Tommy. *I Was Churchill's Shadow* became a best seller:[5] the British people might have turned Churchill out of office six years previously, but they wanted to read every word of what the *Daily Mail* described as 'A more intimate picture of the great man in wartime than from any other source'.

And, suddenly, Walter was a celebrity.

* * *

To a generation used to warts-and-all revelations, it's hard to see what the fuss over publishing Walter's book was about. The solicitor to whom the Yard submitted the manuscript in 1945 considered that it was 'highly improper for a police officer, whose duty it had been to act as personal guard to a VIP, to publish intimate domestic details (e.g. dressing gown, pyjamas[6] etc.)', and doing so was 'a complete breach of confidence'. But none of this constituted an offence in law. He did think that disclosure of comments made by 'a VIP . . . in relation to the affairs of nations . . . might constitute an offence under the Official Secrets Act' – a doubtful judgement considering that Walter revealed nothing militarily or politically sensitive and the war was over; Sir Harold Scott hastily backed away from that one.

In truth – other than that the story unfolded against the backdrop of the war – what Walter had written about Churchill in the 1940s wasn't so different from the kind of thing he'd written in the 1920s. Churchill marching to military music in Chequers' Great Hall or getting guests in a bomb-damaged hotel to fill a bath from jugs and saucepans was the same Churchill who fell in the mud of the drained lake at Chartwell or stripped in the desert for a bath in water from a train engine. The Churchill who wanted to watch the bombs drop on London was the same Churchill who wanted to square up to the Sinn Feiners.

Some of the deletions that Churchill's personal private secretary sought indicate a conviction that Churchill should be portrayed only as the unwavering war leader who'd bestridden the world. For him to be revealed as thinking, even before war began, that he expected to be asked to join the Cabinet smacked to Martin of hubris – cut. For Churchill to say, on becoming Prime Minister, that it might already be too late showed doubt – cut. His emotional reaction to the loss of Singapore, despair – cut. His momentary willingness to die in Carthage, human frailty – cut.

Some of the other deletions that Martin wanted seem ludicrous. Did he, for example, think that Churchill's asking Professor Lindemann to work out the volume of his champagne consumption made him appear a boozer? Was the fact that Churchill had a map room in which to plot the progress of the war something that would surprise anybody and should remain a state secret? Would Britain's relationship with the United States have been compromised by reading that Churchill considered their Secret Service security excessive, or Anglo-Soviet relations be further strained by the revelation of the lavishness of Kremlin banqueting while the Russian people had almost nothing to eat? Perhaps the oddest thing that Martin wanted removed was that Churchill, having forgotten his cigars on VE Day, returned to the Annexe to get one because the crowds would expect it; presumably he thought it could be construed as a calculating action taken only to win public approval – though Churchill's cigar was ultimately as much a symbol of victory as it had been of dogged wartime endurance.

Churchill's objection to Walter's book is hard to understand, and he was never explicit about it. Perhaps the line taken by officialdom was his own, in part anyway. It certainly had nothing to do with his dignity. He never stood on that.

In fact, while Walter was determined to tell his story, the Old Man's dignity was always in his mind. He'd left many of his observations where they were in his notes or drafts when he'd written 'Guard' in the 1930s, and he'd done the same with the original manuscript of 'Shadow'; in both cases anything he thought might cause Churchill hurt – like Clementine's refusing to feed him – he'd left out altogether. Not that this meant hagiography: Churchill had faults and Walter said so.

Walter cared passionately about his writing, but his style was distinctly stiff and he had no ear for the cadences of colloquial speech. He was also vague about when things happened, despite keeping his policeman's diaries (unfortunately lost), meaning that he can't always be trusted about events – curiously he associated the Liberator magneto incident with the downing of Leslie Howard's plane, which took place almost four months later. One of Churchill's major biographers, Roy Jenkins, took Walter to task for his lack of detail: 'Inspector Thompson in his two volumes of reminiscences is good at capturing the heart of the matter but a little less reliable on exact dates, times and places that might have been hoped for from a meticulous detective.'[7]

But there's a sturdy honesty about Walter's prose. Nowhere did he pretend that Churchill told him more about what was happening in the war than he put before the reader. He didn't attempt to be Boswell to Churchill's Doctor Johnson: he recorded what Churchill did, and he didn't attempt to analyse it. But he had a way with an anecdote, especially a humorous one (even Jenkins admitted Walter provided 'shots of detailed colour'), and he did make the Old Man, for all his complexity, appear warm, human and accessible.

As an aside, it's interesting to reflect that what Walter said about Moran could also be said about him, on two counts: just as Moran was writing his diary when he was in attendance on Churchill, so Walter was writing his book (he couldn't otherwise have had it ready for the publisher in the first half of 1945), and just as Moran wrote intimately about Churchill in one way, so Walter did in another. Undoubtedly his answer would have been that Moran wrote for his reputation – and breached the doctor–patient relationship – whereas he wrote out of devotion, to enhance the Old Man's image, not to diminish it. But this begs the question as to why, finally, he went ahead without Churchill's express say-so. It would be a harsh judgement to condemn him. He'd been very patient – he waited nearly six years; others were going into print about Churchill's war years; no doubt he worried that his material would soon be dated and worthless. Ultimately, perhaps, in spite of the rectitude that shaped his entire life, he simply felt as he entered his sixties that he was entitled. Churchill's story, after all, was his story, too.

And he had other reasons, as Harold relates: 'He was proud of what he'd done. He'd guarded the most important man in the world, which Churchill was in the Second World War. He'd been there when history was being made. He wanted that recognised. He was proud of his achievements, a working-class lad from south London. "Thompson hasn't got the education" rankled all his life.'

*　　*　　*

Success breeds success: within weeks of the publication of 'Shadow' Walter was being invited to lecture all over England. It did no harm that Churchill was back in Number 10; Clementine gave him some stamp of approval by coming to the one he gave in Kensington Town Hall. Churchill evidently forgave Walter for going into print; perhaps he was even delighted – somewhere they ran into each other and Churchill told him: 'Thompson, you are doing a wonderful thing for yourself. You are using your brain by writing and lecturing. If only people, when they retire, would keep their brains alive and active, as you have done, they would live for a long time.'

In 1953 Johnson published *Sixty Minutes with Winston Churchill*, a slim volume of sixty anecdotes that Walter had mostly collected together from his previous two books but with a few new ones thrown in; a suitably inscribed copy went to the Old Man. For all its modesty, it was another success. Walter appeared in the first *In Town Tonight* news magazine on BBC television and was invited to lecture in America and Canada. 'He was in his element,' Jan remembers. 'May went with him and appeared on the platform with him – they became a double act. I don't remember them having a social life, they worked so blooming hard.' Two years later an American publisher brought out a compilation of 'Guard' and 'Shadow' (*Assignment: Churchill*), heavily Americanised by a ghostwriter, which was chosen as a book of the month. Five more tours followed – in all, Walter lectured over 400 times in the US and Canada. He and May made numerous TV appearances, including several game shows; on *Tell the Truth* in New York, Walter beat the panel and won $300. On another show, the name of which he couldn't remember, he won a gold wristwatch, 'but expressed my dissatisfaction when I saw the panel look at the script before the questions were put to the contestants'. He had a confrontation with the editor of a local newspaper in a town (unnamed) near Boston after he'd told a questioner after a lecture that it was untrue that he had instructions from Churchill to shoot him if, on their first trip to the US on the *Queen Mary*, he'd fallen into enemy hands – and then saw the headline WINSTON CHURCHILL TO COMMIT SUICIDE. 'I got little satisfaction from [the editor]. All he said was: "After all, that is what he would be doing – committing suicide!" . . . He would not withdraw anything, and I had to send my apologies and regrets to Winston.' Nevertheless, America loved Walter, Nashville and Buffalo to the extent of making him an honorary citizen and a Texan town (which he neglected to name) making him a deputy sheriff for life.

Walter varied the content of his talks: in Churchill's military and political exploits, eccentricities, recklessness, humour and mesmeric use of language he had plenty to work with. But he never left out a tale or two highlighting Churchill's integrity, which, he felt, added 'a magic glow' to everything he did. There was, for example, the matter of the dress that Clementine brought through Customs without paying duty. There was her personal use of her husband's official car over which, Churchill told Walter when he first joined him in 1921, '"the driver has instructions to watch the mileage, inform you and at the end of the month the charge for that mileage will be paid by me". I was informed that there was no need for him to pay, and to my knowledge he was the only Minister with an official car who did pay.' There was the case of Churchill's Conservative opponent – who supported tariffs – driving around Leicester during electioneering in a foreign car. When it was suggested that Churchill, then a Liberal fighting (unsuccessfully, as it happens) as a free trader, should expose this double standard, 'Winston's reaction was angry. "I fight elections on issues and my political opinion, not personalities. I shall make no mention of this in any of my speeches; if it comes to my knowledge that any of my committee should raise this question at any of my opponent's meetings, I will immediately withdraw."' Then there was Churchill's first Budget, in which

he imposed a tax on foreign artificial silk, so as to help the rayon industry in England [against his own free trade principles, in fact]. The manufacturers were naturally delighted. Sometime later, on a visit to the district where the artificial silk was made, Winston was presented with two beautiful dressing gowns, one for himself and one for his wife. He refused to accept them as a gift, demanded an invoice from the firm and paid for them. 'I shall enjoy wearing them equally as well,' he wrote kindly to them.

And then there was May Shearburn's electric copper kettle about which she wrote herself:

I kept it in my bedroom for filling hot-water bottles and making hot drinks. One evening I went to my room and found that it was burned out. One of the maids in dusting had accidentally switched it on and left it so. I told Mrs Hill what had occurred, and she said there was no need to worry as everything was covered by insurance. She sent in a claim and a cheque came back by return to pay for the full amount.

It so happened that I took some letters for signature to Mr Churchill that night and among them was this cheque for him to endorse before we sent it to the bank. He asked me what it was, and when I explained he said very gravely: 'But I am not insured for your possessions, Miss Shearburn. It would not be honest to take that money. Send it back, tell them a mistake has been made, and I shall make good your loss.'

Walter shared Churchill's honesty. As Churchill never carried money, Walter paid out of his own pocket the handouts to ex-servicemen in the street that Churchill wanted to give, as he did taxi fares and tips to doormen and porters. He was scrupulous in the monthly accounts he submitted,[8] and Churchill 'always settled [them] without looking beyond the total sum. I once drew his attention to this apparent carelessness. "I trust you, Thompson," he said. "Otherwise you would not be with me."'

Walter's sense of integrity was as high-minded as his sense of right and wrong. 'An honourable, upright man,' May described him as. He was bloody-mindedly so sometimes – he became a Mason only after he'd left the police, though he'd been advised to join at the Yard decades earlier. 'Freemasonry was big in the police in those days,' says Harold. 'But Dad refused. He thought it was wrong to do that just to get on. He thought you should succeed on merit.' His integrity extended to making a contribution in the community. Even in his teens he was an officer in the Boys' Brigade, and he returned in his thirties to run the Wesleyan chapel unit as well as take Sunday school there. In between, during the First World War, he started a boys' club in Southampton and 'when the wounded poured back from the Western Front I frequently, although tired out from my work, acted as night orderly in different military hospitals around Southampton'. He was, essentially, generous. 'He helped my mother financially when she was on her beam's end,' says Jan. 'He gave us Southways when we couldn't afford to live anywhere. He helped find her a mortgage when we eventually moved, and he put down the deposit. He paid for my wedding, and he gave me away. He really was the best uncle I could have had.' 'Dad was very sympathetic to people's concerns,' adds Harold. 'I could give you a lot of examples. There was a lad at the football club at Greatstone who came from a family with nothing. Dad bought the full kit for him. It was the kind of thing he did.'

In his discarded autobiography Walter described his parents as 'Old Victorians, very proper in everything'. He was very like them; it didn't always make him a comfortable man to be around. A phrase he once used to describe Churchill's character fits him admirably: 'a granite-hard individuality.' Comments Harold: 'I've always thought that Dad and Churchill were alike in their basic character. They were both honest in what they did and said. They weren't always right, but they were quick to apologise. They were very determined to do what they thought should be done. And they didn't care what other people thought if they thought they were right.'

On the other side of the coin, Walter could be censorious. He had, for example, no time for gambling. He liked the Minister Jimmy Thomas when he guarded him but disliked that he was a betting man. Thomas tried to get Walter to place bets for him at racetracks. Walter refused. 'Dad wouldn't have anything to do with gambling at all; he never did,' Harold says. In fact, he did, once – for Churchill, who, in the 1920s when he was recovering from his appendectomy in the south of France, took a fancy to casinos. Walter wrote:

On our first visit I stood with Winston at a roulette table. He staked five-franc chips and won several times. Then, deciding to sit in on a game of chemin de fer, he gave me two counters and told me to continue backing the numbers in the sequence with which he had won until I lost my original stakes. I staked my first chip and won several times. Then I lost and decided not to risk the other. So I walked over to Winston and handed him the winnings, which were quite substantial, together with half the original stake and the unused counter. 'You seem to be a lucky punter,' he said. 'You should have carried on.' But I had had enough of this 'pleasure' [and] I went out into the fresh air and watched pigeons soaring against the silver filigree of a fountain spray.

Walter couldn't bring himself to criticise Churchill, but he noted elsewhere: 'I did not enjoy these visits much. The players showed the strain in their tense faces.'

The broad streak of puritanism in Walter's make-up is demonstrated clearly in his moral attitude. Shown round Cairo on his first visit to Egypt by one of Russell Pasha's detectives, he commented that 'The further east one gets, the more open are the vices of the inhabitants', adding that 'the unpleasant amenities' of the fish market [were] 'booths where in open windows and doorways recline a bewildering variety of women of every type under the sun. I had already been told of the way in which Egyptian youth vitiated its energy and degraded its manhood, but a brief walk down that terrible street of commercialised vice made it impossible to think that the authorities of a so-called civilised country could watch with equanimity the sacrifice of its fresh young manhood to the Baal of sensuality typified there.' When later he visited Pompeii with Churchill, where the 'shops showed by signposts other forms of depravity . . . An uglier aspect of the changeless nature is offered by a mosaic, the gross obscenity of which necessitates its covering by a cloth which is removed only so that "favoured" visitors may see the depths to which Imperial Rome had sunk before its pleasure town was obliterated, even as were Sodom and Gomorrah.' Though he chose not to publish the fact, Walter left Lloyd George's protection because of his womanising. He had taken to the then Prime Minister, who 'could charm anyone in a few minutes with his smile and oratory'. But his opinion soon changed 'when I found out that this hymn-singing Bible-reader did not hesitate to use his magnetic powers on the ladies . . . Disgusted, I was withdrawn at my own request.'

It's difficult to reconcile Walter's high moral principles with his affairs and the fact that he left Kate. Some explanation lies in his dominating personality. 'Mother wasn't worldly; she was very gentle. My father needed a woman who could stand up to him,' Kathleen thinks. From what Marjorie Wigley's daughter Hilary Greenstreet says, her mother wasn't able to stand up to Wally (as she called him) either. 'She was rather naive and very easy-going, and she let him have his way – in the shops everything had to be done his way.'

For both women Walter remained the constant factor in their lives even when he'd gone. 'Mother never felt Father had left her, that she wasn't married to him,' Harold says. 'To the day Dad died she considered him her husband.' On her wedding certificate, Marjorie gave her name as 'Wigley (otherwise Thompson)', an indication to her son, John Tradewell, who runs a marketing company in Bridlington, in the East Riding of Yorkshire, that she considered herself married to Walter. 'She may have called herself Thompson because living together without a wedding ring still wasn't done. But that she described herself on the wedding certificate shows what she thought. Perhaps they would have got married if he hadn't gone back to Churchill.'

It's clear from what Walter wrote that he liked strong women. He 'thought the world' of his mother, who chastised her children with the four-inch-wide leather belt that she always wore, 'and when she unfastened it in front of any of us we knew what to expect'. He worshipped his older sister Alice, who, when a fire trapped her on top of her office block, encouraged other girls to follow her and jumped ninety feet into a tarpaulin – and 'became a heroine overnight . . . reporters besieged our house'. In the First World War he thought 'a tall, handsome young Belgian lady' that the Yard men in Southampton were suspicious of and interrogated for four hours 'by far the cleverest woman I ever encountered' – he was delighted to find out later that she was a British agent: 'I feel sure that the Germans never caught her.' His admiration was hardly less in the Second World War for Madam Chiang Kai-shek, 'a smart, well-dressed and attractive woman' who was not only her husband's interpreter but appeared to be 'the moving force in the relationship'.

May was from that mould – and that was what Walter cherished about her. 'My aunt could handle him,' says Jan. 'She took no nonsense. She ribbed him unmercifully about shooting himself and would laugh uproariously, and he'd look sheepish – but really he loved her doing it.' Adds Kathleen: 'May was nice and I liked her. She was a very strong person, which Mother wasn't. She was the kind of woman my father should have married in the first place.'

In retirement, and inseparable from May, Walter was less the authoritarian; he was chirpier and generally even-tempered and, Jan says, 'impishly humorous'. Walter always had a sense of humour, as some of the tales he told showed, but the intense

266

dedication with which he served the Old Man, certainly during the war years, didn't give it much opportunity to surface. Now he 'almost always was smiling his orange segment smile – straight upper lip and the curved bottom'. Jan adds: 'He was a great one for facetiousness. My aunt used to moan about his sense of humour first thing in the morning. She was one of those people who go around with their eyes shut until they've had three cups of coffee.' Walter didn't, of course, change entirely: he was still a Victorian at heart, 'very strait-laced – damn and blast were his worst swearwords. He thought women shouldn't go into pubs, and May wasn't allowed to get a job. Ma worked in season in the greengrocer's in New Romney, but Tommy wouldn't have a wife who went out to work.' And he remained as quick as ever to get angry, 'but just as quick to apologise. When he did get angry he could be jolly difficult. Then you knew you'd got to watch it. His eyes were very blue and twinkly, but when he was cross they bored into you.'

He never lost his readiness to use his fists. Harold has stories about incidents that happened throughout his father's life, but he tells none with more relish than the one about what happened one day his father was collecting rents in New Romney. 'This woman started arguing with Dad about something, and the upshot was he forgot to give her her change and walked away. Some bloke came rushing out of the house and threw a fist at him, but the one coming back the other way put him flat on his back. Dad was very, very quick off the mark. He was never a man to mess with even in his sixties.'

*   *   *

In late 1955 or early 1956 the Thompsons left Greatstone; the garage and taxi service were no longer doing the business they'd done. Harold, now interested in the application of reinforced plastics in the motor trade, went to the Midlands; Walter and

May, having sold the bungalows, moved to Hill Head near Fareham in Hampshire. They were still at the centre of family occasions like weddings and christenings, and Kate was always invited. 'Mother and Bunny were good friends; they used to ring each other up,' says Harold. 'Mother saw her not as an alternative to her but as part of the family unit.'

At Hill Head, as at Greatstone, Walter and May kept open house. Harvey's children came and went; and Walter still found time to visit his sister Emily Dow. 'We spent every Christmas, Easter and summer holiday with our nana, Emily,' says Linda, Walter's great-niece. 'Around the ages of ten to fourteen or so we would go to Uncle Walter's instead. We got a lot more to eat than at home. I remember he once gave us a pound note to buy ice cream, and he refused to take the change – we didn't know what to do with so much.'

At Greatstone Walter had gardened ('without much enthusiasm,' says Jan), but at Hill Head, where he had a large lawn, he bought a sit-on mower and spent happy hours puttering up and down. He was still lecturing to some 10,000 people a year. The success of *Assignment: Churchill* in the States gave him the idea of putting his entire service with Churchill together in what would also be a biography of the Old Man. No correspondence exists to show that he approached a publisher, but if he did nothing came of it. No doubt as he followed Churchill's career in the newspapers, the photographs of the Yard men who now guarded the Old Man made him nostalgic. Unlike the clean-shaved Walter, the two men now assigned – one, after Churchill stood down as Prime Minister in 1955 – had moustaches, one so fierce that its owner was dubbed 'The Shadow with the Moustache'. Walter must have thought the job a pale shadow of what it had been, for it consisted of little more than dealing with occasional threatening letters, overenthusiastic well-wishers and keeping photographers away from Churchill, increasingly deaf and enfeebled, on his frequent retreats to the Riviera.[9]

In 1965, the year in which Churchill died, May herself went into print – with a four-part series in *Woman* entitled 'Churchill My Boss'.[10] Walter approached his New York publisher with the idea of her writing a book; Farrar, Straus & Giroux showed some interest, thinking there might be something here for their young adult division, but nothing came of that either.

Five years later Walter and May were on the move again, closer to Weston-super-Mare – where Harold and Jean had now moved – to the village of Ansford, near Castle Cary in Somerset, where, Jan says, 'he read a lot, gardened and got under my aunt's feet when she was trying to cook'. He was now eighty. He was still turning out for a few lectures, as long as they were within reasonable driving distance. When Jan and her husband Francis Glass, a naval commander at the Admiralty, were badly injured in a car crash (he subsequently died), Walter frequently drove back and forth the twenty miles to Yeovil hospital.

He had to sell the painting Churchill had given him, 'a lovely garden picture of Chartwell that included a Churchill wall', according to Jan. 'He was sad to see it go, but he was short of funds by the 1970s.' The painting fetched £1,000.

In the autumn of 1977 May was diagnosed with cancer of the spine and was fitted with a harness; in the December Walter was diagnosed with lung cancer and almost immediately afterwards with a brain tumour. Before he was admitted to Wincanton Cottage Hospital (no longer there) just before Christmas, Jan organised a lecture in Wells to the Royal Naval Association. She drove him there. 'I remember a wonderful lecture, all these naval blokes roaring with laughter, and the question-and-answer session afterwards was absolutely brilliant. Driving home, he said what good questions he got – unlike most of those he got asked at

Women's Institutes!' Walter died on 18 January 1978. He had lived eighty-seven years, three years fewer than Churchill; somehow one feels he'd have thought fewer was appropriate. His funeral and cremation were all-male affairs. 'It was a Shearburn tradition,' Jan explains. 'I don't know why. I think it might have had something to do with the army.' May's sister Kit brought her home to Somerton in Somerset, May taking with her 'all the bits and pieces that were precious to her, including a brown leather attaché writing case that had all Tommy's manuscripts and papers'. She died three months later. Kate died the following autumn in Billericay, Essex, where she'd gone to be with her older daughter Grace when she was no longer able to look after herself. She'd moved with Harvey and his family to Bristol when he retired, but as she entered her eighties, 'seeking a little bit of quietness', as Kathleen puts it, she'd then lived by herself in rented rooms in a farmhouse in St George's, the village outside Weston-super-Mare where her younger daughter still lives, before moving into a flat in Weston. When Kit died in 1989, Jan inherited her belongings; the attaché case went into her attic, and then under a table in her sitting room when she moved to where she now lives in Alford, near Castle Cary. And there it stayed until Linda Dow, now Stoker, tracked her down.

There are over 3,000 books about Churchill or aspects of his life and more than a score of biographies. The major lives run between 600 and 1,000 pages, and in none of them does Walter get more than three or four mentions, his presence here or there merely registered, or a sentence of two quoted from his books – as *John O'London's Weekly* presciently remarked in a review, 'Shadow' 'will provide material for historians of the future'. Of the biographers, only Jenkins had anything at all to say about Walter himself: he was just there, the man from Scotland Yard, in the background. David Irving made the error of rolling Walter and his namesake, Churchill's ADC, Commander Charles Thompson, into one person. His old adversary, Lord Moran, even misspelled his name – Thomson.

But Walter was more than the man in the background. Churchill believed in a Higher Authority that kept him alive to fulfil his mission. In practical terms the job was Walter's; that was not only his duty – as much his trigger word as the Old Man's – but his mission. Had Churchill died by whatever means after 1942, the outcome of the war would probably have been very little different from what it was; had it occurred before that, especially during 1940, when he and Hitler engaged in what amounted to chess over the Channel, that might well not have been the case: appeasement still hadn't lost its attraction for some. During the war the Yard told Walter to do his best to safeguard the Prime Minister. Walter tried to do better than his best, and it took over his life – it became his life. In personal terms it cost him dear. He regretted none of it. 'Dad would have sacrificed his life for Winston,' Harold says. 'He'd have taken a bullet – it's as simple as that.' Walter, of course, did take a bullet, though it was self-inflicted and not fatal. The lump of metal, flattened against his hipbone, was among the precious bits and pieces that May took to her sister's after his death.

*　　*　　*

When Churchill died twelve years earlier, Walter, just returned from a lecture tour in Switzerland, found it 'almost impossible to describe the sense of loss' he felt as he listened to the nine o'clock news on the morning of Sunday 24 January.

The following day, when he was talking to the press 'who had descended upon us en masse', May called him to the telephone: a Downing Street secretary wanted to speak to him.

I was told that there was a seat reserved for me at St Paul's

Cathedral for Winston's funeral, and though the official invitation would be coming to me through the mail, it was necessary for those responsible for the arrangements to know in advance those who were able to accept the invitations. This gave me a measure of immense personal satisfaction, the more so when I received the document showing 'The Earl Marshal has it in command from The Queen to invite Mr Walter Thompson to be present at the Cathedral of St Paul in London on the occasion of the State Funeral shortly to be held there'. This document is one of my treasured possessions. I had not been forgotten.

In the early morning of Saturday 30 January I drove my car on to the prescribed route to St Paul's. The whole route for hours before the ceremony was crowded with people. I have officially attended state funerals before, but here was something entirely different. On other occasions I have found people laughing and talking quite loudly to each other, but here was the most uncanny silence over the one and a half miles I had to traverse to reach the cathedral. The people of London – and countless more from all over the world – were waiting to say goodbye to the man who had not only led them through our darkest hours but had inspired them time and time again with the words of grim determination and encouragement. At this strangely silent time, the hearts of all were combined in remembering him . . .

With the special pass in my hands I walked up the imposing frontal steps and took my seat more than two hours ahead of the arrival of the funeral procession. I looked at the pass and thought of all the other special passes I had carried during the war which had ensured smooth and easy passages through guarded and closed buildings in the Old Man's service . . .

When all the seats were taken, most of Winston's main office staff for the war period were there together. It was a significant feeling at the end to be with those who had carried the burden of the war years with him.

The dignified and immensely moving service drew towards its close, and for me the most impressive moments came when Handel's 'Dead March' was played as the coffin was slowly carried the length of the cathedral, from the altar to the open doors. As it disappeared from our view, the pent-up emotions of the congregation were released . . . Tears filled my eyes unashamedly . . . I say unashamedly, for around me kings, queens, prime ministers, dukes and earls, army, naval and air-force chiefs, ministers of state, commoners and nearly everyone, young and old, had tears in their eyes too.

Some months later, our Canadian friends, Doug and Jeanne McLeod, were in England on a short visit, and one evening we decided that the following day we would visit the grave of Winston Churchill. We set out in the morning of a day which was typical of the best that our country can offer in the way of perfect early summer. It was pleasantly warm and the sun shone gently on the soft green countryside as we drove into Oxfordshire . . .

We had to leave the car a mile or so from the church, which afforded us a chance to see this lovely old-world village with its unpaved streets, century-old cottages and – still as it stood hundreds of years ago – the village pump. There was surprisingly little traffic on the main street, on each side of which stood a variety of houses, large and small, each with its garden alive with a profusion of flowers. We walked slowly along the street, and it was impossible not to be aware of an air of tranquillity, and a sense of something unchanged and unchanging through the years. To our left we saw a narrow winding lane ascending to where the little church stood – serenely overlooking the village of which it is the spiritual heart. We climbed the short, steep lane and found ourselves behind a line of people all slowly moving through the quiet churchyard. Finally our turn came and we stood beside the grave, which lies in the shadow of the church tower. It is quite simple. There is nothing elaborate, nothing to indicate that it is the grave of one of the greatest men the world has ever known – just a quiet resting-place where Winston Churchill sleeps beneath a mass of flowers which speak more eloquently than words of the love and admiration in which he was held by so many. The church itself was originally built in the fifteenth century, and largely rebuilt in 1804, but in its shadows time itself seems to stand still.

As he stood there, Walter's mind 'went back over the years during which I had served Winston, and I recalled when danger so often threatened him during the war'. The Old Man had 'adamantly refused to be protected from danger, whether from flying bombs, bullets, shrapnel, crowds, potential assassins or, if you like, his own folly, [but] I loved him, despite his obstinacy, his selfishness and his inconsiderate attitude to those who were close to him. I understood his way in the end. But I know he never really understood – or wanted to understand – mine.'

As Walter turned from the grave, 'I noticed that in a direct line through an opening part of Blenheim Palace could be seen, and I realised that all the members of the Churchill family buried there faced towards the palace'.

In every sense, a journey was complete.

Endnotes

Chapter 1: Getting to Know You

[1] The Metropolitan Police Special Irish Branch was formed in 1883 to combat Fenian bombers who had attacked mainland targets, including the offices of *The Times*. 'Irish' was dropped from the name five years later when the remit broadened to a wider range of extremist and terrorist activity.

[2] The Irish Question had driven Pitt from office, defeated Gladstone and toppled the government in 1885. On the eve of the First World War, the Cabinet drew a 'temporary' border between Ulster and Eire. During the war, Eire turned increasingly to Sinn Fein in the struggle to become a republic. Two years after the Easter rebellion of 1916, Sinn Fein won seventy-three of the Irish seats in the general election, demanded independence, refused to attend Westminster and set up an Irish

Assembly in Dublin. When the Dail was declared an illegal organ-
isation, the Irish Republican Army embarked on another
campaign of murder and violence.

[3] Because army battalions could not be spared for Ireland, 8,000
men, mostly unemployed former soldiers, were recruited for the
new force – called the Black and Tans because of their mixture
of army uniforms and black belts of the Royal Irish Constabulary.
In July 1920 a second paramilitary force, the Auxiliaries, was
formed from demobbed army officers.

On the eve of Barry's execution, the IRA raided several Dublin
hotels and houses, killing fourteen, including six British officers.
In December 1920, after the IRA ambushed two lorries of
'Auxies', killing all but two, Auxies and Black and Tans burned
down part of Cork city centre in retaliation. Later that day the
Auxies, searching for suspects, opened fire on a football crowd,
killing nine. The Cabinet declared martial law in four counties.

[4] As Churchill at this time was the First Sea Lord, development
of an armoured caterpillared vehicle capable of crossing trenches
and crushing obstacles was outside his province and he was ignored.
On his own authority he had the first landship built. After the
war, a Royal Commission inquiring into the invention of the tank
– named after the water tanks they were disguised as before being
sent overseas – stated that 'it was primarily due to the receptivity,
courage and driving force of the Right Honourable Winston
Spencer Churchill that the general idea of the use of such an instru-
ment of warfare as the tank was converted into practical shape'.

[5] Lawrence, an archaeologist and fluent Arabic speaker, was
assigned as an intelligence officer to the British army in Egypt
during the First World War, fighting against the Turks. Becoming

an expert on Turkish movements in the Turkish province that now comprises Syria, Lebanon, Israel, Jordan and the Hejaz region of Saudi Arabia, he was made a liaison officer with the Arabs, becoming the mainspring of their revolution, allying them to the Allied cause. Disillusioned when the Paris Peace Conference refused to recognise a self-governed Arab state and gave Syria to the custody of France, he retired and wrote his memoirs, *Seven Pillars of Wisdom*. Churchill brought him into the Colonial Office to help him try to reach a more honourable settlement and stabilise the region.

[6] After the debacle of the Dardanelles in 1915, when Churchill lost his Admiralty post, he bought a box of oil paints to lighten his deep depression. He had just placed a blob of blue on a blank canvas and was at a loss what to do next when Lady Lavery, wife of the painter Sir John Lavery and an artist herself, drove up. Taking Churchill's brush, she filled in the blue sky in a trice, leading him to the conclusion that painting, like life, was about having 'audacity'. He was to paint for nearly the rest of his life even, to the astonishment of his fellow officers, when he served briefly in the trenches in France.

In 1921 Churchill sent five paintings to an exhibition in Paris under the assumed name Charles Morin – he called in to have a look on his way to the Middle East. In 1947 he would offer other works to the Royal Academy (again under a pseudonym, Mr Winter), two of which were accepted.

[7] Mutt and Jeff was the first successful six-day-a-week newspaper strip cartoon, which ran in America from 1907 to 1982. It involved a tall racetrack punter (Mutt) and his short dimwit sidekick (Jeff). The strip was such a hit that it spawned more than three hundred animated cinema shorts – and Mutt and

Jeff (Cockney rhyming slang for 'deaf') became idiomatic for any pair of tall and short men.

[8] The Cairo Conference had begun with some of Churchill's forty advisers wanting Britain to pull out of Mesopotamia altogether (except for the Persian Gulf with its oil). Lawrence and others wanted the establishment of the Arab kingdom of Iraq, with Prince Faisal on the throne – at whose side Lawrence had ridden against the Turks – with his brother Abdullah on the throne of newly created Transjordan. This was the plan Churchill implemented; it carved away three-quarters of Palestine east of the River Jordan–Gulf of Aqaba divide to form the kingdom of Transjordan. The Cairo settlement failed to resolve the problem that both Jews and Arabs considered Palestine their spiritual and geographic home and now put pressure on the remaining territory. The month after Churchill returned to London, thirty Jews and ten Arabs died in riots in Jaffa. Jewish immigration was temporarily halted.

Churchill's plans for the RAF to be used to cut British military expenditure in the Middle East quickly fell to pieces. Violence in Palestine and Iraq demanded even larger ground forces.

Chapter 2: 'If They Want Trouble, They Can Have It'

[1] During both world wars professional football was abandoned and reverted to amateur status, with pros in army camps turning out for a variety of teams. On Saturday 8 April 1916, Walter played left half for Southampton in a friendly against Portsmouth at Fratton Park, a charity game in aid of the Hampshire FA soldiers' comfort fund in front of 2,000 spectators. The Saints lost seven–nil.

² Suffragettes deliberately got themselves arrested to cause embarrassment to the government. When they began to go on hunger strike in prison, they were force-fed. This caused public outrage – the practice had previously been used only with lunatics. In 1913 the Prisoner's Temporary Discharge for Ill-health Act was passed, its purpose being to allow very weak hunger strikers to be released but then re-arrested on the most trivial of pretexts (often for not registering the address where they recuperated) days later when they were stronger. The measure was dubbed the Cat and Mouse Act.

Churchill had his share of problems with the suffragettes. Like most male MPs, he believed most women would not understand the workings of Parliament and therefore should not take part in the electoral process, but he avoided saying so in public, retorting that 'I am not going to be henpecked into a position on which my mind is not fully prepared'. He was eventually won round by his wife (he almost always took her advice in the end) but not before being attacked by a suffragette with a riding whip.

³ In early 1915, when the Western Front was mired in stalemate and the war effort needed a new impetus, Churchill presented an audacious plan to take Constantinople, attacking across the Dardanelles, the strait separating European Turkey from Asia Minor. Turkey was relatively weak and was likely to fall, creating a domino effect through the Balkans and Austria, completely isolating Germany. The fleet silenced the Turkish forts overlooking the strait, but the admirals decided to await Kitchener's army, which was slow to arrive, and the element of surprise was forfeited. Another static front resulted, with great loss of life. Churchill took the blame.

Chapter 3: Chartwell and Fisticuffs

[1] A. J. Cook, the miners' leader, said he'd settle for anything that Churchill himself thought was fair and sensible, but when the TUC called off the strike the miners felt betrayed and stayed out for up to six months.

[2] 'It appeared,' Walter wrote, 'so an English-speaking Italian told me during our visit to Rome, that the King of Italy dropped his handkerchief as he was strolling through the grounds of the palace one day. Signor Mussolini, with whom he was walking, gallantly stooped to retrieve it, but King Victor waved him aside and picked it up himself. "Majesty," expostulated the Duce, "am I not always at your service? Could you not have let me do it for you?" A trifle grimly, Italy's diminutive monarch gazed back at his august "servitor". "I prefer to pick up my own handkerchief," he replied. "It is the only thing left of mine Your Excellency has not poked his nose into."' The story is almost certainly apocryphal.

[3] The offer of membership of the bricklayers' union began as a joke by union secretary George Hicks and some of his executive, to publicise that tradesmen shouldn't be employed without holding a union card. In fact, Churchill quickly became a competent brickie, practically single-handedly building the long high walls that enclosed the Chartwell vegetable garden, in which he constructed a miniature cottage known as 'Mary's house'. He also carried out numerous smaller projects. Perhaps the union shouldn't have tried to rescind his membership. A few years later, when it wanted to reduce the number of bricks a man was expected to lay in an hour, Churchill argued in the Commons that the new figure was too low, saying he could lay more himself. Challenged by some Opposition Members, he had bricks and

mortar brought into Palace Yard and, watched by many MPs, laid – perfectly – more than the original figure.

Chapter 4: Guilt in New York

[1] The winter of 1929 saw the Churchills in reduced circumstances at Chartwell. In a linking passage of her edited volumes of her parents' correspondence, Mary wrote: 'Chartwell was run down to a low ebb; the big house was dust-sheeted, only the study being left open so that Winston could work there. The charming small house, Wellstreet Cottage (which he had been building and which had been intended for a butler) now became our "slum" haven . . . I remember it all being very cosy.' In 1938 Churchill's finances were again so parlous that he put his beloved Chartwell on the market, before a friend came to his rescue.

[2] The *Evening Standard* wasn't Walter's favourite paper. In the spring of 1925, just before Churchill delivered his first Budget, he abandoned his two-seater in the House of Commons yard, blocking the entrance, rushing away about his business. Walter changed seats, moved it and parked it. That evening's paper carried a story in the gossip column praising 'the skills of Mr Churchill's chauffeur-detective, who combined the role of a sleuth with the skill of an expert mechanic, an aptitude so great that the Chancellor's car is the sweetest-running "bus" that ever entered Palace Yard'. Walter was called to Scotland Yard to explain and, he thought, a serious view would have been taken had he been driving, 'for unemployment figures were mounting and the public would never have tolerated the idea of a "shadow" doing some unemployed chauffeur, or mechanic, out of a job'.

Unquestionably Walter did at least on occasion drive

Churchill's car outside London, if only as a matter of self-preservation. In August 1928, near Lympne in Kent, he ran a motorcycle combination into a ditch – a brand-new machine that cost the two young airmen who owned it £20 to repair. Churchill's motor insurance paid.

[3] Phyllis Moir, a young Englishwoman who had worked in the Foreign Office and was hired by Mrs Churchill as her husband's temporary secretary when he came out of hospital, wrote that the fee was $5,000. As she would have typed the letters about the deal, she is more likely to be right. There were at the time $4 to the pound.

[4] Walter's accident was Harold Thompson's first conscious memory of his father. Aged three, he was at the ground kicking a ball around when the lightning struck. 'Dad went flying across the shed, and he was lying on the floor for some minutes. Then he came to, got on his feet, picked me up and ran home – we lived only a few hundred yards from the Dell. He collapsed on the doorstep.'

[5] Part of the Anglo-Irish agreement was that the Free State should pay land annuities to the British government. Eamon de Valera's Fianna Fail (Soldiers of Destiny) government withheld these payments. Britain imposed a twenty per cent tariff on agricultural imports from Ireland, de Valera countering with a five-shilling-a-ton tax on imports of British coal and a twenty per cent tariff on British cement, machinery, electrical goods, iron and steel.

[6] Churchill and Hitler never met but nearly did in 1932. Having followed his ancestor Marlborough's march to the Danube, Churchill was in Munich where his son Randolph contacted a

friend, Ernst Hanfstaengl, a Harvard graduate acting as Hitler's press secretary, suggesting a meeting. Hanfstaengl tried to persuade Hitler (not yet risen to power) to join the Churchill family for dinner. Having first said he might join them for coffee, Hitler said he was unshaven and had too much to do.

[7] Sarah, Churchill's favourite daughter, joined the chorus line of C. B. Cochran's *Young Ladies* and then became an actress, her wild ways causing her father much distress. Churchill had Walter investigate several young men with whom she had relationships. When she was twenty-two, Sarah fell in love with the much older music-hall comedian Vic Oliver, who was twice divorced; Walter made enquiries about him, too. Sarah bolted to New York, where Oliver was working, and married him on Christmas Eve 1936. Churchill hired American lawyers in an abortive attempt to prevent her. Nowhere in his notes does Walter elaborate on exactly what his 'business errands' involved.

[8] Gaining power in 1933, Hitler aimed to sweep aside the harsh military restrictions and many of the territorial agreements imposed on Germany after the First World War. The desire for peace in Britain was so great that Chamberlain sanctioned Hitler's reoccupation of the Rhineland (and Mussolini's expansionist activities in Abyssinia); then, in March 1938, the annexation of Austria into a 'Greater Germany'; and then the notorious occupation of the German-speaking Sudetenland of Czechoslovakia in September. Believing this was Hitler's final demand, Chamberlain returned from signing the Munich Agreement (with Germany, Italy and France as co-signatories – but not Czechoslovakia), announcing 'peace with honour' at the airport. In March 1939 Hitler overran all of Czechoslovakia, then made demands for Danzig in Poland, as well as the Polish Corridor.

Only now did Chamberlain abandon the policy of appeasement and draw a line in the sand.

⁹ In its heyday Clyno was the third-largest car manufacturer in the UK after Austin and Morris, always selling just below the competition. Between 1922 and 1929, when it went into liquidation, the company, based in Wolverhampton, sold some 40,000 vehicles (and 15,000 motorcycles). Only about a hundred Clynos survive.

Chapter 5: High Risk for France

¹ The Duke and Duchess of Windsor were regarded by many as Nazi sympathisers, following their visit to Germany in 1937 at Hitler's invitation, but there was absolutely no suggestion that they knew anything of any plot.

Support for Churchill's position on Germany was growing before he spoke out for the duke, then Edward VIII, the previous year over the abdication issue. Although Churchill had regularly played polo with him in the 1920s (when Walter's job 'on polo days was to fill two large Thermos flasks with ice-cold Barsac wine and serve it between chukkas'), his steadfastness wasn't to the King personally but to the monarchy, in which he believed as passionately as he did in empire. Howled down in the Commons, the worst political mauling of his career forced him to leave the Chamber.

When Germany invaded France, the Windsors fled from Paris to the Riviera, then to Spain and then to Portugal. A 'defeatist' interview with the duke received wide coverage. Churchill got him out of the way in 1940 by making him governor of the Bahamas. US intelligence reports released in 2003 indicated that

Germany considered the duke 'no enemy of Germany' and 'the logical director of England's destiny after the war'.

2 Some 60,000 German refugees entered Britain in the 1930s, mainly Jews and left-wing opponents of Hitler. The government, fearing some of them might be spies, interned abut half, holding them in various camps all over Britain until they appeared before tribunals. Those classified as 'A' class stayed in internment; 'Bs' were allowed to leave, with restrictions on their movements; and 'Cs' – the overwhelming majority – went free. Two days after becoming Prime Minister, Churchill had all 'B' class aliens arrested as well as 2,000 others, who hadn't been classified, living in coastal areas.

When Mussolini declared war on the Allies on 10 May, 4,000 Italians with less than twenty years' residence in Britain were also interned.

3 'Come then, let us to the task, to the battle, to the toil – each to our part; each to our station. Fill the armies, rule the air, pour out the munitions, strangle the U-boats, sweep the mines, plough the land, build the ships, guard the streets, succour the wounded, uplift the downcast, honour the brave. Let us go forward together in all parts of the Empire, in all parts of the Island. There is not a week nor a day nor an hour to lose.'

4 Nearly 900 volunteer craft of all shapes and sizes and 40 British, Dutch, French and Belgian destroyers, minesweepers and patrol ships finally ferried 338,226 troops, mostly British but over a third of them French, to safety.

5 The House of Commons at the time wasn't wired for sound recording and this speech, while reported in the newspapers, was

heard on radio read by an announcer and only in part. In the 1970s the actor Norman Shelley (Colonel Danby in *The Archers* before his death in 1980) claimed to have impersonated Churchill when he was too busy to go into the BBC to record a number of speeches delivered in Parliament, including this one. There has been controversy ever since. A 78-rpm disc found by Shelley's son in 2000 has his father's recording of the 'Beaches' speech, but the label is dated 7 September 1942, over two years after Churchill delivered it in the House. Assuming the date is correct, Shelley must have made the recording for some propaganda purpose.

The issue is further confused by the fact that after the war Churchill rerecorded a number of speeches that were commercially released with others that were broadcast. In 1990 an American speech research group tested twenty sold under Churchill's name. They concluded that three from 1940 – 'Beaches', 'Finest hour' and 'Blood, toil, tears and sweat' – were different from the rest.

Chapter 6: Exhaustion on the Home Front

[1] The idea for cheap household air-raid shelters is attributed to John Anderson when Home Secretary. The first 'Anderson shelters', basically a small 'shed' of corrugated steel with a curved roof that was placed in a pre-dug hole in the garden and covered in soil, accommodated six people. The first were delivered in February 1939 – free to those earning less than £250 a year, £7 to everyone else. Over 2.25 million were distributed. In August 1940 Churchill ordered a ten-person shelter for Chartwell, which cost £15.

[2] During the brief period in which Churchill used Down Street station, Walter thought there was a symbolic closeness between

Churchill and the country because so many Londoners took to the underground as a shelter. At first the government had forbidden the stations to be used for the purpose, but people bought a 1½d. ticket and refused to come up. Eventually canteens and even libraries and entertainment were provided. The togetherness of Prime Minister and people during the Blitz was closer than Walter at the time knew – two-thirds of Londoners refused to use the shelters, preferring, like Churchill, to be in their own beds, though most at least brought them downstairs.

[3] The Cabinet War Rooms as well as his map room, with its thousands of maps, books and planning paraphernalia, and his next-door office were opened to the public in 1984, left as they'd been when Churchill was last in the Annexe in 1945. Other areas of the Annexe had been stripped and kept by the Treasury for use as storage. In 2003, after years of negotiations, restoration work began on the Churchills' kitchen and other rooms, and a new learning and conference suite was installed. In January 2005, marking the fortieth anniversary of Churchill's death, a museum devoted to his life was opened.

[4] Siren suits (Churchill's 'rompers') got their name from the sirens that heralded an impending air raid. They became popular because they were easy to pull on over night attire – even Princesses Elizabeth and Margaret had them. So did Clementine Churchill, though hers were tailored and rather more chic than her husband's. 'His famous siren suits were worn for comfort, not style,' Walter commented, 'although he was quietly pleased to have set a fashion.' A little later in the war, Churchill had lightweight rompers made for visiting North Africa and the Middle East – and in old age had others, including one in chalk stripes and another in red velvet.

[5] The continuous offensive on London lasted until the all clear on Sunday 11 May 1941, which signalled the end of the final and worst raid of the war, but the industrial centres and ports suffered concentrated attacks for a while longer, although these usually lasted for only two or three nights at a time. Altogether 40,000 people were killed and 86,000 injured and 2 million homes were destroyed, over half in London.

[6] Lindemann, born in Germany of an American mother, was a member of the Royal Aircraft Establishment in the First World War and organised London's balloon barrage. A leading physicist, he became Professor of Experimental Philosophy at Oxford. Teetotal and vegetarian, he always wore a bowler, even on a warship. Churchill called him 'The Prof', and everyone followed suit. Lindemann, Churchill said, had a 'beautiful brain'.

[7] Chartwell was initially guarded, according to Churchill's quixotic wishes, by the 70th Buffs, a battalion of young regular soldiers aged between sixteen and a half and conscription age. A number of such battalions were formed following Dunkirk, after which, according to Professor Charles Arnold Baker, OBE: 'The War Office, having other concerns, lost sight of them. They acquired unwanted old officers and corpulent NCOs. The soldiers turned up on parade when it suited them, deserted and sold their clothing and equipment when they wanted money, and hit NCOs if they gave an unpopular order. Eventually somebody noticed; all the officers and NCOs were sacked and the 70th Buffs got a fire-eating colonel. A stern regime was instituted. In a year, absences were reduced from sixty to seven per cent. At this point Churchill became interested, and the 70th Buffs [into which Arnold Baker was transferred as a platoon commander] went to Chartwell because he wanted to see how such a unit had

progressed and because he did not want to disturb other formations.'

At Chartwell the 70th 'pitched camp in a wood above the house, ran a telephone line round the outer fences to connect the guard posts, diverted traffic with bogus "road closed for repairs" signs and, armed to the teeth and twice a day, searched every nook and cranny – even the loos and Churchill's bedroom, at least once with him in bed in it. He visited them and every week sent them a barrel of beer.

'Walter Thompson originally sited the guard posts.'

The 70th were at Chartwell for three months before being replaced. The battalions of 'young regulars' were disbanded once Britain went on the offensive, by which time Arnold Baker was in MI6 'busy catching spies in Belgium and Norway' (personal communication). In May 1941 men from the more conventional unit guarding Churchill's home were warned about gossiping in the Westerham pubs about when he was due to visit.

Chapter 7: Winnie, Franklin and Joe

[1] The Lend-Lease Act of 11 March 1941 resulted in America providing $50 billion to 38 countries. Over $31 billion came to Britain, most of the rest to the Soviet Union. Virtually bankrupt by 1945, Britain was eventually asked to repay $650 million.

[2] The pact had been a matter of convenience from Hitler's point of view: he always intended to invade Russia, and Churchill had communicated as much to Stalin; Hitler wanted the raw materials in the Urals and the Ukraine. Why he turned on Russia when he did is a matter of conjecture (the decision saved Britain from further pummelling by the Luftwaffe, which turned to the

war in the east). Probably he was encouraged by the enormous casualties that little Finland had inflicted on the Red Army when it invaded in October 1939. The efficiency of the Red Army, from which Stalin had purged 10,000 senior officers, was cast into serious doubt. The rest of Europe regarded the fifteen-week Russo-Finnish conflict, which Stalin waged to secure his Baltic flank, as something of a sideshow and offered no assistance. Walter had a particular interest in the affair: he had guarded the Finnish leader Marshal Mannerheim when he'd come to London in the 1920s.

[3] No one knows how many people died during the Second World War, but the total was ten to twelve times greater – something between 50 to 60 million. The greatest total losses were sustained by Russia, 20 million (half of them civilians); China, 10 million; Poland and Germany, 5.5 million each; and Japan, 2 million. The number of British killed was around 350,000, a third of them civilians. Just under 300,000 American military died.

[4] In September 1940 Japan had signed a tripartite pact with Germany and Italy, tying its fortunes to the Axis. But the war it fought was its own, quite separate from Hitler's, in pursuit of its expansionist plans – it had been making incursions into Chinese territory since 1931 (China and Japan had been at war since 1937) and had its eye on American and colonial territories. The pre-emptive attack on Pearl Harbor in Hawaii was intended to destroy the US Pacific fleet. Japan assumed that Allied governments would quickly accept a peace settlement.

[5] That the south-west Irish ports were denied him was particularly galling to Churchill. The Anglo-Irish Treaty of 1921 that he'd largely been responsible for negotiating allowed the Royal

Navy to maintain bases there. When the constitution of Eire took effect in December 1937, Southern Ireland, a republic in all but name, claimed the surrounding waters as national territory and received Britain's agreement in April the following year – against Churchill's opposition.

It's worth pointing out that citizens of Southern Ireland were free to join the British forces during the Second World War and over 40,000 did; many more worked in British factories. Allied airmen shot down over Eire were quietly repatriated, Allied over-flights ignored and Axis airmen interned.

[6] Over the war years, Walter destroyed hundreds of cigars sent to Churchill. 'No chance could be taken. But there was one exception, towards the end of the war, when an American soldier in uniform came to Downing Street and asked to see the Prime Minister. After being told by the doorman that it was not possible, I saw how downcast he looked. I asked him if I could help. He was smoking a long cigar, and told me very brightly that he had ascertained where Winston bought his cigars; he had been to the store and purchased two. One he was smoking, the other he wished to give to Winston. I asked him to wait and telephoned the store, which confirmed what he said. Winston was in conference, and he could not see him, but I said I would see that he received the cigar, and if he would give me his address he would receive a personal letter. When I told Winston, he was very touched. "I will write to him personally and I will smoke the cigar," he said. I know he did both.'

[7] In November 1940 Walter wrote an official letter, which went up the line to the Commissioner, saying that when Churchill went to Chequers he wanted the normal practice of informing the Chief Constable of Buckinghamshire to be stopped. Further,

Churchill wanted no information about any of his movements to be given to any police force. The superintendent who forwarded the letter to the Commissioner wrote on the bottom: 'I do not know whether this request by the Prime Minister relieves the CC Bucks of responsibility.'

[8] Walter's namesake, Churchill's ADC Charles Thompson, didn't like being left behind either. He even offered to replace the steward.

[9] Rushed into service, the Churchill tank suffered mechanical troubles. Early in 1942 the Prime Minister went to see seventy or eighty being put through their paces on the Sussex Downs. Walter: 'The testing-ground was a difficult one and, for a time, the tanks were on their best behaviour. Then one or two started to ease up . . . An officer standing by me said: "Of course, it would happen like this today. The tanks are all right, but the gearboxes are always giving trouble. They are not strong enough."' The rectified Churchills proved their worth in Tunisia, where their ability to climb hills was invaluable.

[10] British and Russian forces jointly entered and occupied Persia in June 1941 to protect the supply route for Western aid to the Soviet Union and to deny German access to the Anglo-Iranian oilfields. Shah Reza Pahlavi, a German sympathiser, was made to resign in favour of his son, who was given British advisers.

[11] Up to May 1943 U-boats took a great toll of Allied shipping, in the Irish Sea, the Mediterranean and the Arctic, but primarily in the Atlantic. Hunting in packs, U-boats accounted for 142 Allied vessels in one 12-week period of 1942. Surface raiders like the battle cruisers *Scharnhorst* and *Gneisenau* and the long-range

Focke-Wulf Condor fighters that could reach far out into the Atlantic also took their toll. Over 21 million tons of Allied shipping was sunk during the war, two-thirds by U-boats. From 1943 new radar equipment, new anti-submarine techniques and very long-range aircraft forced Admiral Dönitz on the defensive. The U-boat fleet ceased being a serious threat.

[12] Walter's unpublished notes say Churchill also painted two pictures in the grounds of the villa in Marrakech when he was recovering from serious illness at the end of 1943 – 'I should know, because I erected his easel and helped to mix his paints.'

[13] 'Where are my eggs?' Churchill frequently asked – his latest box of Enigma intercepts, a description that stemmed from his having once said that the cryptanalysts at Bletchley Park were 'the geese who laid the golden eggs but never cackled'.

The Enigma enciphering machine for radio transmission was invented in the early 1920s and employed commercially in Germany before being adapted for military purposes. An electro-mechanical computer that generated apparently random number groups, it was copied by the Poles – who sent two copies to both the French and British in 1939.

With daily codes changed and numerous different codes used by different services, the Germans remained convinced throughout the war that their signals were secure. But the British constructed deciphering machines, The Bombes early in the war and the Colossus later and thus had access to almost all radio transmissions between the German High Command and the various field headquarters.

Nowhere in his history of the Second World War, written in the late 1940s and early 1950s, does Churchill mention Enigma or Ultra. The story wasn't revealed until 1974.

Chapter 8: Pain and Loss

[1] Bureaucracy doesn't stop for war, as extracts from correspondence relating to Walter's double move shows.

On 20 February 1941 L. H. Langmaid from the Ministry of Works and Buildings wrote to Eric Seal, Churchill's principal private secretary: 'I am sorry to bother you personally with a very small matter, but it concerns a removal charge incurred by Inspector Thompson for the transfer of his effects on the 1 July last from Richmond Terrace Mews to College Mews. As the matter was urgent, we assisted at his request by getting the work carried out by one of our contractors, Messrs White & Co, at the cost of £2.10s. Inspector Thompson now feels that he is not liable for this charge and refuses to pay the account, stating that he would refer the matter to you. Perhaps you will kindly say if there are any special reasons warranting this expenditure being met from public funds.'

On 25 February Seal replied, saying he had spoken to Walter and 'Have a certain amount of sympathy' for his case. 'There was very little furniture in the [Admiralty] garage and the Inspector therefore brought up some of his own furniture from his home ... When Mr Churchill became Prime Minister, the Admiralty garage naturally had to be vacated and it was therefore necessary that the Inspector's furniture should be taken to the Prime Minister's garage in College Mews ...' On 3 March Langmaid wrote back: 'I, too, am sympathetic in regard to Inspector Thompson bearing the cost of this enforced transfer, but it is inevitable that when his chief removes he must follow suit. We do not accept any of the costs incurred for the Minister's transfer and to me it appears rather a personal matter between Inspector Thompson and his chief.'

The saga continued. Seal wrote to F. J. Root at the Ministry of Works and Buildings: 'I would be disposed to agree with Langmaid's views were it not for the fact that Inspector Thompson tells me that he had to provide a great deal of his own furniture for the Admiralty garage ... He says that when he went there the furniture consisted of one armchair, one kitchen table and one chest of drawers, and that he had to provide the furniture shown on the attached list, marked "A". When he moved to the Prime Minister's garage in College Mews he found slightly more furniture, as shown on list "B" ... I think it is reasonable that the State should pay the cost of moving his furniture. If it is maintained that he need not have taken additional furniture to College Mews, I think he would be justified in claiming for the return of his furniture to his own home. So far as I know, he has put in no claim for the cost of bringing his furniture up in the first place.'

The issue was resolved by 23 May, when the Ministry of Works and Buildings wrote to Downing Street to say Walter had paid the bill and been reimbursed from the Police Fund.

[2] In 2003 the Winston Churchill Center in Washington DC answered a question on its website asking what had happened to Walter after 1940. The writer understood that he had been killed in the Blitz. The reply posted gave some details but included that 'Thompson left under a cloud involving the waving around of a firearm at Chartwell'. Walter's son Harold e-mailed a correction.

[3] Like the Luftwaffe in 1940, Bomber Command concentrated on daylight bombing but lost so many aircraft that it switched to night raids. Initially relying only on dead reckoning, squadrons often missed their targets. Two technical aids were developed: radio navigation and, later, the more sophisticated H2S radar system that was carried by the Pathfinders, which flew ahead of

the main bombing streams to locate and mark targets with coloured flares.

There were calls for H2S to be fitted on all bombers – when Pathfinders were lost, so was mission efficiency – but the government was reluctant to widen usage in case the system fell into enemy hands. According to Harold, his brother went to a War Cabinet meeting to put the case.

The Pathfinder Force flew over 50,000 sorties against nearly 3,500 targets. Nearly 4,000 lost their lives.

[4] In an interview in the 1970s, ex-Detective Sergeant Roy Richards, who served very briefly as one of Churchill's protection officers after Walter retired the second time in 1945, said that Walter carried a 7.65-millimetre Menta hammerless semi-automatic, not a .32 Webley. He had loaned the Menta, his personal property, to Walter on his reappointment to Churchill in 1939. When Walter handed it back at the end of the war he told Richards, 'It has been everywhere with me' – from which Richards concluded that Walter carried the Menta daily as his weapon of choice. What Walter meant was that he took the Menta as a spare – just as Churchill took a .38 Webley as a backup to his Colt.

[5] It isn't generally realised that civilian flights carried on during the war, even at the height of the Battle of Britain. Flights from neutral Portugal were by tacit agreement: they carried neutral diplomats, diplomatic bags, prisoner-of-war mail and the British newspapers – information for German intelligence.

Howard, who had been in Spain and Portugal on a lecture tour for the British Council, bore some resemblance to Walter in height and build, at least from a distance, wearing a trilby. Chenhalls, corpulent and a cigar man, was not unlike Churchill, although taller and younger.

One can speculate that if the Germans shot down the Lisbon flight because they believed Churchill was on it, then British Intelligence – and Churchill – might have known what was going to happen by deciphering Enigma communications. If that is true, they took the decision not to give a warning for fear of alerting the Germans that they'd cracked the code.

There are other possibilities for the downing of the DC3 by a squadron of Junkers Ju 88s: for example, the aircraft might have been mistaken for a military one. It's also possible that Howard was the target – his propaganda work had come to the attention of Goebbels, and Haw-Haw had threatened him by name in his broadcasts.

The three remaining DC3s on the route resumed flying within the week, but at night, with cabins blacked out.

[6] In 1950 General Lahousen, the German Chief of Secret Operations, confirmed that Hitler had ordered an assassination attempt in Teheran. The order came down through Field Marshal Keitel and then Admiral Canaris, Chief of Intelligence.

Chapter 9: Death's Door, D-Day and Doodlebugs

[1] Nugus/Martin Productions have probably made more programmes about the Second World War than any other independent television company in the world. Their output – which includes such series as *Secrets of World War II*, *Heroes and Weapons of World War II*, *Gladiators of World War II* and *Last Days of World War II* – is seen in the UK on the BBC, The History Channel and UKTV, The Biography Channel, Discovery and Civilisation, as is their wider output, which includes *The Century of Warfare* and *World War I in Colour*.

Nugus/Martin's 800 documentaries have been translated into fifty languages and are seen in prime-time slots on hundreds of historical broadcasters worldwide. In April 2005 the company had a record 108 programmes on British television in one week across all channels.

[2] Lord Moran's *Struggle for Survival* was objected to by Clementine before publication, and after extracts appeared in the *Sunday Times* Churchill's son Randolph wrote angry letters. Though his diary was hailed as a literary masterpiece, Moran, then eighty-four, was heavily criticised by the medical profession. He justified himself by saying that Churchill's health affected the outcome of the war.

[3] Aviation fascinated Churchill. In 1909 he created an air arm for the navy that eventually became the Royal Air Force. When he was thirty-eight, in 1913, he decided to learn to fly – dangerous at the time, with one death in every five thousand flights. Some weekends he went up as often as ten times a day. 'He frequently made flights in machines which were nothing more than crates with canvas, bamboo and wire to hold them together,' Walter commented. He had several lucky escapes; once he bent an under-carriage on landing; on a second occasion, when his plane crash-landed, his co-pilot was knocked unconscious. Clementine begged him to give up, and he gave in. He never did get his pilot's licence. During the Second World War he took over the controls of at least one other aircraft, the *Berwick* flying boat, on the flight from Washington to Bermuda in January 1942.

[4] Acronym for Supreme Headquarters Allied Expeditionary Force. SHAEF moved to Granville in France on 1 September 1944 and then to Versailles on 20 September, with an advance

HQ at Reims, from where the Allies accepted Germany's surrender on 7 May 1945.

[5] Churchill thought of the idea of floating harbours during the First World War, but a similar thought occurred to a civil engineer, Hugh Iorys Hughes, in 1941. Churchill certainly drove the idea, with a memo to Lord Mountbatten on 30 May the following year: 'They must float up and down with tide. The anchor problem must be mastered. Let me have the best solution worked out. Don't argue the matter. The difficulties will argue for themselves.'

The two Mulberrys were needed until the harbours at Cherbourg, Le Havre, Dieppe and St-Malo, heavily fortified by the Germans, were taken. That they were conceived, made in pieces (by up to 45,000 men in 8 months at sites all around Britain) and towed across the Channel almost defies comprehension.

Each, when finally put together, weighed nearly a million tons and involved the laying of 146 caissons (the largest the height of a five-storey building), 33 jetties and 10 miles of floating roads.

Mulberry A, on the American beachhead, was wrecked by a violent storm after only four days, but Mulberry B (nicknamed 'Port Winston') worked for 10 months, landing 2.5 million men, 500,000 vehicles and 4 million tons of goods.

[6] Churchill was in a danger he didn't know about at Montgomery's headquarters – two German paratroops were hiding in rhododendron bushes yards from him. Neither, in fact, posed a threat. Both were armed but cut off from their unit; cold and hungry, they were happy to give themselves up two days after the Prime Minister's departure.

[7] Sources vary widely about how many of the 35,000 mass-produced V-1s came Britain's way – a figure of up to 9,500 is

given, with about half knocked out by fighter planes, AA guns or barrage balloons. Over 2,300 hit London, causing up to 6,000 civilian deaths and 18,000 serious injuries.

About 5,000 V-2s were fired, mostly aimed at London, Antwerp and Liège.

Chapter 10: Things Catch Up with Walter

[1] On the roof of the Annexe on the night of 10 May 1942, when 1,000 incendiary bombs were dropped on central London and the Chamber of the House of Commons was destroyed, Walter 'could see flames rising, some of which came from the area where Miss Shearburn, previously Winston's secretary, was living [almost certainly in his flat in College Mews]. Winston, who had been walking around, came over to me, looked in my face and said: "Are you scared, Thompson?" "Yes," I replied . . . and Churchill agreed to go down.' What Walter didn't tell him was that it was May he was scared about.

[2] BBC files of the time are incomplete. The only entry about Mary Shearburn is in 1944 when she was Assistant in the Defence Adviser's Department (Home Guard Unit).

[3] Stationed in Cyprus, Flight Lieutenant Thompson in December 1960 made a splash in the English newspapers after rescuing eleven seamen from a Yugoslav cargo ship aground on a reef off Famagusta. He volunteered to be lowered to the deck and strapped himself to the mast to catch the helicopter safety harness so that they could be winched up.

Chapter 11: Parting of the Ways

[1] Neville Bullock made the news three years ago when the original letter containing Britain's final ultimatum to Germany before the outbreak of the First World War, and the German reply, were sold at auction for £2,400, almost twice the estimated value. While with Churchill at Potsdam, Bullock found the letters in Hitler's Berlin Chancellery – after it had been looted by the Russians.

'There were hundreds of Russian troops around and they exercised tight control, challenging everyone,' he says. 'But I found I was able to move about because of the red band around my cap – to them it meant a high-ranking officer. I had no right to be where I was. There were papers scattered all over the place – the one in English with the British government crest just caught my eye.'

Bullock sold the letters for a small sum when he returned to England.

Chapter 12: Brought to Book

[1] New Romney was then a busy municipal borough. Following local government reorganisation in 1974, most functions moved to Shepney District Council in Folkestone.

[2] The original Cinque Ports of Hastings, Romney, Hythe, Dover and Sandwich were established long before William the Conqueror as a united naval force. After 1066, William found it advantageous to deal with the Cinque Ports, giving them tax exemptions and the right to make their own by-laws in return for a commitment to maintain a fleet. Later, Winchelsea and Rye became Cinque

Ports, which together became so powerful as to be almost an independent state. Their privileges were withdrawn and their power ended when Henry VII created the first true Royal Navy, but the ancient title of Lord Warden has remained as an honorary and ceremonial office within the gift of the monarch.

[3] At the Churchill Archives Centre in Cambridge, the file Personal: Staff: Correspondence O–Z dated 6 June 1945 to 13 December 1951, which includes correspondence with Walter, is closed except for certain folios.

[4] Churchill had once been a Freemason, belonging to the United Studholme Lodge in the St James's area of London, but resigned in 1912. His only recorded Masonic contact afterwards was a visit to Royal Naval Lodge No. 59 on 10 December 1928. However, as Warden of the Cinque Ports he was an honorary Freemason and therefore entitled to support Walter's and Harold's application. The New Romney Lodge, which then met in the back room of the Broadacre Hotel, no longer exists; it was incorporated into the Romney Marsh Lodge at Dymchurch.

[5] Exactly what the sales figures for 'Shadow' were I've been unable to find out; Christopher Johnson has long gone out of business, the *Bookseller* of the period carried no detailed listings and Book Trust has no record.

[6] Only once does Walter mention pyjamas. Churchill always wore a silk vest in bed, as Walter repeats on numerous occasions. Randolph Churchill wrote a letter to *The Times* saying that his father never wore pyjamas in his life. In fact, Randolph appears to have been friendlily disposed to Walter. Eight years ago Jan Glass met his daughter Arabella at WeightWatchers and, when

she said who she was, was told: 'Tommy? We were brought up on stories about Tommy!'

[7] Jenkins was positively peevish about what Walter wrote regarding Christmas 1939, when 'the war had been in progress for nearly four months and the terror and devastation had fallen very far short of the prophecies that had preceded hostilities . . . Many were able to spend the time in having a welcome break. [But] at the Admiralty, Christmas Day was like any other day. The First Lord carried on in his usual manner. He worked from early morning until dinnertime. The staff were at their posts. There was no relaxation there. He did unbend a little on Boxing Day. He worked for fourteen hours and spent three hours in a local cinema!' Rather as if Walter's job was to provide a future biographer with the material he desired, Jenkins commented that 'there is room for doubt whether "local" meant Westerham, a more natural meaning, rather than the West End of London. Nor does Thompson record the name of the film.'

[8] In January 1932 Walter's expenditure on Churchill's behalf in New York was $36.75.

[9] And, of course, looking after Churchill's painting equipment. Both George Williams (1945–55) and Edmund Murray (1947–65) were in their thirties when they were assigned. Murray, himself a painter, tried and failed several times to have works accepted in the summer exhibition of the Royal Academy. Once he showed Churchill three canvases. Churchill judged one very good, one very, very good and one excellent. 'They are,' he said, 'much better than mine – but yours are judged on their merits.'

[10] May originally wrote a three-part series for the Amalgamated

Press's *Good Taste* magazine in 1951; in the event they were
unable to publish: the material was submitted to Churchill for
his sanction, which was not forthcoming – Churchill said he'd
seen several manuscripts giving the background to his wartime
life and he felt that the market was being flooded. Subsequently
May was one of forty people who contributed a chapter to a
book, *Churchill by His Contemporaries,* edited by Charles Eade.
In September 1953 the Amalgamated Press wrote complaining
that some of the wording was the same as in their unpublished
series. On Churchill's death, Amalgamated (now Fleetway
Publications) wrote again (erroneously stating that the original
material had been commissioned for *Woman and Home, My Home*
or *Woman's Weekly*), saying they wanted to approach the family
or the estate to agree publication. Odhams Press, however, to
which group *Woman* magazine belonged, were now interested
and came to some arrangement with Fleetway. May's fee of £1,000
was the equivalent of the average annual wage at the time.

Index

Note: 'WT' denotes Walter Thompson, 'C' Winston Churchill, 'WW1' and 'WW2' World Wars One and Two. A subscript number appended to a page number indicates an endnote. Subheadings are in chronological order.